WARRIOR OF GOD

JOHN HUS AT THE STAKE

WARRIOR OF GOD

THE LIFE AND DEATH OF JOHN HUS

Paul Roubiczek and Joseph Kalmer

NICHOLSON AND WATSON
LONDON

First published in 1947 by
Ivor Nicholson & Watson Ltd.
26 Manchester Square
London W.1

Made and Printed in Great Britain by
Love & Malcomson, Ltd.
London and Redhill

CONTENTS

PAGE

INTRODUCTION 1

BOOK ONE : IN THE STREAM OF TIME

DEATH OF AN EPOCH 7
THE YEAR OF SALVATION 13
AN UNKNOWN STUDENT 21
EDUCATION THROUGH CHAOS 31
NATION AND CHURCH 42
MESSAGE FROM ENGLAND 53

BOOK TWO : THE SUMMONS

HESITANT BEGINNING 67
OBEDIENCE TO GOD BEFORE OBEDIENCE TO MAN .. 76
THE FIGHT FOR THE UNIVERSITY 85
NATION AND FAITH 97
THE KING RIDES INTO THE CATHEDRAL 108
STORM OVER INDULGENCES 121
PRAGUE UNDER INTERDICT 135
IN THE HIGHWAYS AND HEDGES 151

BOOK THREE : THE TEST

CHRISTENDOM IN SESSION 165
JOURNEY TO DEATH 180
THE END OF FREEDOM 188
THE POPES FALL 200
DEAF EARS 216
THE FIRST DEATH 231
THE SECOND DEATH 246
BOHEMIA IN FLAMES 260

INDEX 267

LIST OF ILLUSTRATIONS

PAGE

John Hus at the Stake .. .. *Frontispiece*
The Council of Constance in Session .. .. .. *Title page*
King Wenceslas IV 11
(*Reproduced by kind permission of the Cambridge University Library*)
Sigismund, King and Emperor 35
John Wyclif 55
Pierre d'Ailly 63
Jerome of Prague 89
(*Reproduced by kind permission of the Cambridge University Library*)
Pope Gregory XII 123
Pope John XXIII 137
Hus before the Council (woodcut) 164
Frederick of Brandenburg 167
Jean Gerson 175
Frederick of Habsburg 207
Cardinal Zabarella 221
Zizka 245
(*Reproduced by kind permission of the Cambridge University Library*)
Poggio Bracciolini 251
Pope Martin V 261
John Hus at the Stake (woodcut) 265

All the illustrations, except the Frontispiece and the two woodcuts, are from
Jaques Lenfant, Histoire du Concile de Constance (1714)

The Frontispiece is from
Litomericky Kancional (1510-1514)

The two woodcuts (pp. 164 and 265) are from
Processus Consistorialis Martyrij Jo. Huss (1520-1530)

The picture on the dust cover (Hus as preacher) is from a late 15th century Czech manuscript,
The Conflict between Christ and Antichrist

AUTHORS' NOTE

The authors have, unfortunately, not been able to provide a bibliography for this book. They succeeded in leaving Czechoslovakia only shortly before the beginning of the war and during their flight all the relevant notes were lost. Only the manuscript itself, which was already in England, could be saved. As Czech, Latin, German and French sources were extensively used in addition to English, and the authors had later no access to the continental libraries, all attempts to reconstruct the bibliography have proved inadequate and it seems best to abandon the idea. The authors, however, will willingly give any information as to their sources to those who may be interested.

We should like here to express our cordial thanks to Mr. Lawrence Wolfe, to whose initiative the publication of this book is due: to the University Library, Cambridge, and to Dr. Victor Fischl, Press Attaché of the Czechoslovak Embassy in London, who have been of very great help in procuring the illustrations: to Dr. S. F. Winter, who prepared the Index: and above all to Miss Ruby Hobling, for her invaluable help and inexhaustible patience in the translation of this book.

Paul Roubiczek *and* Joseph Kalmer.

Cambridge and London.
May, 1946.

INTRODUCTION

"The Middle Ages had given birth to such a 'faith,' that there was no hope for liberty of speculation until by rival 'faiths' belief in the infallible church had been undermined."—G. M. TREVELYAN. *England in the Age of Wycliffe.*

BY general consent of historians the year 1492 marks the end of the Middle Ages and the beginning of Modern Times. It is a chance figure and is useful as a symbol because the discovery of America opened a new world in a literal sense. But the stimulus to this discovery was not a matter of chance. There was, indeed, a new world; a radical change had been in progress from the end of the fourteenth century. This could be traced back to a spiritual and economic transformation; to an empiricism which, alien to the complex catholic foundations of mediæval thought, superseded scholasticism; and to the undermining of the feudal system by the bourgeoisie still struggling at this time for their rights as the Third Estate. In the German Empire this epoch was marked by Wenceslas of Luxembourg's assumption of the role of arbitrator between the predatory nobles and the townsmen.

The growth of prosperity aroused in the middle classes a desire to be free of feudal lords, whether kings or nobles.

The armed protection that these overlords could give the trade of the towns had grown ever more questionable since, with the invention of gunpowder, the knight in armour had given way to the mercenary, while plundering by taxation grew ever more certain. It is not surprising that the middle classes finally sought to protect themselves by setting up their own mercenary armies.

When one god falls, others follow. The fact that the feudal powers did not prove invincible increased the already existing doubts of the scientific system which bolstered them up and in turn received their support. This scientific system was an exceedingly rigid one and its rigidity was due to age. The curricula of the universities reveal the astonishing paucity of the body of knowledge with which that age made shift. It is, therefore, not difficult to imagine that a desire for spiritual independence emerged with the demand for political independence. But it was not yet absolute freedom of thought that was demanded: such an idea had not yet been formulated in men's minds.

Hus strove constantly for the right to seek instruction and to demonstrate the correctness of his thinking. Indeed he, and with him the whole of the bourgeoisie, sought first of all freedom of discussion, the right to debate with impunity. This demand had its inevitable effect ; church and state opposed any opening of the way to doubt of their divine institution. The course of events was also influenced by the increasing abuse of religion by the church and of the church by the state, which used it ever again as a political commodity and instrument. Feudal submission was finally swept away by the irresistible force of conscience. It was in the nature of the times that spiritual disruption meant, too, ecclesiastical disruptions. And that clerics like Wyclif in England, and Hus in Bohemia, were the protagonists in the fight for freedom of thought was due to the fact that revolutionary strivings at that time had no terminology other than that of religion. The social movements which developed in the train of the religious—Wat Tyler followed Wyclif as Zizka followed John Hus—were a sign of the deep unrest among the "people": and the people were more than nobility, clergy and the Third Estate.

But the fight was fought with spiritual weapons and at first the issue was only religious freedom. "So long," says the Czech historian Jan Herben, in his book "Hus and his Followers," "as Hus was castigating church abuses in a general way, he met with sympathy and even praise, but the moment he turned against the immoral life of the priests themselves he was suspected of heresy. And a real heretic, as regards church history, he became soon afterwards when, following his long theological doubts and disputes, he sought information of the English heretic Wyclif, and thus entered upon . . . the road travelled by all reformers. He found that the church tenets conflicted with the Gospel, which was to him a source of religious perception. Finally, at the Council of Constance (1415), Hus parted with Rome not merely on account of a few dogmatic articles but also because of the mediæval principle, according to which the Christian must, in matters of faith, submit to papal decrees in all circumstances. Hus did not refuse to submit either to the Pope or to the Council of Constance, but he opposed to the authority of the church a new principle, that of the personal intellect and personal conviction of the Christian, supported by his conscience. Hus, therefore, declined to retract his real or supposed errors ; he asked to be both taught and convinced by arguments. This was altogether a new idea—for it signified new principles and new rules of life in the mediæval darkness. And herein, too, lies the enormous significance of Hus."

The church met the attack with its proven remedy. The argument of Hus, "I am humbly ready to retract anything that shall be proved erroneous to me according to the scriptures," was answered with death at the stake. Thus the burning of Hus was the signal for the first revolution for a spiritual end. Since then they have never ceased; only the methods have changed.

The middle classes are seldom bellicose. Inclined to seek allies to do the fighting for them, they need the support of classes outside their own ranks. Mercenaries can be used in a war for political aims, for freedom of trade. Wars for conviction are not waged by mercenaries. The Hussites could fight victoriously—victoriously until their own ranks were divided—because at a time when there was as yet no industrial proletariat, artisans and peasants rallied to their new standard. The artisans with their numerous highly specialised journeyman organisations, and the peasants who, though free in name, had become serfs, formed the social classes whose needs could not much longer be soothed with promises of salvation in the next world: they were crushed beneath the ever-growing burden of tithes for the church, taxes and corvées for the nobles. A large part, probably the majority, of the priesthood abused its privileges, neglected and maltreated religion. Hus was the son of peasants, he knew how his class was oppressed. Thus it could be no academic struggle that he led. He pledged his heart's blood and his conscience. He finally paid with his life itself for his political impotence.

Apart from his peasant origin, which enabled him to tap the source of sheer inexhaustible national strength, the infantry of the nation, so to speak, Hus brought to the fight another advantage. He came from a linguistic frontier region where the areas settled exclusively by Czechs or Germans merged into each other.

Civilisation is always the work of foreign conquerors or colonists. Civilisation was brought to Bohemia by the Germans. Seldom have colonists agreed to leave a country when their mission is ended. It is human nature to cling to advantages won, particularly those of an economic nature. The Germans who had civilised Bohemia held the key positions and were not inclined to give them up to the native population, to let themselves be deprived of their privileges. In the days of Hus the Roman Catholic Church in Bohemia was always called the German Church. The struggle for the Czech instead of the Latin sermon and the struggle for a Czech preponderance at the University of Prague were struggles for a national church, a national school. Hus, who had national feeling, and came from the linguistic frontier, gained both these ends in his lifetime. He also recognised the limits that must be set to the nation's claims if they were to bear fruit. When he repeatedly declared after his victory that he preferred a good German to a bad Czech, it meant that for the sake of justice he strove for national freedom but regarded it as a means to a supra-national justice and order.

Hussitism had become more than the first historical move in the direction of revolt against the hierarchy of the Church. More was at stake, although disguised under different names, than church doctrine and deviations from it : substantially the issue was freedom and the individual search for truth, and as Hus launched this struggle, the dates of his life and death are more important than those of stories about America and the predatory expeditions of the Spanish Conquistadores. In his treatise " De Trinitate," Hus writes : " From the earliest days of my studies I have abided by this my rule that as soon as I learn to know sounder opinion, with joy and in all humility I abandon the earlier one." That is the beginning of modern thought. Threatened with death by burning at the stake he cried out : " Instruct me ! " That is the beginning of modern thought. And for these reasons Hus stands at the well-springs of modern times. He was a warrior of God : he fought for divine truth alone. But he thereby unconsciously began that fight for human dignity and freedom which characterises the new age.

To-day, we probably stand at the end of the epoch which we call the Modern Times. It therefore seems important to be clear about its beginnings in order to recognise wherein its significance lies. Human freedom, which recently seemed victorious and secure, is once more threatened and once more called in question. It grew in detaching itself from the religious soil but threatens to die now that soil is destroyed. The struggle of Hus, who unconsciously united divine truth and human freedom, can perhaps teach us how they may consciously be united.

A word about the paradoxical conditions that made his struggle possible in such an age as his. When Charles IV died, Wenceslas, his successor, continued in the main the foreign policy of the House of Luxembourg. The ties with the court in Paris were maintained and indeed should have been strengthened by the marriage of Anne, Wenceslas' sister, to the King of France. This was also the wish of the cardinals who supported Clement VII, the " French Pope," after the schism. But then Rome intervened and the cardinals who supported Urban VI paved Anne's way to the English throne. At the end of 1381 she arrived in London and was wedded to Richard II, the son of the

Black Prince who had won the Battle of Crécy against John of Luxembourg, Anne's blind grandfather, and taken as his crest the three vultures' feathers in the helmet of the King of Bohemia, France's ally.

The English made a gift of fifteen thousand pounds to the Bohemian court for the bride of their sixteen-year-old king, but Prague did not become the ally of the English crown in the struggle with France : the Luxembourgs did not wish to fight one Pope for the sake of another but to end the schism in the church. Nothing remains for the English but the memory of " good Queen Anne " since the Queen died without issue : the Czechs received more—the moral foundations for the Hussite struggle, " Wyclifism pure and simple," as Professor Trevelyan calls it. The Czech students who visited Oxford must certainly have brought back to Bohemia not only the doctrines of the English reformer but also news of John Ball and the Peasants' Revolt which took place the year Anne arrived in England, of the leader Wat Tyler, and of the Lollards. These early social movements may have made little impression on Hus himself : political aims were too remote from him. But not from the Hussites who led the first national revolution against the Church of Rome and a hundred years before the Reformation showed that for the sake of religion a whole people may rise in revolt.

The abundance of ideas of the Hussites not only on religious but also on political regeneration cannot here be discussed. But we may remember in an age which is again striving for a peaceful form of co-existence for the various nations that George of Podebrady, the only Hussite king the Czechs ever had, was the first who wished to follow up the decaying Holy Roman Empire with a kind of League of Nations. In the sixties of the fifteenth century, three hundred years before Kant, four hundred years before Victor Hugo and four hundred and fifty years before Wilson, George of Podebrady suggested a League of Christian Princes that reminds us of yesterday and to-day in the modernity of its proposals. These were not carried out but the idea continued to live on among the people and has often found political and poetic expression. And the name of John Hus has remained so alive among his people that after the re-creation of the Czechoslovak State there was a rebirth of Hussitism if only on a slight scale. At that time T. G. Masaryk wrote in his book, " The World Revolution " :

" Many demand in the name of progress that the religious question be left in quiescence, and assert that we cannot return to the Middle Ages. This is an abundantly confused and unprogressive point of view. Nowhere to-day does the religious question mean a simple resumption of the old church forms. It is alleged that the modern Czech does not believe as Hus did and that Hus was nearer to Rome than to us. True, the modern Czech no longer believes what and as Hus believed, but does he believe as Rome? True, we do not believe as Hus did, but Hus and his followers are an example to us of moral determination, certitude and religious sincerity. Hus began the fight against the worldliness of the church, and the nation followed him: his fight for a higher morality and religion, sealed with the sacrifice of his life, was the fight against the moral decadence of the church, the priesthood and the papacy."

The many elements in Hussitism that are worthy of study may justify this new book on Hus. An age of constant ferment and change like our own may be able to recognise new aspects of the martyr's life, may be able to interpret it anew. The facts that we relate may be of service in this.

BOOK ONE

IN THE STREAM OF TIME

DEATH OF AN EPOCH

THREE hours after sunset on the evening of November 29, 1378, Charles IV, King of Bohemia, Emperor of the Holy Roman Empire of the German Nation and third ruler of the House of Luxembourg, died in the castle of Prague. He had reached the age of sixty-three. The same night a fire broke out in the Hospital of the Knights of the Cross. It raged unopposed as everyone had thronged to the Castle. Those of the sick who were able to rise from their beds fled into the sharp frosty night : the rest perished in the flames. Aroused at last to the danger, the people of the neighbouring streets fought to keep the fire from spreading to their houses. The dead were buried hugger-mugger, for preparations for the funeral of the ruler allowed of no distractions.

Gorgeously attired, the Emperor lay in state for eleven days. In the daytime the people came to stare at him and listen to the Masses that were being said in all the churches and monasteries of Prague. At night they congregated in the Cathedral to take part in the last service of the day.

The funeral procession did not begin until December 11. Five hundred and sixty-four men, clad in black, paced before the coffin, holding aloft wax candles weighing two pounds apiece. A hundred and fourteen of them had been provided by King Wenceslas IV, son and heir of the dead Emperor, a hundred and fifty more by the citizens of the Old Town and New Town, the old and new parts of Prague, which formed independent cities in those days, and three hundred by the Guilds. They were followed by the Canons with their trains, the pupils of eighteen parish schools, monks of all the monastic orders, and seven thousand Masters and scholars of Prague University.

The proud climax of the procession was the array of banners of the ten lands ruled by Charles. Each banner was escorted by three horsemen with clothes and saddlecloth in the colours and with the emblems of the banner. Behind them a knight bore the helmet and the naked sword of the Emperor, held in reverse as a sign of mourning.

Then came the man who was the occasion of all this pomp. The Emperor, wrapped in a purple cloak embroidered with gold, lay on a bier draped with gold brocade. White gloves had been drawn on his hands, and rings on his fingers. The imperial crown lay at his head, the Lombard crown to his right, and the Bohemian to his left. The orb, with cross and sword, was also to his left, and within reach of the dead right hand was the sceptre. Twelve knights held a golden canopy over the bier.

Wenceslas, the eldest son, heir to the Empire, followed. Beside him walked his ten-year-old brother Sigismund, who had already been ruler of Mark Brandenburg for some months. Behind came the wives of the princes, with no fewer than a hundred ladies of the court. At a suitable distance the wives of the richer citizens followed in twenty-six carts with a due display of wealth.

Five hundred noblemen of Bohemia and Moravia followed beneath a sea of banners.

The procession lasted until December 15, wending its way from Hradcany, the hill of the new castle, over the Small Side, the most fashionable quarter of Prague, and the Old Town and New Town to Vysehrad, the hill of the old castle. Before the Town Halls and before the monasteries the people paid homage to the mortal remains of their sovereign. In every church Masses were sung. Five hundred candles burnt in Saint Jacob's Church and five hundred in the Cathedral of Saint Vitus.

There was a sharp frost when the procession set out ; seventeen days later the nobles and citizens came wading through melting snow to the Church of the Virgin Mary, where the Emperor lay in state. The crowns, the orb, the sceptre, the sword and the imperial banners still lay beside him, although soon to be handed on, people expected, to his son, with imperial honours. Who could have foretold on that December day that Wenceslas would never become Emperor ?

The Middle Ages had found their last splendid embodiment in Charles IV : he had brought fresh might and dignity to the office of German King and Emperor after a long period of decline, and he had secured this to his heirs by increasing the power of the House of Luxembourg. Life promised fair for Wenceslas ; born on February 26, 1361, he was scarcely two and a half years old when he was crowned King of Bohemia on June 15, 1363 ; and, still a boy, he was crowned King of the Germans on July 6, 1376. Charles' authority secured him an unchallenged recognition seldom accorded to a new ruler in those days. When Charles died Wenceslas had only to go to Rome to receive the imperial crown. His coronation as Emperor elect took place in Aix-la-Chapelle. Only the Pope, however, could crown him Emperor. But Wenceslas never made the journey to Rome, although the Pope urged him to do so. He decided upon it, made hesitant preparations and abandoned the enterprise at the last moment. That was typical of his whole reign. He never saw anything through.

Charles had indeed pondered well all that could be done while he lived. A year before his death he had divided his heritage. Wenceslas had received Bohemia, Silesia and parts of Bavaria, Saxony and Lusatia. Ten-year-old Sigismund had received Mark Brandenburg six months before the death of his father and was claimant to the Hungarian throne as a result of his betrothal to Mary of Hungary. For John, the youngest son, the new Duchy of Goerlitz had been created from parts of Upper and Lower Lusatia. Moravia had been left to Jost and Prokop, his brother's sons. Charles believed that he could die with a quiet mind, having set his house in order. The power of the House of Luxembourg seemed assured by all that human providence could do.

But the problems of the past and of the coming eras alike proved beyond the powers of Wenceslas.

It was maybe his misfortune that he grew up without a mother. Anne of Schweidnitz, Charles' third wife, had died within a year of his birth, and from his third year the little king had his own household. Petrarch declined Charles' invitation to undertake the education of Wenceslas. The teachers provided by the Emperor for his son were certainly good, but they did no more than instil into the young king a fund of knowledge above the average of his days. This enabled him to find enjoyment in theological discussions ; but perhaps this very fondness for scholastic debate prevented him from seeing the fundamentals lying beyond the details. The finest spirit, too, must be spoiled by court flattery from early childhood, and Wenceslas grew vain as better men would have done. He had also inherited a fondness for display from his father.

Charles IV had committed a basic error when he allowed his son the extreme honour of two coronations without the logical sequel of a share in the responsibility of rule. If under the guidance of Charles, a master of statecraft, Wenceslas had learnt the intricacies of government, he might perhaps have developed a sense of fundamental realities.

Family relations, too, were by no means happy. Wenceslas was not only the liege of his brothers but also their guardian until they came of age. He espoused the family cause whenever and wherever opportunity occurred. Ingratitude and hostility were the only response. Repeatedly attacked by brothers and cousins, he finally turned against them, but in spite of bitter experience was always ready to forgive and forget. This readiness to be reconciled was abused again and again.

Wenceslas was not a good man, but he was kindhearted. Fired with the best intentions, he at first attempted to rule, but as soon as things began to go wrong he only made them worse : he would then take refuge in hunting, which he passionately loved, and for weeks would neglect the work of government. At such times he was more concerned with getting hounds, and particularly Italian greyhounds, than with anything else, and his agents scoured Europe for them. He used to take his largest greyhound to his bedchamber in the evening. It is even alleged that Johanna of Bavaria, his first wife, was bitten to death by one of them.

After her death he was afflicted with a mania for drink, which has been attributed to an unquenchable thirst resulting from an attempt to poison him. Soon his life was nothing but an alternation between outbursts of drunken wrath and fits of repentance. He would fly into a rage and, in the face of all reason, make autocratic decisions fraught with fateful consequences. Sober again, he would try to make good the ill he had done. His thin, delicate, finely knit face gives a wrong impression. He went to ever coarser excesses, and needed increasingly weak and subservient courtiers. The company of the old nobility made demands he could not meet : he surrounded himself instead with petty knights and burghers. He did indeed genuinely love the common people and they remained true to him to the end, but his choice of favourites was governed more and more by his fear of strength of character. Thus he not only drove the disappointed nobles to rebellion : he was also involved in petty intrigues by petty advisers.

There is no truth in the stories invented about him afterwards to blacken the picture of the only too lukewarm patron of John Hus. Charles had three daughters before Wenceslas was born. It was easy enough to assert that he was a cobbler's son substituted for a daughter so that there might at last be an heir to the throne. He is said to have fouled his baptismal water, while the house in which the water had been warmed was burnt by God's wrath.

At his coronation as King of Bohemia at two and a half years old he polluted the altar, say the legends, which also relate that he was a monster, a horror to all his contemporaries, going through the streets at night violating the citizens' wives and knocking the heads off statues. A cook who had roasted a joint unsatisfactorily was himself roasted by Wenceslas on the spit, according

WENCESLAS
ROI
DE BOHEME.
B. Picart In. 1712.

to other stories, and when out hunting he is said to have shot monks.

Not a word of all this can be proved. In actual fact, as an occidental Haroun al Rashid he would go out in disguise to buy bread, and if he were cheated he would have the baker fined or given corporal punishment and his bread distributed to the poor. He did the same with butchers, tradesmen of all kinds, and artisans. He once worked for a whole day in a vineyard. The result of this day's work was the first social reform by Wenceslas; the employer had to give his workers an hour's break at midday.

In the first two years after the death of his father, Wenceslas was a good ruler. From filial piety or from recognition of his own shortcomings, he made use of the advisers of Charles IV. But Archbishop Ocko of Vlasim and the Bishops Albert of Sternberg and John of Neumarkt were too old to ensure the continuance of good rule. They all died in the same year, 1380; and then Wenceslas stood powerless in the face of times whose complications his father himself would hardly have been competent to master.

The order created by Charles IV for long remained apparently intact, cloaking the work of destruction being wrought by the weakness of his successor. Only after fifteen years did it become clear that it was crumbling.

Wenceslas was perpetually involved in conflicts. First of all his quarrels with the Archbishop assumed ever more threatening forms. At the beginning of March, 1393, Wenceslas, King of Bohemia, wrote to John Jenstejn, Archbishop of Prague: "Archbishop, give me back the castle of Roudnice and my other castles and keep clear of my country Bohemia. If you raise your hand against me or mine I will drown you and make an end of the dispute. Come to Prague!"

The Archbishop naturally hesitated to accept this blunt invitation. He did not lack good will to make up the quarrel; he had already set out from his stronghold of Roudnice and was on his way to Prague when the king's letter reached him in a village near the city. He took fright at it and turned back. However, the king's counsellors who had delivered the letter reported that Wenceslas' intentions were of the best; the letter had been written in a fit of rage, but in the meantime better counsels would have prevailed. They begged the Archbishop to comply with the king's orders since he alone could settle the quarrel that kept the country in perpetual disquiet. They themselves undertook that no harm would come to him. And thus he finally consented to go.

A treaty was indeed prepared and it seemed as though everything was in order. The king, solemnly attended, went out in great state to meet the Archbishop, who was attended by his official, Nicholas Puchnik, the Vicar-General John of Pomuk, and other ecclesiastical dignitaries. He was also protected by a small armed force.

The two processions met in Small Side, not far from the famous bridge erected over the Vltava by Wenceslas' father. Here stood the Maltese Church, the Romanesque towers of which, fortress-like, bore witness to the power of the Church. It was night. Flickering torch-light fell upon the two rulers as they approached each other.

Hardly had Wenceslas caught sight of his old enemy than he

was overcome once more with rage. " Archbishop," he rebuked him, " you have excommunicated my advisers without my knowledge. You have confirmed the appointment of the Abbot of Kladruby. You have imputed heresy and false doctrine to my Chamberlain. You have asked nothing and acted on your own powers. You shall make amends to me for this."

The Archbishop was disconcerted. In an attempt to save the situation he bowed his knee to the king. But the king only imitated the gesture mockingly. He pointed to Puchnik, to the Archbishop, to Pomuk and others. " You shall drown, and you and you." He ordered them to be seized.

" To the Chapterhouse with you. I want to find out who is the ringleader."

A scuffle ensued, and in the confusion the Archbishop, with the help of his men, succeeded in fighting his way through to his palace. The same night he fled, escaping down the Vltava by boat from Prague, and he reached one of his castles near the frontier unmolested.

Pomuk, Puchnik and a few other ecclesiastics, however, were seized. The king himself accompanied them to the Chapterhouse of the Prague Cathedral. There the aged Dean Bohuslav attempted to oppose him, but the king beat him on the head with the hilt of his sword till he collapsed, streaming with blood, and was thrown into prison. A long interrogation began, but no-one confessed anything, perhaps because there was nothing to confess. The king suspected a conspiracy between the Archbishop and the rebellious Bohemian nobles. He kept asking about the ringleaders, but learned nothing. Wenceslas grew more and more enraged and commanded the prisoners to be taken to the Town Hall of the Old Town. There in the torture chambers the obstinate had before now been made to talk.

Here was waged once more that struggle between temporal and ecclesiastical power which recurs throughout the whole of the Middle Ages ; always undecided, always threatening, it was ready at any minute to discharge itself in blood. But this strange outbreak had arisen from singularly unworthy causes, as unworthy indeed as the representatives of the two powers who here confronted each other.

John of Jenstejn was by origin a typical Prince of the Church of those days. Belonging to the old nobility and early destined for the Church, he was even as a boy master of seven rich benefices which permitted him all worldly magnificence. When at twenty-eight years of age he became Archbishop of Prague he attributed it to the Virgin and vowed to reform his life ; but he rapidly fell under the spell of the free and full-blooded life of the Court, to which he belonged as Chancellor. He was one of the gayest of the young nobles of the Empire. A fearful shock was needed to rouse him to a consciousness of his spiritual mission. Archbishop Ludwig of Magdeburg, who led much the same life as he, died a terrible death. A fire broke out at a great feast. Surprised in the midst of a dance, Archbishop Ludwig carried his lady through the crowd to save her. But the stairs broke under him and he was killed. John saw in this the punishment of God which hung over his own head.

He suddenly became an ascetic, scourging himself night after night until he collapsed amidst his own blood ; he fasted to the extreme, slept only three hours, and in the cold on bare boards with the Bible as his pillow. But his body was not equal to the burdens he laid upon it and he became sick, embittered and irascible. He was numbered amongst the most devout men in the whole country, but his devotion had little in common with true religious feeling. He was not deeply concerned with reformation of the dissipated clergy ; he laboured rather to get the Visitation of Our Lady observed as a holy day. He was concerned with pomp and power. He wrestled bitterly to build up the power of the Church at the expense of the Throne. He rejected no means ; he excommunicated, threatened with interdict, simply to obtain the pettiest worldly advantage for the Church, whose sublimest weapons were blunted in squabbles about money, position and privilege.

Wenceslas, on the other hand, who might legitimately fight for it, did not know how to safeguard power. As genuine power slipped through his fingers he contended ever more doggedly for small claims, needing wealth and sinecures to bind to him the greedy parvenues with whom he surrounded himself. His outbursts of rage, normally disastrous, were here still of service to him. He could encounter the Archbishop in this realm, where both understood how to deploy their forces. We see here indeed the age-old struggle between king and Church finding its outlet in the pettiest of squabbling.

This time it was once again a question of trifles. The Abbot of Kladruby, holder of a rich benefice, was on his deathbed. Wenceslas forbade the election of a new Abbot, wishing to create a new bishopric to give to a favourite. The Archbishop was determined to prevent this encroachment on his power. To forestall the king, John of Pomuk sent to Kladruby a signed confirmation of the appointment of the new Abbot before the old one was dead. A blank was left for the name to be inserted after the election had taken place. Thus there was a new Abbot in office before the king had learnt of the death of the old one.

Such disputes were frequent. The Archbishop excommunicated the royal Underchamberlain, Huler, who had protected the Jews, burnt a student of theology and executed a priest. The sentences were not unjust according to the law of the times ; existing documents tell only of the crimes of the priest, who had stolen from a country church chalices, crucifixes and even monstrances containing relics, and spent the proceeds on harlots in Prague. Priests, however, came under the jurisdiction of the Church and not of the secular authorities. Jews, much-wooed victims, were indeed under the king's jurisdiction but the Archbishop wanted them persecuted on religious grounds. In all these instances the actual bone of contention was immaterial ; power and money were the real issue.

The prisoners in the king's hands had to pay for the sins of the Archbishop. Late on the following afternoon Wenceslas himself went to the Town Hall to watch the torture. " Who is the ringleader ?" he demanded again and again.—Was the Archbishop alone or was he in league with the dangerous nobles ? He finally believed that some of the prisoners had nothing to confess. He dismissed them after they had promised to reveal nothing of what was taking place and in future to work against the Archbishop. His anger flared up anew with Puchnik and Pomuk. Torture after torture was used on them. As they lay on the rack and were still silent the king snatched a torch from one of the torturers and thrust it into their sides. The smell of burnt flesh brought him to his senses, and Puchnik, too, was able to buy his life with promises. Probably he had nothing to confess ; the conspiracy with the nobles could hardly have begun at this time.

But the king had gone too far. John of Pomuk was beyond speech. But if released to die in safety he might nevertheless betray what had happened. In the king's eyes he was mainly to blame. He had signed the Kladruby document. Rage and revenge had kept the king's hand steady as the flame had eaten into his living flesh, and under their sway he stopped at nothing. Pomuk's hands were bound and his mouth held open with a wooden gag ; head and feet were bound together so that his body was bent to a wheel. Thus was he borne in public procession through the streets of Prague, across the Old Town Square, through the narrow alleys to the famous bridge, and there, on the same day, March 20, 1393, at nine o'clock in the evening, he was thrown into the river. He was indeed drowned by Wenceslas.

The people looked on with timid misgiving at this strange procession. Did they murmur against the king for it ? Did they murmur against the Archbishop ?

John of Pomuk too was not of heroic stature. He did not become a priest till lucrative offices beckoned and then he used his power to trade in still more lucrative ones. Legend reports on his death : " Hereupon the river dried up and when the people could no longer grind their rye and had no bread they began to murmur against the king."

But the Vltava has dried up often enough and the watermills been idle ; and the people certainly raise their voice when they have no bread.

The Church abused its power too publicly for the people, in spite of their piety and superstition, to lament the death of a dignitary of the Church. Even the legend does not report that the people were angry until they began to seek someone to blame for their hunger. The terrible death of Pomuk was only one small sign of storm in tempestuous times.

It had no significance ascribed to it until the Hussite movement, which began shortly after it, had ebbed. Three hundred years later Pomuk was canonised as John of Nepomuk. His figure is surrounded by a host of legends. He is said to have been the Queen's confessor. The king wanted to tear from him secrets of the confessional and he was cruelly murdered because of his heroic refusal. The Vltava laid bare his body to enforce his burial in the Cathedral, and for three nights a light appeared above the corpse of the martyr until it was found. Mild little miracles were wrought by his tomb. But these legends were invented a hundred and fifty years later by the Jesuits who designed them to erase the memory of a greater man than Pomuk. To help people forget, to Pomuk were assimilated the features of this greater man ; he alone had been the Queen's confessor, he alone had had the strength and purity of character to go to death for his faith. And when Catholicism, saved once more, erected statues of John of Nepomuk in every town and village of Bohemia, the statues too had the features of the greater man. They looked like John Hus.

But the hour of John Hus had not struck when John of Pomuk, intriguing Vicar-General and hunter of rich benefices, was drowned in this ghastly fashion, a victim of petty politics and not a martyr to a great faith.

The king's anger seemed to have brought peace and quiet to the land once more. The king himself slid back into yielding penitence. He besieged the Archbishop with messages, deeply distressed at what he had done, and begged the Archbishop to return that he might make amends, nay, bend his knee before him. And he threatened that if the Archbishop did not come, he would in despair do many an evil thing which would fall on the head of the Archbishop.

But the Archbishop over-estimated his own power. He appeared to yield, conceded what he must, and then slipped away to Rome to ask the Pope's help against the king. An interdict on Bohemia, banning all the offices of the Church, and intolerable for the people, would force Wenceslas to surrender. The Pope, however, decided in favour of the king.

Boniface IX, who then ruled in Rome, was himself in the utmost difficulties. The Church was in confusion ; it had no longer one head. In Avignon there was an Antipope. The entire Catholic world was split. Rome or Avignon, which would win ? All that was certain was the Church was in the greatest danger. What did the Pope at such a time care about the troubles of an over-zealous Archbishop ? Wenceslas on the other hand could help the Pope. Perhaps he might yet decide to come to Rome for his imperial coronation. And the Pope who crowned the Emperor was the true head of the Church. The Holy Roman Empire still included Italy and Burgundy, and its ruler was still, in name at least, the highest lord of Christendom. The glamour of the holy crown could still, even on an unworthy head, unite again the crumbling world of the Middle Ages. The Pope had just performed an act of grace conferring a special distinction on the king ; the Jubilee of 1390, celebrated in Rome, was re-celebrated in Prague in 1393, the year of Pomuk's death, because many Bohemians, the king among them, had been unable to make the pilgrimage to Rome. Ceaselessly the Pope spurred the sluggish king on to the step that would have saved both of them ; the Archbishop, too, was his instrument in this purpose.

The terms of the Prague Jubilee Year were particularly favourable. In every Jubilee Year the pilgrims received plenary remission of their sins. The indulgence granted in Prague was to be as complete as that granted in Rome in 1390. It was only necessary on certain days to visit four churches specially appointed for this purpose, the people of Prague fifteen times, foreigners seven times. After this they had to go to confession, and finally lay on the altar of the Vysehrad Church the sum they would have expended on the journey to Rome, the amount being fixed according to wealth and position. Half of the money remained in Prague for the extension of the Vysehrad

Church and others ; Prague too kept the free-will offerings that usually flowed into the Church. The sale of indulgences, too, one of the main sources of income of the Pope, was on this occasion to be for the benefit of the Church in Bohemia. Finally, the clergy had to yield a tithe of their takings to Wenceslas to defray the cost of his journey to Rome.

This Jubilee Year saved Wenceslas for a while. It began badly in the midst of strife on March 16 ; the Archbishop refused to proclaim the solemn opening of the Jubilee. Wenceslas, however, made immediate use of it to buy absolution for all the injuries and wrongs done the Archbishop and Pomuk ; these sins were forgiven him. When the Archbishop came to Prague at the beginning of April, he tardily performed the solemn opening of the Jubilee Year. Prague awoke to the consciousness of her honour. Once again, however, Wenceslas seemed to be at a disadvantage ; priests said that the Jubilee Year had only become effective with the Archbishop's opening of it and that Wenceslas' absolution was therefore invalid. But again the Archbishop had to yield, and much against his will admit that indulgences were valid from the beginning of the year. When he went to Rome to prepare humiliations for Wenceslas and Bohemia, Prague was wrapped in the gaiety and splendour of the rare festival. And what had begun so badly ended for Wenceslas with a stroke of luck. He discovered that the Papal Legate was embezzling the money earmarked for Rome ; he confiscated it and himself sent it to the Pope, thus putting him under a firm obligation.

The bells of Prague rang solemnly over the town. In slow procession the pilgrims drew towards the hill of Hradcany, where the great cathedral was approaching completion. They passed out of the town to the monastic church of Brevnov, over the bridge to the New Town, founded by Charles IV and already widespreading and beautiful. Here was the Corpus Christi Chapel, a round Gothic structure, the third halting-place of those seeking pardon. The pilgrimage ended on the hill of Vysehrad, in the vast basilica dedicated to St. Peter and St. Paul. This was about to be enlarged and embellished. But it had not much longer to stand; the Hussites would soon raze it to the ground.

Enthusiastic preachers cried the sale of indulgences. Only a short while before, voices had been raised against such sales, which meant simony, a confusion of money and repentance, of business and faith; and fresh sins instead of forgiveness of old ones. But the general enthusiasm swept aside doubts ; one priest alone, Magister Wenceslas Rohle, spoke of fraud, but even he only in secret. Clergy and laity alike saw a new chance of stemming the oncoming tide of disintegration ; simple and sophisticated alike pinned their hopes to this festival that showed their two masters, king and Church, in unity. They willingly conformed, anxious to be able to believe once more without any shadow of doubt. With sins forgiven the old life might return, that old secure life to be found only in the bosom of the one redeeming church.

In the midst of the procession there was seen with the rest a lean, shabbily dressed student whom few knew. He listened with bliss to the sermons announcing salvation. Sins had tormented him ; now they slipped from him as he offered up four groschens on the altar. It was his last money, and he would have to live on dry bread for many a day. Yet such a sacrifice seemed small for such grace.

The name of this unknown man was John Hus. Nineteen years later, on another such occasion, he was to unleash a storm that would shake the whole Kingdom.

THE University of Prague, where Hus studied, was at once the mainstay and the glory of Bohemia. Founded by Charles IV in 1348, on the model of Paris, it was the first university in central and eastern Europe, and secured to Prague the dignity due to the residence of the Emperor. The University was organised as four "nations." This had at first a regional but no political significance, only revealing what a centre Prague had become. The Bavarian "nation" included students from the whole of southern Germany, the Tyrol and Switzerland, the Rhineland and the Netherlands; the Saxon, students from northern Germany, Scandinavians and Finns; the Polish, students from Poland, Prussia, Lithuania, Silesia and Thuringia; the Bohemian, students from Bohemia, Moravia, Austria, Hungary, Croatia and Transylvania. The University was in itself a large world. In 1389, when Prague numbered eighty thousand inhabitants, seven thousand belonged to the University according to very cautious estimates. Others set the figure much higher. The figure is an unusual one for those days.

This numerous world was also a powerful one. Completely autonomous, it had its own government and laws and was subordinated only to the king and the Pope, under whose patronage the University stood. But the Pope and the king themselves had to woo the vote of the University as they would that of a great power, for it carried decisive weight and influence. In the dispute between the two Popes, soon to reach a settlement, the voices of the Universities of Paris and Oxford, Prague and Padua, were often far more important than those of the rulers of the countries where the universities were situated. Hus was such a significant figure only because for a while the University of Prague stood at his back.

On January 3 of every year "Quodlibet," the great public debate of the University, began. It often lasted an entire month. The debate was attended not only by all the Masters and scholars but also by the king and the Court, the Archbishop and the chief dignitaries of the Church, any outstanding foreign visitors and selected guests from among the merchants and officials of the town. This was no empty formality; it attested the great significance of the University for Prague, for Germany and indeed for the whole of Europe. And the distinguished audience did not merely listen with patient endurance to day-long discussions of the most abstract problems but followed them with interest ; scholarship then was closely linked to daily life. The University was, indeed, a child of the Church. But teaching, building and mounting guard at the very sources of ecclesiastical life, it could often exercise an influence which placed it even above the Church.

At the time of John Hus, however, Prague University was declining in importance. New German universities in Vienna and Heidelberg, Erfurt and Cologne, and a Polish university in Cracow had drawn away many scholars of Prague. But in Prague itself this decline long remained imperceptible. For John Hus, the poor peasant boy, the new world which he entered there was overwhelmingly great and powerful. He vanished into it like a drop of water into an ocean.

Detailed as is our knowledge of his life once his political career had begun, we know little of his youth. Why should records be kept of a life that did not seem marked for any special tasks ? We do not know the age of the student who in 1393 bought an indulgence. July 6, 1369, is regarded as his birthday, but the year is uncertain and the day the result of a misunderstanding. " Birthday " for the Hussites meant the day of death, since death for them was the birth to the life of the spirit. A later age which had forgotten this notation accepted the term " birthday " literally. We do not know when Hus first came to Prague. His name first appears in the University records in 1391, but he must have been in Prague for some time. A few remarks of Hus himself are our only source for his life as a student.

He was poor. Thus at first he learnt only the reverse side of Prague's splendour. As his name appears in the records, accommodation must have been provided for him ; every student had to attach himself to a Master and dwell with him in one of the great lodging houses, the " scholars' halls." But this did not mean that his material needs were assured. The Masters were not in the habit of using the proceeds of their often rich foundations for their scholars. Those who could not pay had to go begging ; and they were not even allowed to keep what they thus obtained. Food or money, it had to be handed over to the Master, who gave back only a meagre part.

Hus's stony road to the heights began in the very depths. Like all poor scholars of his times he must have slept on the bare ground and made his way, dirty and ragged, one of the hosts of wretched people who plagued the rich. He was even without a spoon at times, for he himself wrote : " When I was a hungry scholar, I made a spoon of my bread as long as I had peas, and then I ate my spoon." From time to time however he could gain a little by performing small offices in the Church. The reformer began as a beggar and server.

Legend indeed paints in a heroic background. Hus, it is said was reading the story of St. Laurence to a circle of comrades. He suddenly put his hand in the fire. Startled, a friend snatched it out. Hus reproached him : " Why are you frightened by such a little thing? I wanted to prove that I had sufficient courage to bear but a small part of the sufferings that St. Laurence endured." We are hereby supposed to learn his early consciousness of his vocation and of the death at the stake that lay before him.

This legend is certainly no truer than all the others that evolved later. As server he came into immediate contact with the Church, but took no interest in the offices he performed. "When as a scholar," he confessed later, " I sang vigils with the others, we merely ground them out in order to get through them, for others pocketed the money and ploughed and harrowed with us." This does not betray religious feeling, but only a sense of being exploited.

He joined with more liveliness and fun in the extraordinary student customs of his age, as he himself once more reveals. This age, it must be remembered, not only built the Gothic cathedral but also decorated it with devilish faces, obscene offspring of a secular imagination. The students, for example, used to mock the Christmas festival in a grotesque procession. They chose from among themselves " a Bishop of the Innocents," dressed him up comically, set him backwards on a she-ass and led him into the Cathedral of St. Vitus. There the Mass was burlesqued. The " bishop " received a bowl of soup and a jug of wine. He ate and drank. Then instead of candles, his fellow students carried a huge torch before him as they conducted him from altar to altar. He stopped at each one, raised his leg, and " consecrated " the altar. Once this ceremony was over they all turned their skin coats furry side out and, miming animals, danced wildly. Hus, too, took part in this. " While I was still young in years and understanding, I myself made one in this wild rubric." This does not suggest any deep reverence for the Church. That this mummery, a survival of pagan times, was regarded only as a joke and not as blasphemy also shows the lack of any gulf between religious and daily life. Hus brought the breath of daily life to his profession, which was for him a profession and not a vocation. He simply took the most promising way to prosperity and comfort for one lacking wealth and position.

More revealing than these few confessions about his early student years are the reports of Hus's early youth, scanty though they are.

Hus came from Husinec, a village in southern Bohemia. His parents, poor peasants, wanted their son to have an easier life and sent him to the grammar school in the nearby market town of Prachatice. This town had grown rich from its situation at the end of the " Golden Way " to Passau, a trade route even in the Roman days. Prachatice grammar school, which was connected with the monastery, went back to the thirteenth century, when Otakar II of the House of Premysl presented the market centre to the Prague foundation of Vysehrad.

Prachatice developed into a town when the Provost John, a son of Otakar II, distributed the land among the beneficiaries and licensed them to levy duties on goods using the Passau road. The citizens of Prachatice then contributed to the support of the grammar school, in which Hus paid for his education and bread by acting as server.

Prachatice was until recently still to some extent a German town. In those days it was perhaps mainly German, but, as later on, surrounded by purely Czech villages. These villages were peopled largely by free peasants who served as frontier guards; as such they were immediate subjects of the prince of the province or of the burgrave except where nobles had seized the frontier roads in order to exact tolls.

When John, first of the House of Luxembourg, came to Bohemia he had to secure his kingdom by gifts to the native nobility. These times saw the building of " The Castle of Hus," to which the village of Husinec and twenty-two other villages belonged and from which the boy John later took his name. It was built in the year 1341.

A brief glance backwards will best show what a change this meant for the peasants who till then had enjoyed freedom in this part of the country at least.

One of the earliest sources of information about the life of the Slav people is a remark of Constantine Porphyrogenetos, Emperor of Byzantium, who said of the southern Slavs in the tenth century (and his words applied to the Czechs of the previous century): " These peoples have no princes except old men called Zupans, as is the case among the other Slav peoples." Feudalisation followed on western, that is German, lines. This was most clearly evident in the fact that military service, till then a popular duty and right, slowly became a privilege. In the twelfth century the Zupans or eldest members of the clans were already called " nobiles," to distinguish them from the younger males of the clan, the " druhones." The difference meant initially that the " nobiles " were, so to speak, professional soldiers while the " druhones " went to war only when summoned by their " graf." But " graf " at that time was still a title attached to an office and not a hereditary one. Princes of the ducal houses were called " duces," but sons of the " graf " only became " grafs " if they succeeded to the office.

But the development of a nobility owing their position to service could not be held up and as the patriarchal nobility assumed offices and the serving nobility received estates, the margin became blurred. The citizen Huler, for example, was made Master of Worlik under Wenceslas. Under the House of Luxembourg the title of " baro " was first used in Bohemia. It was restricted to the holders of court offices. All the other nobility were called " nobiles." There still remained the free eldest members of the clans, now called " Vladicones," but by the second quarter of the fourteenth century they had already disappeared. Their place was taken by a new hereditary class of knights and landowners from whom military service was due. One had now to be born to military service ; the old clan organisation had collapsed.

With this went the freedom of the peasants. The old community house had been replaced by the house of the nobleman. Grain, meat, bread and beer which the member of the clan could formerly take from his farm freely he could henceforth only obtain by surrendering his raw products. In addition, the lord had the right to purchase all the peasant's produce, former communal amenities like pastures, hunts, the cutting of wood, fisheries, mines and beehives now belonged to the lord, along with the rights of grinding, slaughtering and distilling. In the fourteenth century all memory of the clan as such had perished. The land belonged exclusively to the lord ; the peasant had merely a piece assigned for his use and not even his son's inheritance was sure. Although usually permitted, it was never recognised by the nobles as a right. Thomas Stitny, the Czech moral philosopher of the fourteenth century, sought to base his theory of the freedom of mankind on the sentence : " Though the goods may belong to the lord, the human being belongs to God ! " The lord's ownership of the land was no longer attacked ; nobody even cast doubts on his right.

But does the rise of feudalism alone suffice to explain the

decay of the clans and the enslavement of the peasants? Certainly power was an important factor, but not the only one. The development of the mines, especially in the thirteenth century, brought to the country money that sought a use. The ecclesiastical ban on interest forbade the increase of possessions by lending. To circumvent this, the worldly minded, with the pious in the vanguard, purchased copyhold deeds and peasants' services. Such deeds were transferable and thus the peasants passed continually from the ownership of one lord to another. Often several capitalists in one village combined, as when, for example, John Hus and three others together bought a copyhold. This perpetual change of master wrought a complete estrangement between lord and subject.

The decline had already set in in the eleventh century. As the payment of their rent often compelled the peasants to take long journeys to the seats of their oft-changing lords, the tillage of the ground became endangered. The burdens imposed by the count—levies for the building of castles, roads and bridges—were so crushing that often the free peasant simply abandoned his farm. To avoid the unlimited demands of the public authority he would often voluntarily accept thraldom, thereby freeing himself from corvées for the province. By the twelfth century the small holding had almost disappeared. Originally the free peasants had paid the lord a tax in return for armed protection; towards the end of the twelfth century this no longer represented a source of income, as nine-tenths of the free peasants had become thralls. The burden of war was borne now only by the lords. This was not due to their concern for their subjects, but only to lack of possessions which prevented the peasant serving in war, for the warrior had to equip himself and the peasants now had nothing left but their slavery.

This was the society into which John Hus was born. The peculiar conditions of the frontier regions meant that memories still lingered in his homeland of a time when the soil belonged to all. Hus grew up among Czech peasants who consciously and bitterly saw their rights being curtailed by the ever stronger nobles, the German king and the rapacious Church, which they also called the "German Church." They enviously watched the German colonists and citizens who with self-government and their rights intact grew richer and richer. There was an atmosphere of social and national tension among the Czechs which Hus was to understand as no other learned man had ever done.

School opened up to him a new world. He entered the town, which aroused reverent admiration in the peasant, despite his grudge against the town dwellers, and he entered the sphere of the Church which commanded universal devotion ; he suddenly belonged to the circle of the privileged.

At Prachatice the precious salt coming from Passau to Bohemia was unloaded, and from here the grain and malt, corn, brandy and furs were sent from Bohemia to Germany and the West. Merchants from far countries could here be heard telling their tales of the wide world they knew so well. And these breath-taking strangers treated with reverence the monks to whom Hus already half belonged. It would mean many years of hard work, but he nevertheless was sure that he would not remain a simple peasant.

He successfully climbed to a higher social level. Ambition, at first material and later spiritual, gave the peasant boy, the humble server, the necessary strength to make his way in a new world that once had seemed unattainable. He would never be ashamed of his origin, he would never forget the peasants, the beggars, the humiliated and down-trodden ; yet he had nevertheless a strikingly high respect for all form, whether scholastic or social : it was respect for what he had achieved through hard and bitter struggles. Goaded as he was by reforming zeal, he never aimed at any revolutionary undermining of the established order ; he sought rather to adapt the new to what already existed. He never went as far as his nobly born fellow fighter Jerome, who, born to what Hus had to strive long years to attain, was the more able to do away with it. But this very respect for externals saved Hus from losing himself in them ; his achievement, with its national and social roots, overflowed into the realm of the intellectual and the religious.

For this, too, the ground was prepared in the Prachatice school. True, only the scantiest foundations of knowledge were taught here. Grammar, rhetoric, dialectics, the three sciences of the trivium—the Latin studies of a modern junior grammar school go further. One advantage not usual in such schools was that here were taught some mathematics and astronomy, subjects already belonging to the quadrivium. The modest limits of the material taught in those days can most plainly be seen from the fact that mathematics, the commonest of these subjects today, did not go beyond simple arithmetic. Astronomy consisted of learning by heart a set of verses which served to memorise the holy days. For time then was not fixed by dates, but by the holy days. June 16, 1415, was reckoned as the Sunday after St. Vitus ; June 26 was the Friday before St. John the Baptist, and so on. There being over a hundred holy days in the year, their memorisation was no doubt a great feat of memory, but hardly seemed to merit the name of astronomy.

And yet this astronomy is a good symbol of the methods of this school. Science must not be measured by the standards of today. It had a different aim. The mother tongue was completely dropped in favour of Latin and books were rarities ; this lack had to be made up by learning by heart and as it was in a foreign language material had to be more deeply and completely memorised than today ; knowledge had to be accurately pigeon-holed in the mind, always ready to hand, and details were therefore of greater importance. Education was, above all, a training of the memory and a systematic extension of its scope, preparing the scholar for scholasticism. Hus was here well schooled for this tremendous force, and all his life long he never escaped its spell.

Scholastic knowledge today seems dry, rigid and unintelligible ; it did not aim at the extension of empiric knowledge, the widening of experience or the mastering of reality. Its aim was not therefore more limited and was indeed more daring than that of learning today ; it aimed at nothing less than the union of knowledge and faith. The truth had been vouchsafed : it was comprehensively and finally laid down in Holy Writ, which proceeded from divine revelation. The human mind had only the task of grasping this truth ever more clearly and accurately by meditation, inquiry and discussion. Much knowledge and experience seemed irreconcilable with the Bible, and it was the task of science to bring to light the harmony which must exist. To the limited human mind it seemed that many passages of the Bible were contradictory ; it was the task of dialectics to solve these apparent contradictions. The entire labours of the Fathers of the Church and of mediæval theology were directed to this end : its ideal was the gathering up of all knowledge in one " summa," a systematic exposition of all theology. Scholars should collate all that was available in order to complete the structure and at last set up, in place of the conflicting ideas which had emerged in the course of time, one all-embracing and right explanation.

The way to this end was, above all, debate. In endless arguments the most important theological questions were analysed with a hair-splitting subtlety which we are unable to follow now. The famous scholastic problem of how many angels could stand on the point of a needle, they being incorporeal, is their typical expression. Yet these very debates were the expression of a magnificent faith, the faith that in living speech and discussion the soundness of explanations and arguments is best revealed ; living human expression is thus made the instrument of divine revelation. A trained memory was indispensable for such intellectual work, and even devout Catholics were to admire the ability of Hus and Jerome to stud their speeches with quotations from Holy Writ and the Church Fathers, quoted from memory and without reference to the books.

It is certainly true that in the time of Hus cracks were beginning to appear in the scholastic edifice ; new forces were at work ushering in new times. Scholasticism as the spiritual expression of the Church had already performed its task, spread over centuries, of gradually bringing the barbarians who had destroyed the antique world to the point where they could receive the new culture. In the fourteenth century scholasticism began to be a hindrance ; to the contradictions of the Bible were added the innumerable contradictions in the works of the Fathers of the Church ; to the explanations of the revelation were added the explanations of the explanations ; at the same time the spirit, bound to a rigid truth, became fossilised. The further inquiry proceeded, the more people clung to external details ; the stream of life, too disturbing, was excluded, and the magnificent structure of scholasticism gradually was transformed into a wall cutting off knowledge from life. Finally, vital experience burst the barrier of ever more abstract subtleties.

Hus was one of the moving spirits in this. But it was not without its significance that he had first learnt scholasticism in a provincial school to which the new breath of the times had not yet penetrated ; for he derived from it that inner certitude, that unshakable knowledge, which gave him the tremendous daring to oppose the Church and to accept all the logical consequences in defence of his teaching.

In spite of the slender evidence there can be no doubt that Hus left school with the most important traits of his character already beginning to develop. But the encounter with Prague must at first have shaken him. The difference between the two towns was too crass. Prachatice, which had appeared magnificent to the peasant lad, had its one square and its one church ; the University alone was larger than the whole of Prachatice. Prague, the hundred-towered, was one of the wonders of the world of those days ; even the Italians reported with bated breath of its wealth, its splendid buildings, the brilliance of its teeming life, nourished from all countries. And once again Hus, though he might be compelled to beg, belonged to a privileged circle, which the richest and most distinguished vied with each other to enter ; such a transition could undermine a strong character. In addition, the poverty which had scarcely oppressed him in Prachatice, where he could easily visit his parents, became here in the loneliness of the great city a cruel torment. Welcome any mummery that could make him forget it. Life was a painful business ; there was need to flee it, not to expose oneself to it. The depths in which he had to beg a living were particularly terrible, because at the same time he belonged to the circle of the elect ; the career that was to lift him out of his miseries became his only concern.

Hus was hardworking, but he was obviously so only because he must speedily earn money. Nothing at first suggested any particular talents. In his examinations, as the university records reveal, he was always placed somewhere in the middle of the list. His mind was still turned to worldly things ; he later revealed that he loved fine clothes, rich food and amusements when he was no longer in need and thus was certainly already a Master. He reproached himself : " What pain it is to me that before I was a priest I used frequently to play chess, thus killing time and rousing myself and others to anger through this unhappy game." Or : " I, unhappy creature that I am, will have to pay for it that I had beautiful clothes in abundance, misled by the common vices, estranged from God by a spirit of pride." Certainly in these later memories the over-sensitive conscience of the reformer may be seen, but there is no reason to doubt that for the poor student and the more prosperous Master these were the most important things. Need and poverty had made them especially desirable for him. The fact that he spent his last penny on an indulgence shows that he felt himself to be a sinner, but this feeling, as the great success of this sale of indulgences shows, was a general one. It does not reveal religious feeling, but simply that the reformer was not yet awake.

In the year of Pomuk's death, the Jubilee Year of 1393, Hus won his first academic distinction ; he became Bachelor of Arts. He had to pass difficult examinations and fulfil the complicated formalities of the Middle Ages. He had also with infinite pains to raise the money for the heavy fees, the usual present for the examining Master, and the traditional celebration. Did he notice the course of political events, did he perhaps stand at the side of the alleys through which Pomuk was dragged ? Or was he too deeply absorbed in his own troubles ? However this might be, the age offered the future reformer a most effective object lesson.

The times were drifting towards chaos. Even the strong hand of Charles IV, the great mediator, had no longer been able to settle the conflict. He had, however, been able to keep it in check. Under the feeble rule of Wenceslas, the war of all against all flared up, ravaging the whole of Germany. Any claim, be it never so ill-founded, was settled by war ; the division of estates among brothers, the usual practice in those days, led almost invariably to fighting. The innumerable German princes, whether secular or ecclesiastical, were continually at loggerheads. The most serious armed conflicts sprang from quarrels between the princes and the towns. Here it was clearly visible that a period of transition had set in. The firm framework of the mediæval world was tottering ; the feudal system that had for centuries safeguarded order in Europe was nearing its inevitable collapse. The cities began to take the place due to them in a world in which money was playing an ever more important role.

War, too, which now reigned everywhere, was changing its aspect. The knights did not keep pace with the new armies. Too proud to enrol themselves in standardised units which must obey, they found a last refuge as robber-knights. War was waged by mercenaries, hired by either side, who avoided dangerous pitched battles and, when they could, by-passed the towns, well shielded behind their walls. Their main activity was to ravage the land of the enemy ; the peasants, unable to protect themselves, were the first to suffer in any quarrel. Wars dragged on interminably, never decided. There was scant opportunity for chivalry and daring deeds. Soldiering had become a mechanical profession which simply cost so and so much, and it was through their pockets that large numbers of town-dwellers learnt to know it. Money was above all to be found in the towns and naturally the powerful shifted the heaviest burden on to the shoulders of the weak. Money was exacted with ever-increasing ruthlessness from the common people. Instead of heroism and glorious battles, the suffering and misery of the simple folk, more and more apparent in town and country, were the fruits of war.

In the year 1393 this general malady descended too upon Bohemia ; this richest, best governed and most stably organised part of the heritage of Charles had remained so far sheltered from all fighting. The conflict with the Archbishop was only a faint prelude ; a year later the Bohemian nobles had risen against Wenceslas, led by his cousin Jost, Margrave of Moravia. The king, in name the ruler of all the countries between France and Poland, between the North Sea and Central Italy, was brought to Prague a wretched prisoner, and as the towns rose in his favour was dragged off to southern Bohemia and Austria. War, the general evil, had a more terrible significance for Bohemia, this rich land accustomed to peace, and in this war, moreover, the issue was a German kingship, now in the lowest depths of abasement. An important symbol of the declining Middle Ages.

The first time the Empire felt the shame of it and Wenceslas was quickly freed by an imperial army. " But the king," an old chronicle reports, " was double-faced, like a two-edged sword, letting the one side or the other have the advantage." He concluded treaties and broke them ; he quarrelled with his friends, was reconciled to his enemies and betrayed them again. Vacillating and undecided, yielding yet truculent, he soon dissipated the help of the Empire. Decline could no longer be staved off.

The Luxembourg family abandoned themselves to bitter senseless fratricidal strife ; an orgy of treachery and cunning, of fraud and perfidy, began. Wenceslas invited Jost to negotiate and treacherously took him prisoner. He quarrelled with his brother John, whose intentions were patently honest, and called for help on his brother Sigismund, his most dangerous enemy. Then he had to make up his quarrel again with Jost, who was thinking only of revenge. John died suddenly, obviously poisoned. Was it thanks to Wenceslas or Sigismund ? We do not know. Jost's younger brother always helped Wenceslas, who now handed him over to his enemies for the sake of Jost. Wenceslas's chief advisers were cruelly murdered, apparently at the instigation of Sigismund. But then Wenceslas made his peace with Sigismund and protected the murderers of his friends. There is no crime that was not committed in these wars—and as speedily forgotten.

Thanks to these family traits of character the wars of the Luxembourgs meant a crescendo of the wars ravaging Germany—a crescendo in which all the prophecies of the Apocalypse seemed to be fulfilled. Wenceslas was, in spite of all, the best of them. No means was too base for him when he was attacked, but he was always ready to be reconciled and even to make great concessions. Jost, on the other hand, was nicknamed the Great Liar even in his lifetime. He swore far too often by his expressive beard and never kept a vow. He was inordinately ambitious and greedy, very learned but faithless, cunning, treacherous, and a master of the art of forging money. The most dazzling and crazy figure of the House of Luxembourg was, however, Sigismund, first Margrave of Brandenburg and King of Hungary and later, after Wenceslas, German king and emperor. All reports praise his beauty and his tall slim figure; a long forked beard, well-tended but no less suitable than Jost's for perjury, gave dignity to the well-chiselled face. He was the hero of the tourney, a great hunter and drinker, without moral inhibitions but different from Wenceslas, cultured and captivating, a fine and fluent speaker in seven languages—German and Latin, Czech, Hungarian, Polish, French and Italian. As a lad, soon after the death of his father, he caused an uproar in Prague by having his mistress live openly in his house. He was often separated from his second wife, Barbara, Countess of Cilly, but they were always reconciled, too like each other to be able to live apart for long. She was as beautiful and dissolute as he, frankly going man-hunting while he was chasing women. The greatest magnificence alternated in their lives with the utmost misery. Sigismund ran up vast debts and would borrow the pettiest sums without ever repaying anything.

As a boy he had already begun an endless jobbery with Jost over his possessions. Brandenburg was early pledged, and then parts of Hungary. Then Neumark was given up to John and at the same time offered for sale to Jost and the Teutonic Knights. When Sigismund needed money he would promise Wenceslas help and Jost the Empire, and anything else that he intended to steal from Wenceslas. And Sigismund always needed money, whether to bolster up his perpetually threatened power in Hungary or because money simply flowed through his fingers. He rightly recognised the Turkish danger and desperately and vainly threw himself against the barbarian assault. He would later for once rise to his great task, but for the time, lack of money, ambition and faithlessness made him ready for anything, whether it were fraternisation with Wenceslas or the most senseless alliance against him.

Sigismund was not even sobered when in 1400 Wenceslas was deposed from the German throne. The Empire was making a last attempt to set its house in order and the threatening chaos called for extraordinary measures ; in place of the incompetent Wenceslas, Rupert of the Palatinate was elected. He was an honest and energetic prince who should have been able to rule competently. The general disintegration had proceeded too far, however, for one man alone to be able to stem the tide ; the well-intentioned and energetic Rupert failed as miserably as the sluggish and incompetent Wenceslas. Above all, he was never in a position to discharge his task completely, for instead of one king Germany now had two. Instead of the peace all longed for, there had simply come a split in the royal power, and thus the great symbol that had dominated the Middle Ages was not re-established but still further degraded. But for that very reason the Luxembourgs had to hang together if they wanted to keep the crown for their House. As Rupert proved unavailing, Wencelas might have regained power with the help of Sigismund and Jost. But Sigismund now demanded such a high price for his help that the negotiations could not but break down and Jost used this occasion to ally himself with Rupert against Wenceslas. While a part of Germany and Italy was still faithful to Wenceslas the Luxembourgs welcomed even the rival king himself if they could use him to help them extort anything from Wenceslas. In the spring of 1401 large armies closed in on Prague from all sides, looting and laying waste Bohemia and besieging the city for weeks on end. And when Wenceslas was in a position to ward off this assault, the fruit of manifold betrayals, and a tolerable peace had been attained, Sigismund struck his blow and took Wenceslas prisoner.

The last bonds holding the state together were now burst asunder in Bohemia. Complete chaos reigned. Sigismund had the crazy plan of taking Wenceslas a prisoner to Rome and having him crowned emperor in order to save the royal and imperial crowns for himself. But first of all Sigismund used his victory to extort money from Bohemia cruelly and ruthlessly. Wenceslas's treasury alone was robbed of a million gulden, Sigismund not even drawing the line at carrying off his gold and silver plate. Then with his captive he went through southern Bohemia to

B. Picart del. 1712.

Vienna. But his Italian plan got no further. Bohemia was in open revolt. A number of the nobles suddenly went over to the side of Wenceslas, the towns rose in arms, the Prague New Town, true to Wenceslas, fought the Old Town which followed Sigismund. As in the Empire all were against all. Sigismund forced Wenceslas to sign a treaty handing over to him all his towns and castles, but the orders wrested from Wenceslas under duress were not obeyed. Thereupon Wenceslas was handed over once again to the custody of the Habsburgs who were always striving to jolt the Luxembourg pride and they held him captive in Vienna. Sigismund went to Hungary and there with Wenceslas's money recruited twelve thousand mercenaries, mainly half-savage Rumanians and Jazyges. With this frightful army he fell upon Bohemia, burning, murdering and plundering. Prague in the meantime was being terrorised by a robber-band led by the hatter Trinkaus; the streets and squares of Prague were no longer safe even in daylight. Jost chose this moment to desert Sigismund, make an alliance with the insurgent Hungarians and place himself at the head of Wenceslas's followers. The Luxembourgs' orgy of hatred and treachery had reached its climax. The Bohemian Empire was tottering.

Listen, Hus, and learn: your nation is bleeding to death beneath these fearful blows. The social problem and the national are one: the Germans, who belong to the wealthy classes, do not suffer so terribly: and it is they who have called in the army that lays waste the land: the downtrodden and wronged to whom your pity is due are the Czechs. You were a peasant, you were a beggar: you are a Czech: from these fibres of your being must flow the words that will bring help.

This dissolution of the state, however, was not the most baleful of the Apocalyptic signs. The second great power of the Middle Ages, the Catholic Church, which even more deeply than the state permeated daily life, was split and shaken to its very foundations. There were not only two German kings, but also two Popes, two mutually hostile Vicars of God on earth fighting each other in a far from Christian fashion. It was the age of the Great Schism. The position of the Roman Catholic Church had already been threatened when the Pope resided in Avignon, neglecting the Catholic world to the advantage of France. Here too, however, Charles IV had seemed to create order out of chaos, forcing the Pope to return to Rome. When this Pope died it had been possible to carry through the election of an Italian Pope who would remain in Rome. Then, however, the rescue revealed itself simply as an aggravation of the evil. The

French party rallied and elected an Antipope who was to reside in Avignon. And hardly had he been elected when Charles died.

No one was strong enough to combat the schism. The indecision of Wenceslas merely squandered each opportunity that offered. Europe was divided into two hostile camps : Germany, parts of Italy, Hungary, Bohemia, England and Poland acknowledged Rome ; and France, Scotland, Spain, Naples and Savoy followed Avignon. Here, too, the death of Charles marked the decline of the homogeneous world of the Middle Ages. In vain did devout Catholic congregations appeal for a council that would restore unity, feeling this schism to be intolerable. For them the dual papacy destroyed the meaning of Catholicism : Christendom no longer existed but Antichrist's rule. Yet for decades no council was called. The Popes, fearing for their power, shrank from no means, however unscrupulous, to prevent it. Schism continued.

The power of Rome nevertheless remained tremendous. This was plain in the Jubilee Year of 1390 under Pope Boniface IX, celebrated in Prague three years later. A huge crowd of pilgrims from Germany, Bohemia, Hungary, Poland and England streamed to Rome. Vast sums were brought in by the sale of indulgences to the devout in these countries who could not make the pilgrimage. Hus spent his last penny on one. But this proof of how deeply the Church, in spite of the schism, was rooted in the people reveals most clearly the irresponsibility of the leaders of the Church who were continually undermining and jeopardising its power. All these solemn ceremonies, this devotion and faith, nourished a papacy that had lost its religious meaning. How could the Pope otherwise cling to his office and not make every sacrifice to heal the schism? " Rome does not seek any sheep that does not yield wool " ; an immeasurable sum of faith and piety was squandered for gold and power. Boniface simply amassed money.

In this respect the rival Popes were one ; there was no office in the Church that could not be bought—and wherever possible the same office would be sold by both Popes. An enormous burden of taxation was laid upon the Catholic world ; ever higher grew the payments that had to be made in advance for benefices or even the next presentation of them : nomination became dearer and dearer ; annates were exacted with increasing rigour, the Pope insisting on the first year's income from any benefice.

When Olbram of Skvorec succeeded the unhappy John of

Jenstejn in Prague in 1396 he had to pay the Pope 5,515 gulden; by purely monetary standards this means some £2,750 today, or about £10,000 in actual value. This sum was so large in proportion to Olbram's income that when he died in 1402 he still owed 582 gulden, although the Pope was by no means a patient creditor. Nicholas Puchnik, John of Pomuk's fellow sufferer, was then appointed, but he died before his induction into office. Nevertheless his sponsors had to pay the sum in full; and in the following year the Pope received once more the payment of the new candidate. This was quite apart from the bribes that were necessary to get an election confirmed. Prague was still a fairly new and cheap office and in both cases there was no rival candidate to drive up the price. John of Nassau is said to have spent seventy thousand gulden in an unsuccessful bid for the Archbishopric of Mainz. This figure, although not authenticated, is quite probable since another source even speaks of three hundred thousand gulden; it is certain, however, that he laid out 7,433 ducats and 6,700 rhenish gold guldens for bribes in Rome, that is, three times as much as the Archbishop of Prague had to pay. All these benefice-hunters bought their offices in order to make money by them. The sums they spent and a due profit had to be squeezed out of the common people. Thus to the burden laid on them by the state was added the crushing burden of church exactions, and the latter were even more difficult to evade since their payment was enforced not only by might but also by conscience.

In the fateful year of 1393 it seemed as if the schism had been healed. The Pope in Avignon died and the French king, supported by the University, tried to prevent a new election. He was anxious to free himself from the heavy burden that Avignon had begun to represent. But the Cardinals, concerned only with the preservation of their power, forestalled him and immediately elected the Spaniard, Petrus of Luna, as Pope Benedict XIII. Benedict had indeed to vow that he would withdraw if any opportunity of settling the schism offered itself, but in fact he clung energetically to his office; he held on to it in spite of the king's besieging Avignon and later on every appeal to his vow remained in vain. Thus through him above all, who was personally purer and nobler than the other Popes, the re-establishing of unity was rendered still more difficult. In its turn the schism made it more and more impossible to arrest the process of degeneration in the Church. The saving council for which people longed had faded once more into the remote distance.

Listen, Hus, and learn : the religious problems in Bohemia too, coincide with the social and national one. The state taxation which cripples the people is dwarfed by the exactions of the Church. The poor people, the Czechs, are again the victims. And the rich, powerful Germans, who must lose power by any change, strive against a reformation of the Church which they rule ; they oppose such an innovation as sermons in Czech. But above all, and this is more important than any social or national consideration, the people, devout and God-fearing, find themselves thrown back on the instrumentality of a Church who uses a language they do not understand, whose morals they must despise, and whose demands for money they cannot satisfy. The Church, whose services the people need, no longer opens the way for them but bars it and brings it into doubt and contempt. It destroys the people's link with the God they cannot do without. With their last strength the people try to satisfy the demands the Church makes upon them, but in vain. The man who will point out to the people the immediate way to God without this mediation of the Church will be the liberator of the nation.

The religious chaos was much more deadly than the political. It became ever more apparent that the schism was undermining the very roots of Christianity. If a prince or a bishop did not obtain from one Pope or his agents whatever he wanted he simply appealed to the other one, who gladly granted anything to increase his own power. Thus Austria long adhered to Avignon in order to gain a privileged position for herself in Germany. In the west of the Empire the frontiers of the two spheres of influence were completely fluid. Candidates of Rome and Avignon fought each other for the benefices they had both bought. Italy had forgotten the meaning of peace. These were indeed struggles for power such as there had previously been and which would survive the schism, but they also received from it a sinister background. Excommunication and interdict became common weapons. The one Pope blessed those whom the other cursed. The whole Christian world found itself excommunicated and under interdict, each Pope cursing his enemy and those who followed him. The struggle for power thus undermined faith, the very foundation of the mediæval world. Every Catholic was suddenly blessed and cursed simultaneously. As the princes switched over their allegiance from one Pope to the other, the blessing of Rome and the curse of Avignon would be exchanged for the curse of Rome and the blessing of Avignon. Yet no one could decide which Pope was definitely the right one. This was harm that could not be made good.

This was clear in Bohemia in particular where order had once again been restored for a short time. Wenceslas had succeeded in escaping from Vienna and now he, the powerless, despised and betrayed king, was hailed everywhere as the liberator. After Sigismund's reign of terror the whole of Bohemia thronged rejoicing to Wenceslas and even Jost was from now on his honest ally. Wenceslas's position was more favourable than ever before. He was no longer bound by any troublesome treaties, he need not give up his power to an imposed council of nobles. Sigismund's claims were null and void ; for the first time for years he could rule again as a true king. Once again, in alliance with the Habsburgs, Sigismund fell upon Moravia but Jost defended it well. Sigismund had to return to Hungary for a long stretch and the Habsburgs dropped out of the struggle. After the death of Puchnik, the Pope, an enemy of Sigismund's, appointed an Archbishop who supported Wenceslas. In 1405 Bohemia was once more firmly in his hands.

This return to peace and quiet was, however, only superficial. Bohemia had already been too deeply stirred for order to return as long as the schism continued. The apparent quiet merely meant that the religious discontent which had long been fermenting could finally and irresistibly be brought to a head. Religious conflict, reinforced by social factors, broke out and as the socially and religiously discontented in Bohemia were almost exclusively Czechs it gained an irresistible momentum. The part played by national feeling made this revolt unique. For the first time in modern history a united nation was to rise in arms. It was fighting for its faith, but national feeling, particularly strong for social reasons, was also engaged. For the first time the overwhelming and fateful strength of national feeling was revealed. John Hus personifies the fusion of these three compelling forces. He finished his studies in these years of confusion. In 1396 when the death of the Archbishop revealed prevalence of simony in the church only too clearly for Prague, he became Master of Arts. In the meantime he began his studies in the Faculty of Theology in order to prepare himself for the Church. In 1398, when Wenceslas returned from an unsuccessful journey to the Empire where he was trying to consolidate his power (he was never again to tread the soil of the Empire), Hus began to teach. This opened to him the way to the career he had laboured to achieve. For Hus obviously had a gift for oratory. Once he had an opportunity to make his mark through public speaking, he began to emerge from the mass of the other Masters and came ever more quickly to the fore.

In the year 1400, when the king was deposed, Hus preached his first sermon as a priest. Thus he was ready to unite in himself those under-currents in the Church in Bohemia which prepared the national uprising, and to give this its ultimate religious aim transcending nationalism.

Now he was gradually to develop to a full consciousness of those reforming trends through which he was later to reach complete fulfilment.

A GREAT crowd had gathered before the Tyn Church in Prague. The vast Gothic nave of the church was too small to hold all the people, but those who could not get inside remained patiently standing before the entrance, above which the figure of the Saviour seemed to be blessing them. They listened intently in dead silence, and every word of the sermon could be clearly heard. " When Christ sent his preachers forth He said : ' Freely have ye received ; freely give.' But they, as soon as they have a parish, immediately set up coffers for the money they carry off from those who listen to them. On their begging missions through the towns and villages, often lasting two or three months or more, they preach nothing so urgently as, ' Give, give, and we will pray for you.' Thus they seek their own good and not Christ's. Oh, what will God say on the awful Day of Judgment to those who have snatched the alms from true beggars and the poor and given it to those who were not in need."

The excitement of the listeners found vent in one or two cries of assent and murmurs of " Yes, the mendicant monks are just like that." But all quickly relapsed into silence. Again the words of the preacher rang forth, strangely muted by the Church walls which hid him from the crowd in the square.

" No monk may hope for salvation simply because the founder of his order was a holy man. I might as well hope that St. Augustine would bring me to Heaven through his own holiness without any good works on my part. It is not the saints who have made holiness but holiness which has made the saints ; thus holiness must be loved no less than the saints. The graves of the saints bring in gold, of course. I verily believe that if St. Francis were to reproach the friars for their evil works they would condemn him and they would never recognise him as the founder of their order. So far, alas, have they fallen away from the purity of their foundation and their original poverty."

The preacher was not John Hus but the Augustinian monk Conrad Waldhauser. He was the first to castigate the avarice of the church and the substitution of outward forms and observances for inner holiness. Charles IV, the " parsons' emperor," had summoned this Austrian to Prague in 1358, for the church which he had made so great that one third of the soil of Bohemia belonged to it was beginning to show signs of degeneration. It needed this zealot to hold up to it the mirror of a truly religious life. People streamed to him ; Conrad was surprised for, as he himself said, in all his sermons he denounced the pride, avarice and sumptuousness of the people of Prague. They listened to him. A chronicler commended him thus : " Among the many good things which this man did, one was particularly great and memorable. The women of Prague laid aside the magnificent mantles and other richly decorated robes which they had hitherto worn, and daily, simply clad, came to listen to the words of this great teacher and preacher. Through his holy sermons the morals of the people in our land were improved."

But nothing improved the morals of the Church. The Dominicans and the Franciscans who, " it was generally known in Prague, had never loved each other, but had rather fought like hungry birds of prey for the corpse of mankind," suddenly united to attack Waldhauser.

In Prague there were at this time eighteen monasteries and seven nunneries, apart from the parish clergy who were not touched in this first attack. St. Vitus alone had three hundred clergy attached to it and in Prague there were altogether far more than a thousand. The monasteries and nunneries were independent of the Archbishop, being immediately subordinated to the Pope. Waldhauser thus challenged an immense power which no one before him had dared to attack. His reproaches were more than justified. Rich possessions yielding large incomes guaranteed the prosperity of the foundations, and yet they exploited the believing and self-sacrificing people in every way possible. People had to pay for confession and communion, for the sight of relics and for every prayer. The monks flattered them till many would make over their entire heritage in return for a son being received in the monastery. The richer the monks grew the more they extorted from the simple people who found life unthinkable without the blessing of the Church. Waldhauser's attacks were an unheard-of piece of daring ; the most generally recognised and most rigid authority of the age was for the first time made aware that it could indeed be attacked. It gathered its strength bitterly for the counter-blow.

A drama was unfolded that would often be repeated. A Papal Legate came to Prague ; the monks lodged a charge against Waldhauser in which his misdeeds were set forth in a number of articles. His virtues were distorted to sins, trifles magnified to vast proportions, and the whole charge bolstered up with lies. But Charles IV and a severe and holy Archbishop still kept watch over the life of the Church. A factual refutation of the charges sufficed. The monks were not able to lay their hands on this forerunner of Hus who aroused the consciences of the people to the scandals of the Church.

Soon it was plain how deeply the people were moved ; when Waldhauser went to the Archbishop's house to answer his accusers, a huge crowd accompanied him. With difficulty he prevented the first outbreak of religious disturbances in Prague. The monks had failed in their attack ; more people than ever before thronged to Waldhauser and till his death he could preach and teach unmolested. He died in 1369, which was probably the year of the birth of Hus who decades later would fulfil the mission of Waldhauser.

The struggle in the meantime did not abate. Six years previously Milic of Kromeriz, a high Church official, had renounced the world and taken up the fight. " He left his goods and chattels and all his benefices and sinecures and the Cathedral Church of Prague," wrote Matthew of Janov, who in turn would take his place, " and followed completely in the footsteps of Jesus Christ in that he chose to bear the shame of Jesus the Crucified and rather to be the lowest in the house of God than to have riches and the glory of the daughter of Pharoah." His Archbishop attempted to restrain him. " Master Milic, what can you do better than help your Archbishop to feed the flock entrusted to him ? " But Milic would not allow himself to be led astray and chose the way of the Apostle.

Again a crowd such as no church could hold listened enthusiastically to the words of a preacher. And his words pierced their hearts all the more deeply because Milic preached in the vernacular, an unconscious but decisive step forward. He preached in Czech ; a new and fervent appeal to feeling was added to Waldhauser's passionate denunciations. " Simony, hypocrisy, greed and other such vices are rife among the clergy," he cried insistently. " If the church now has peace and earthly riches in abundance, she is thereby robbing herself of spiritual riches." And then, " Has not love grown cold and injustice gained the upper hand ? " He announced that Antichrist had come and that the end of time was approaching.

This pessimistic mood was not attuned to the happy reign of Charles IV but to the ever more apparent decay of the Church. There was still only one Pope but he resided in Avignon and served not God but the King of France and Mammon above all. Fresh taxes were constantly being introduced and church honours sold ever more frequently by the Pope himself to foreigners, which caused bad blood. And the parish priests, who were no better than the monks, followed their example ; baptism and marriage, communion and extreme unction were only to be had for money and still more money. The corpses of the poor lay unburied for days on end until a rich man could be found to pay for the funeral. The people were devout ; they loved to go to church and to make frequent communions. They would come to church, however, and find the doors locked ; the parish priests did not live in their parishes and were often away for months on end without appointing a deputy ; they skimmed through Mass, neglected to preach and above all refused to give frequent communions. They drank and diced, brawled and chased women, and their parishes were only too glad when they kept their own concubines, since then at least they left other women in peace. They were inexorable in their collection of dues, however, and excommunicated people for small delays in payment ; the highest spiritual penalties were even used as threats in the drawing-up of leases. It is true that some of the clergy, with the Archbishop at their head, fought against these abuses, but it was an uphill fight and brought little success. Above all the parish priests on whom the people depended sank more and more into vice and excess. How could the Archbishop succeed when the canons of the Cathedral on the Hradcany openly received notorious courtesans ? What could the simple people believe but that the end of the world was approaching when the guardians of the faith they loved above all turned Prague into Sodom ? The Apocalypse became a threatening and terrifying reality.

All hearts went out to Milic. Untiringly he hastened through the town, rapt and fervent, always ready to preach, advise or help. He owned but one shabby cloak. His admirers gave him furs ; he always gave them away again immediately. He feared neither cold nor poverty ; the word of God was all in all for him. Many days he preached five times. When Waldhauser died Milic learnt German in order to be able to tend his parish. He unstintingly administered the communion of which the other priests were so sparing. He visited prisoners and the sick, widows and orphans, the poor and the wretched. He took money only from those who could spare it and he took it only to give to others. " In him," says Janov once again, " there was a spring of love and sympathy for all mankind that welled from the depth of his heart. Who, having to speak or do with him, did not derive love and gentleness of spirit from him ? From him no one ever went away uncomforted."

And so he too succeeded in breaching the Sodom of Prague.

He was drawn to the "Prague Venice," the most degraded quarter of the town where the prostitutes lived. And here too the minister of God was recognised, and two hundred prostitutes were converted step by step and became penitents. The Emperor Charles gave Milic some ground and pulling down the ramshackle tenements he built instead a large home and a church which was called Jerusalem. His zeal and labours knew no bounds. "I saw," Janov attests, "that he who owned nothing, having given away all for Christ's sake, nevertheless clothed and fed those two hundred penitents from his own hand, providing them with all their daily needs. To do this he sold his very books. Then he begged and borrowed from the rich, unabashed by refusals, hard words or mockery; the whole day he went here and there, ever labouring to find ways and means to satisfy without stint the needs of these poor frail women. With how many tears, with what loving care did he watch that they should not slip back; with what patience for their weakness, with what pity, did he pour out the stream of his mercy and perform the acts of charity to them. Who could worthily number or describe all these?"

Such great strength aroused great opposition. Waldhauser had upset the trade of the religious orders; Milic generously and zealously satisfying the true religious needs of the people might well make the priests fear that their own costly and rare performances might appear in all their glaring meanness. Once again a charge was formulated under numerous heads, and this time there appeared several of those articles which were to bring Hus to the stake. Milic described the revenue of the Church as usury although it was sanctified by a long tradition; he demanded that priests should own no private property; he openly preached that there was "no truth in the Pope, the Cardinals, the Bishops, prelates, priests of the orders and parish priests" although they alone led the people along the way of truth; for him the Bible and the writings of the Fathers stood above the institutions of the Church.

The priests themselves unconsciously betrayed how far the Church had already strayed from pure Christianity. They were especially offended by Milic's demand for frequent communions, rightly dreading that the expression of a living faith would bring down the edifice of the Church. On the other hand, the charge that he was ready to appeal to the secular arm against the Church was probably correct. He is alleged to have said that if the Pope excommunicated him he would defend himself through the Emperor. The Archbishop too sought help from the Emperor, for the decay of the Church had gone so far that only secular intervention could arrest its progress. But Milic's most damning piece of work in their eyes was his greatest. " He had on the site of a brothel, moreover, built a church which he named Jerusalem and here he founded a congregation of prostitutes and asserted that they are to be preferred to all holy virgins." The repentant sinner meant no more to the Church than the ninety and nine just men. For the first time the word " heretic," which was to open the road to the stake, was used.

But things had not yet gone so far. The charge skilfully intermingled truth and falsehood in a form that was bound to have its effect on the Pope, and a Czech who knew the magnitude of the danger carried the charge to Rome. For now as always the prophet's destruction was encompassed by his own countrymen. But in 1367, Milic, too, went to Rome, where the Pope had returned for a short time from Avignon, and his forceful personality carried conviction even to the Pope. While he was in Rome the monks exulted : " Behold, oh ye faithful, he will soon be burnt." But Milic returned with unsullied honour and was allowed to go on preaching. A peaceful end, however, was not to be vouchsafed him. Seven years later, thanks to the efforts of his enemies, a papal bull was issued against him. He again went to the Pope, now in Avignon, and again he cleared himself of the charges against him ; he then fell seriously ill, however, and died in exile. In despair Janov exclaimed : " Thus by the grace of Jesus Christ and by the merits and works of Milic, Sodom has been brought back to its old dignity, rich in the word of Christ and the teaching of salvation. But for this he has received nothing but blame, reproach and endless persecution from his fellow-Christians in this same city of Prague. By various means and by charges of heresy they succeeded in driving him from the the House of God and finally from his fatherland into exile."

This Matthew of Janov, whose writings are the finest memorial to Milic, continued the struggle. What his predecessors had only gropingly performed, guided by individual experience or by feeling, he now repeated in full awareness of all that was at issue. He consciously experienced that transformation from a conventional to a true Christian which even in the case of Hus can only vaguely be seen. " I confess that I have wavered from the days of my youth as to what I should choose and hold firm to ; whether I should strive for benefices and honours, as alas I have done, or whether I should bear poverty and shame outside the tents ; whether I should look for a peaceful and comfortable life in the present, living with the crowd on an equal footing and at peace, or whether I should bind myself to the holy evangelical truth. But it has pleased the Lord Jesus to tear me from the ranks of the Antichrist and to free me, the most degraded slave of his passions, from the flames of Sodom although I fought against Him. He led me into great mourning and tribulation and shame, and only thus did I become poor and contrite and began with trembling to admire the truth of the Holy Scriptures; and I saw how necessarily and inexorably, little by little, in general and in particular, they were being fulfilled. And a kind of fire entered into me and into my heart, a fire which I could feel even with my body, new, strong, strange but yet sweet. And it has continued to this day, burning ever more as I lift my heart in prayer to God and our Lord Jesus Christ the Crucified."

He was as unflinching in his denunciations of the Church as were his forerunners. But to one thus converted the symptoms of decay seemed to have an even greater significance. "Antichrist has come and is ruling," he announced, and the whole Church was for him the embodiment of the Antichrist. He castigated the individual sins of the priests, but he saw a decline from pristine Christianity even where the Church was exercising her office without abuse; the church organisation itself was a contradiction of the Bible. "I tell you all, and let him who can grasp it well, that I, before the Lord Jesus, have searched the Scriptures and now am of the opinion that all the works, ceremonies and traditions of man will be shattered to their very foundations and will come to an end; and God alone will be exalted and His Word alone will stand to all eternity."

The first conscious reformer was speaking. Janov saw the "abomination of the desolation of the holy places"; "the mingling and the confounding of the fleshly and the spiritual, of the temporal and the eternal." "They wish to own earth and Heaven together in all ease." Human laws and ordinances have more authority than the laws of God and "the cross and its shame" are forgotten. "We blush more at the slightest misdemeanour in the presence of those set above us than if we sinned tenfold against Jesus Christ in our thoughts, words or deeds. People speak more calmly and securely about the power of Christ than they would ever dare do about the power and special privileges of His prelates."

The Christian, he said, was weighed down with a countless host of rules about fasts, times for prayer, the psalms to be sung, all of which were fixed in detail; this he described as nonsense. "No one can invent or set up a law applicable to every person, every state and every condition"; in the spirit of Christ people find for themselves the application of the general rule to each individual case. Man is betrayed and misled when he seeks "his justification in human promises, indulgences and epistles to the congregation instead of seeking his justification in God." When they need money they promise anything ; this is, however, a mighty snare since men believe that "they can thereby be blessed and receive remission of their sins without meet fruits of repentance and divine love ; therein they flatter themselves, trembling not at the countenance of justice nor hastening directly and immediately to the crucified Lord Jesus." The poorer people were driven to despair ; "their confidence is broken since they feel too weak to receive such great and costly promises." And the established Church, moreover, hindered and persecuted those who showed forth the Gospels in their lives, teaching and seeking to bring it nigher to the world.

But what could be expected from a Church divided within itself? The priests waged feuds with the monks, the Dominicans with the Franciscans, and in the meantime schism was flourishing in high places. There were now two Popes, and thereby "the great Babylon, the fleshly Church," had fallen into three parts ; "to the East the Greeks, who had separated themselves from the Roman Church on account of the endowment of the Pope, to the West the French, and to the South the Romans. Nowhere is there a notable certainty of the existence of Christ in one of these parts." Blasphemous abuse was carried on with the goods of Christ to the exaltation of self. The Pope himself was Antichrist since he would be reverenced as God on earth. "Thus did the heathen emperors who believed that they were God on earth and held themselves worthy to be reverenced of all men as by birth and fate set up above all."

Janov set forth several specific demands for reform that went beyond those of Hus. He was against the adoration of the saints. "Because they are of this world, they surround the bones of the saints with silk, gold and silver ; but they abandon the poor saints while they are alive and do not take them under their roofs. Because they are proud they prize the glorious saints in Heaven, but those who live with them they hate and despise because they cannot bear their humility and lowliness."

He was not against pictures in the Church, "such pictures are the writings of the laity" ; but he was against the adoration of these pictures which the Church ordered. "The people are to be taught to believe devoutly that there is divine strength in the holy statues and pictures. Thus, according to their assertion, God has in these days, passing over His saints and His elect, turned towards images of stone, thus permitting among His Christian people the entrance of heathen idolatry. The people hasten to show their adoration with genuflexions and candles and other outward shows and have little or no reverence for the Body of Jesus Christ there present." He demanded that pictures commanding special adoration, especially such as had miracles attributed to them, should be removed from the churches "for then it is indeed to be feared that a diabolical deceit may already have crept in to mock the people"; he denounced the clamour for miracles. "They demand more miracles than the Jews and show thereby that they are a still more perverted and stiff-necked generation than the Jews at the time of Christ. Is it not known that true miracles have long since ceased to be performed." Faith for him was a fervent spiritual conviction; if there were still miracles faith would be no merit.

And he took up his stand with the Czech people. He defended their desire for Czech sermons and frequent communions. "There is now a great hunger stirring in the world, not a hunger for fleshly meat but for the Word of God and for the sacrament of communion with the Lord Jesus. This glow of devotion, this hunger and thirst for a frequent enjoyment of communion, springing from devotion, has been aroused by the Holy Ghost." And he drew steadfast confidence from this. "Gradually a new people will arise, new men created in the likeness of God, and from these there will arise just priests and clerics." Christ had begun greatly to hasten this work of regeneration in the previous fifty or sixty years, and a new generation was growing up to complete the work.

The people understood him, but the Church did not. It was severe to pious zealots, indulgent towards the wrongdoers in its own ranks. In 1379 there was a visitation of thirty-nine Prague parishes, and unbelievable things came to light. Six parish priests did not live near their parish churches; one of them, the priest Kojata of St. John's Church in Podskal, had neglected the vicarage to such an extent that it collapsed during a storm. He did not even trouble about repairs but had it pulled down and the materials sold; nothing but a heap of rubble remained at the side of the church. The money thus gained Kojata put into his own pocket and went the round of the taverns. An inveterate dicer, he often lost all he had, including even his clothes, and could be seen at night running naked to the house of his concubine with the catchpolls at his heels. The trade in bogus relics flourished; at that time St. Vitus possessed among others the hand of Lazarus, some hairs of Mary Magdalene, the swaddling clothes of Jesus, the table cloth of the Last Supper, part of the ropes which had bound Jesus, a third of the veil of the Virgin and the sponge which had been handed to Jesus on the cross. But the Church glossed over all these evils and scarcely a punishment followed the visitation. A fine of five groschens was prescribed for concubinage, dicing, debauchery and whoring, and even for theft. The priest Kojata remained in office and, indeed, was soon a canon of Vysehrad, and thus had not to go so far at night to his beloved.

On the other hand, those who wanted to purge morals were rigorously persecuted by the Church. Janov felt the strength of her arm. As the Pope had proved unsatisfactory in the case of Milic, Janov was summoned to appear before the Synod of Prague. And this time the Church gained its ends ; they had correctly sized up their opponent. On October 18, 1389, they succeeded in extorting a recantation from Janov. He declared that pictures of the saints do not give rise to idolatry, that they should not be destroyed but adored, and that they could work miracles. He announced that daily communions must cease. He bowed to the sentence when he was forbidden to preach or hear confessions for six months. At the same time the parish priests Jacob and Andreas also recanted, Jacob of still more heresies, as that the Virgin cannot help, that the saints in their heavenly home cannot help and that prayers for the dead are futile. And for ten years he was forbidden to preach since he had mocked at a picture of the Virgin.

Matthew of Janov went the furthest of the forerunners of Hus. Many of his demands were not taken up again until Luther appeared. At the same time he was the most inadequate. The charges made simultaneously against the parish priests showed that the reform movement was reaching ever wider circles. Janov's recantation threw back the movement that he had brought so far forward. He did indeed lament : " Wretch that I am, I was forced by their turbulent cries at the Synod to agree that believers in general should not daily partake of communion." Though the whole world might stand against him, Hus would never be coerced by threats and cries. Janov never quite overcame the vacillation which he himself confessed ; unlike Milic, he always retained his benefices ; in his writing the severest criticism of the Church is coupled with complete submission to it, new and extreme views with praise of the hierarchy, revolutionary democracy with conservative views. He was simply a scholar and no man of the people ; the people stood behind him but he made only theoretical use of their support; this part of his learning he translated least of all into life.

The most important source of energy of the Bohemian reformation, national feeling, still remained unconscious, untapped. Janov recanted, but continued to work at the same book in the same fashion; but when it was demanded of him for correction in 1392 he handed it over. Then he had to keep silent when in 1393 the bells of Prague rang out to summon the people to join the pilgrimage for remission of their sins. A stream of enthusiasm welled up to save the Church, and only one person dared secretly to speak against it. Those whom Janov had betrayed stood apart or clung once more to the time-honoured forms of devotion.

The new generation which Janov had foreseen was standing ready. There was Hus, who would later die for his faith. And there was Jacob of Stribro, nicknamed Jacobellus on account of his small stature. He was a pupil of Janov's, the toughest and most stubborn of them all. To him the Hussite movement would owe its uniting symbol, the chalice. There was John of Reinstein, later to be called the Cardinal because at the risk of his life he went to Rome to defend the cause of Hus. There were Stanislav of Znojmo and Palec, who would betray Hus one day, and Marcus of Hradec, who would remain ever true to him. They were all ready, and the soil was ready, the seed of the new had been sown. But the word that would germinate it, summoning all these men to their work of liberation, was not spoken. Matthew of Janov had indeed nourished the seed, but he had also buried it deeply.

In 1365, considerably earlier than in any other country, England became involved in a national conflict with the papacy. The Pope resided in Avignon and thus stood under the influence of France, with whom England was waging an interminable war. In the interests of France the Pope suddenly made claims to tribute which England had for decades no longer paid. Parliament forbade the export of the money which only benefited their enemy. But the reasons which Wyclif, on behalf of Parliament, adduced for this and a later decison contained, apart from juridical and political argument, ideas and accusations of a plainly reforming and even revolutionary character. They were more radical than anything that had been thought or said elsewhere.

The tribute was exacted because the Pope had raised an interdict which he had earlier imposed on England. This raising of the interdict, quite apart from the question of whether it should ever have been imposed, was simony, " since it is not permitted to confer spiritual benefits in return for temporal goods." The Pope was a successor of Christ who had ordered poverty for His disciples, and it was the duty of England to see that he obeyed this religious law. Moreover, he was only a human being who could fall into mortal sin, and therefore it was better to look to Christ, the true head of the Church, and give the money to the poor. The king also exercised greater rights over the native clergy than were conceded to him, for the Church owned a third of the land ; and how could this remain outside the jurisdiction of the head of the state ? Wyclif said he would undertake to prove that " such temporal goods may justly and meritoriously be taken from the Church, though never so securely held by human law too." Particularly reprehensible was the sale of church offices to foreigners. This was not only wrong in itself but money was thereby carried to the enemy, and excessively much money into the bargain. The taxes paid to the Pope in return for Church offices came to " five times as much as the income from all monies which flow in to the Crown from the whole kingdom." At the same time true merit was deprived of its meed in this way, for " agents of that sinful town Rome promote many a wretched man to a benefice of a thousand marks a year whereas learned men can scarcely obtain one worth twenty marks." In a word, to spend money thus was a sin, but not to refuse to give it. Every payment was nothing more than alms, but alms should be given to those in need. The riches of the Apostolic See, however, were famous throughout the world, while the parishes of England were growing poorer and poorer. So an end to all payments! Wyclif recalled to the Pope the words of St. Bernard: "If you will be a master, you must lay aside your apostleship; and if an apostle, then your mastership." He spoke a language the world had not yet heard.

It was of great importance that a link was forged between England and Bohemia. France and England both aspired to the hand of Anne, the sister of Wenceslas. He gave her to Richard II of England. The House of Luxembourg was already friendly with the French royal house without this new union, and by it Wenceslas hoped to gain England's support in his struggle for power in Germany. In addition, it brought him in a hundred thousand gulden in ready money. Wenceslas' political hopes, however, proved illusory. When the fight for the German crown began in earnest this marriage was already a thing of the past. Anne died in 1394, Richard was overthrown in 1399, to die of starvation. This marriage nevertheless had exceptional significance, playing a decisive role in the development of the religious struggle in Bohemia. The pious Queen Anne was herself "a kind of heretic," Wyclif gloried in saying. With her she brought to London the Gospels in Latin, German and Czech, an event so unheard of that it was mentioned in all the chronicles. In the same spirit she smoothed the way for close contact between the Universities of Oxford and Prague, and thus the books of Wyclif reached Prague.

Among the countries of the then catholic world Bohemia occupied a special place. Christianity here took root late, and even then in its Byzantine form. Not until about the year one thousand did Rome completely prevail after some previous temporary victories, and certain orthodox features were even then still maintained. When in 1197 a Papal Legate came to Prague in order finally to establish the celibacy of the clergy he hardly escaped with his life. Celibacy became general only in the thirteenth century. Even Charles IV had to issue stern decrees against the use of Czech in church services. Until then not only were Czech sermons common but also the use of the Slav instead of the Latin liturgy. Not until 1344, when Prague was raised to an archbishopric, did all traces of the eastern

B. Picart Inv. 1713

IEAN WICLEF.

c

church finally disappear. Among the people, however, there remained unsettling memories. The apparent absorption of Bohemia into the Catholic world was superficial. It was not just chance that the Waldensian sect, one of the first to preach a return to the purely apostolic life and the rejection of all the outward forms of the Church, succeeded in spreading as far as southern Bohemia and here, in the immediate homeland of Hus, it survived longer than elsewhere.

Prague as a bishopric was under the archbishopric of Mainz. Charles IV brought forward two reasons why this connection should be severed ; one at least was readily accepted. The Czechs were separated from their Archbishop by a ten days' journey through the high mountains and the thick forest of the Bohemian frontiers, and along robber-infested roads. This made business with him difficult and dangerous. The East was now far too important for such a state of affairs to be tolerated any longer. The second argument, the difference between the Czech and German languages, which was here for the first time attested in documentary form, Charles had to state upon oath, so little was then known of the Czech nation.

A living national consciousness was indeed lacking at first. Even the Czech kings of Bohemia invited German colonists into the country and made them great concessions. The demand for Czech sermons was at first not a national but a practical religious demand. But in every reformation national feeling plays a decisive role. The Church, indeed, which had accepted celibacy only a century previously and had won power and riches in an unusually short time, had no internal stability and degenerated more rapidly than in other countries. The counter-forces were thereby the more decisively aroused. But this advantage could not immediately be exploited, for complete familiarity with scholasticism was indispensable for anyone wishing to exert an influence in the sphere of religion. Every form of faith had to be scientifically confirmed to be accepted. The young University of Prague, however, had not yet completely established itself, and the scholastic sciences were still foreign to the people of Bohemia. Behind the still unconsolidated Church in Bohemia there stood the majestic structure of the Church as a whole ; emotional and spasmodic attempts at reformation could not in the long run compete with the overwhelming impression it made. Janov's recantation had such a shattering effect because there was nothing in Bohemia at that time to take the place he left empty. Everything in the country was in a state of flux ; the readiness for the new was there, but this could not easily crystallise into a formal and effective movement.

What was lacking in Bohemia was abundantly present in England. Thanks to her island situation a strong national consciousness had developed early. Parliament, the first in modern history, gave visible expression to the nation, and as the Pope resided in France, national feeling was early quickened by religion. Over and above this, England possessed the weapons that carried weight in the religious world of the Middle Ages. The University of Oxford had existed since 1214 and had a high scholastic reputation. Here the world-shaking controversy between realism and nominalism was first unleashed and in its acutest form. Thus the necessary conditions existed for John Wyclif, the great teacher of Hus, to be able to give the first determined and clear expression to the reforming spirit of the age. He was the father of all reformations.

How far England had outstripped the rest of Europe was shown most strikingly when the great schism occurred. The whole of Europe was alarmed, overawed by the incomprehensible. Now indeed the reformers received their real urge and their justification. Wyclif on the other hand was jubilant. It had long been obvious to him that the Pope was Antichrist on earth, and now at last the world would see it too ; Christ Himself had cleft the head of Antichrist in order to destroy him. Wyclif declared that God would no longer tolerate the Pope in His Church, and therefore had split it between two heads so that the fraud of the Antichrist might the better come to light. From this cleavage of the Popes, he said, a great good had already developed ; while the Antichrist was weakened, believers were strengthened to utter many evangelical truths which they would have not dared to express if he still had had his old strength.

His demands touched the very foundations of the Church. They will be briefly expounded here, since they also form the comprehensive framework within which Hus developed his activities.

Wyclif regarded as superfluous and harmful the whole hierarchy, the innumerable archbishops and cardinals, and indeed the papacy as a whole. And he considered a holy layman or simple priest as more worthy of respect than an impious Pope. He regarded any worldly possessions as fatal for the Church, distracting her from her true mission and transforming her into a creation not of God but of Cæsar. A property-owning body of clergymen was for him irreconcilable with the idea of priesthood. It was not for nothing that Christ, who might have had all, remained poor, rejecting all worldly dominion. This dominion was the business of the laity, whose duty it was on the one hand to defend the Church, but also to mount guard over her purity. The secular powers should make use of the schism to lead the Church back to her pristine state. The mediæval service, the chants which ruined the meaning of the words, the innumerable ceremonies, all of which usurped the centre of the stage instead of the sermon, which alone was important—all these were un-Christian for him. It had gone so far that men would rather break the commandments of God than neglect the smallest ceremonial. He hated the cult of the saints who crowded out Christ, the many holidays, the adoration of holy pictures and the fraudulent relics, and claimed that it would be sensible if the faithful believed more in the living works of holy men than in dead jugglery over their graves. He opposed all that served the clergy's desire to "increase their fictitious powers and maintain the false obedience and the subjection of the people to them." He was concerned with true inward faith; he wished to restore the efficacy of the Holy Scriptures in their purity. And as there was nothing to be hoped for from the clergy who would not thus undermine their own worldly power, he crowned his work with the first complete translation of the Bible into English. Holding fast to the Bible, he assailed the very kernel of the teaching of the Church, even rejecting several sacraments which seemed to him not to have been instituted by Christ Himself. Confirmation, the ordination of priests, and aural confession seemed to him to serve only the priest's desire for power. Absolution pronounced by the priest confirmed the faith of the penitent in externals and diverted his attention from the true inward repentance which alone could save him. "We are not absolved if God does not see that we grieve in our hearts for our sins and are firmly resolved to turn from them from henceforth." Even extreme unction could only help, but could not bring salvation, and he stated that it was an un-Christian assumption that no one could be saved without it. And like the favours of the priests, their punishments, excommunication above all, were empty. A believer could only exclude himself from the congregation of the faithful by his sins. The whole conception of the sacraments had been extended to the point of blasphemy. He accused priests of claiming that they had more power from Christ than He ever would give to Paul and Peter, and boasting that they could remit or retain sins at will, that they could send to Heaven or Hell, as it might please them, forgetting that it was not they but God who redeemed or damned.

In granting indulgences, abominable enough without this, the Pope even had the presumption to claim that he could " command the holy angels that without delay they carry to eternal rest souls departed from their bodies," and people had become so stultified by this that they were more concerned with buying costly indulgences than with obeying the commandments of God. People finally believed, Wyclif continued, that the priests were God's plenipotentiaries, able to pass judgment on each sin as it pleased them and for twelve denarii to sell the blessing of Heaven, authentically and legally sealed. But the prayer of a layman destined to bliss was better than the prayer of a prelate who was damned. The priests only offered the people the outward sign of the sacraments, but the spiritual grace therein, which we do not see, was given us by God. In those days these were dangerous and subversive utterances !

The greatest outcry was caused by Wyclif's interpretation of the sacrament of communion : because of this he was accused of plain heresy, as Hus was wrongly later on. The point at issue was this : the Church believed that the bread, the host, after consecration, retained the outward characteristics of bread but in reality had been transformed into the body of Christ ; Wyclif maintained that the bread remained bread, the transformation into the body of Christ being understood symbolically only.

The vast scholastic apparatus was set in motion by both sides to prove ever afresh the one opinion or the other. This distinction, which has lost its clear outline to modern thought and experience—for the word " symbol " had for Wyclif a much more corporal meaning than it has today—had a more revolutionary effect than all the attacks on the Pope.

The priest believed already that he could forgive sins, that he could consign souls to eternal bliss or damnation ; when, in addition, he created the body of Christ with every consecration of bread, he gained an immeasurable conception of his own powers. The priests boasted that by the celebration of the sacrament they could at will create God or God's body and therefore were greater than the Mother of God, since she could bear God only once. This is no invention, but a claim frequently made at this time. Services became complete idolatry ; the people believed only in external miracles ; when the priest broke the host they believed they could see bleeding flesh ; enraptured they sank to their knees not before God but before the priest, the magician, who had changed bread into living flesh.

" The consecrated host that we see on the altar is neither Christ nor a part of Him, but an effective symbol of Him. None may see Christ in the consecrated host with his bodily eyes but only with his faith," Wyclif contended. Christ only manifested Himself in the sacrament to those who partook of communion in the true spirit : the sacrament was only a help and God helped only those whose feet were on the right path. The priest could do nothing by his mechanical performance ; many a priest was sunk in mortal sin, and his deeds were a desecration, a mockery of God which damned him. The act was effective where it fell on fruitful ground, and this God alone could decide and bring about. The believer could only hope to partake of this grace through a Christian life. Neither he nor his priest could compel it or buy or sell it : it was the Christian life alone that was the test. In the place of idolatry Wyclif would substitute an inner piety of living ; in the place of the mediation of a degenerate Church, immediate contact with God.

But all these daring demands were not the most decisive. Through them Hus was encouraged and made sure of himself, but he was only to adopt them partially. In many respects he lagged far behind Wyclif. He did not fiercely attack the adoration of the saints, nor the mediæval church services to which, on the contrary, he gave a new spirit. He had a far greater understanding of the place of art in the Church, whether picture or music, and he was far more deeply dependent on feeling. In the sacrament of communion, too, he only fought against the abuses within the Church and not against her doctrine : only because he acknowledged Wyclif was he accused of this most hated of all heresies. Hus adopted from Wyclif above all the emotional approach, seeking with simpler means the same inner deepening of faith. The only concrete demands he made were directed against the decay of the Church and were for the most part nothing new for Bohemia. And yet Hus could make these demands far more effectively than any of his forerunners because he based himself on Wyclif : for Wyclif's achievement lay in the fact that he had given the demands for reform a complete and magnificently logical substructure. Here Hus found on the one hand the important practical support of the nation, of which Wyclif's political writings had made him aware, and on the other hand the theoretical support of a scholastic system which at long last could measure itself against the Church.

The foundation of this system seemed a paradox. Wyclif and Hus adhered to the older trend of scholasticism, realism, and not, as seems more appropriate for reformers, to the newer, nominalism. Realism, and we must not be misled by the term, consisted of a literal interpretation of the ideas of Plato who gave the universal the same existence as the individual. This means that a general notion like horse or tree was not for him a mere abstraction but as real an object as any specific tree or horse which we see or own. What today passes for a mere notion is in realism—and hence its name—a tangible reality. It would therefore seem more probable that reform would start from nominalism, which makes the universal simply a name, a notion and thus corresponds roughly to the modern outlook. The specific existing tree is the reality, the general idea on the other hand only an abstraction. At the Council of Constance, which defeated Hus, he was scornfully told that only the real donkey might be believed in and under no circumstances the donkey in general.

But this paradox is only apparent. The reformation was for the restoration of the strength and fervour of faith in the face of a Church grown too worldly and external. How certain faith must be when the simplest conception has a real existence : how firmly real must then be the objects of faith, God and the Holy Ghost, the soul and its immortality. If once the rule of abstract ideas were established, it would not stop short even of these highest ideas of all. It was no accident that the Renaissance, with its completely different way of thinking, started in Italy at that time. Realism harked back to times in the Church when her life was purer and simpler. Hus and Wyclif wanted no new doctrine but only the restoration of pure Christianity : they looked back not only to the Bible but to the Fathers of the Church, who were realists. Their efforts were at first reactionary. That this reaction swiftly changed to revolution further clarifies the contrast between realism and nominalism. It was the progressive spirits of the Church who were nominalists. They were soon forced to admit, however, that nominalism paved the way for an empiricism which was hostile to the Church, and which, if logically pursued, outstripped the Church altogether. Thus they were forced to fossilise nominalism at an early stage so that it should not be developed to undesired lengths. To them, above all, the Church owes the laying-down of dogmas which were meant to cut short any further development. Till then the discussion of many articles of faith was freely allowed ; in this, too, the reformers could appeal to the past.

It was significant that at the Council of Constance the nominalists, led by d'Ailly and Gerson, of Paris University, were the opponents of Hus and Jerome although they were striving for the same thing as far as the reform of the Church was concerned : they could at no price allow free development since nominalism freely developed could not but cut the very ground from under their feet. For the sake of their religious and material existence the originally progressive party had arbitrarily to oppose any further progress. The originally reactionary realists on the other hand found themselves involved in a struggle with the official Church which had accepted nominalism. Desiring reaction, they found themselves suddenly in the midst of revolution. They had no fear of progress or fear that the existing might totter, for the realism for which they fought embodied an age in which the Church was better and firmer. They alone, therefore, had at their command the energy necessary really to set the reformation going. And for long they themselves did not notice that their reaction had been transformed into revolution—Hus to the end of his life did not quite understand—but as they were fighting against the official Church they were fighting for freedom of thought and freedom of conscience; they appealed, in fact, to the conscience and the judgment of the individual, for they did not recognise the existing laws; they showed him the direct road to God and thus overflowed the edifice of the mediæval Church. It is true that they, far more exclusively than their opponents, based themselves on the Bible but as they opposed the current exegesis they paved the way for the subjective and individual interpretation. Nominalist thought built a bridge to our own times but it was the reactionaries Wyclif and Hus who fought for the freedom that made the enjoyment of this thought possible.

But to them too the idea of freedom was still infinitely remote, and above all freedom of will. Men who abide in God can do nothing that is not laid down by the will of God. But realism led Wyclif to a new interpretation of this idea: he contrasted the visible Church with the invisible Church. Every man, he declared, was predestined to salvation or damnation by the will of God: from the beginning of time this fate had been laid down inexorably. Those predestined to salvation formed the true Church of which Christ was the head. Confusion had entered through the visible Church, for the damned might find themselves within the Church and the blessed outside. But as no one to whom God had not revealed Himself could know whether he was chosen or damned and as he could only hope that he was pre-elected, he had to do his utmost to live in Christian fashion. If he succeeded, then it was probable that he was pre-elected since "by their fruits ye shall know them." Man's efforts changed nothing, but a Christian way of life spoke for membership of the true Church. All signs were indeed uncertain and vague: the pre-elected might sin, but they awakened thereby

B. Picart del 1723.

c*

to fruitful penitence ; the damned, too, might do good, but they soon sank again into evil. The final truth was hidden from mankind and therefore none should abandon hope. The visible Church ought to coincide with the invisible. All confusion and decay arose only from the fact that the visible Church was mixed and yet was taken for the true Church. Only those therefore should be priests in whom the signs of a moral life were plainly to be seen. Only because laymen belonged to the invisible Church could Wyclif appeal to the temporal powers to reform the visible Church ; only because a Christian life was a sign of the decision of God could Wyclif demand it unconditionally from the priests. The invisible Church, no abstraction but a reality, made demands for reform a powerful reality in the Middle Ages in spite of the absence of freedom of will.

This basic idea, the doctrine of predestination, built up into a system with a vast amount of scholarship, with all its endless detail and innumerable implications, was taken over by Hus in its entity ; he changed nothing, he left nothing out and he added nothing. By his popular and gripping language he merely charged the learned apparatus with vital life. In this transformation we see reflected the original moral strength of his personality; and this alone, and not his intellectual achievement, was his greatness.

Wyclif's figure is not one that can readily be used as a symbol : he remains immured in scholasticism. The impact of life, however, was necessary to make the dry bones of scholastic learning live. Wyclif nailed his twelve articles, soon to be rejected again, to the church door in Oxford, and then retired to his parsonage in Lutterworth, availing himself of the protection of Parliament and of powerful nobles in order to work and write. A peasant revolt that broke out was laid to his account but he, like Luther later on, repudiated it, although he had written : " If a temporal lord does not do by those beneath him as he would wish to have done unto himself, he fails in love and therefore in his lordship. Consequently, his subjects are released from their subjection to him."

A Synod was summoned in London, his teaching condemned, his followers persecuted and he was called to Rome but did not go. A collection for indulgences called forth the indignation of his followers ; he took up the fight with his pen only. True, Hus did not always intervene in the fight. Hus, too, did not go to Rome ; but Hus made known why he behaved thus and his life was always in accordance with his doctrines. We do not know whether it was Wyclif's severe illness which thus fettered him or whether he did not indeed place his writings above the fate of his followers in that he did not intervene. He died in 1384, in peace and safety, while the first blows were already falling on those who confessed his teachings, but he had completed the translation of the Bible. The great effect of his writings might justify this attitude, but it remains unknown whether this relation between his work and his life really existed, as his state of mind during the vital years of his active life remains veiled in obscurity. His intellectual achievement was greater but the seed he set came up not in England but in Bohemia where the personality of John Hus gave the reformation its quickening impulse.

This may be due to the fact that the island situation of England which accelerated the demand for reformation also facilitated effective counter-action by the Church. The Lollards, the followers of the teachings of John Wyclif, were cruelly exterminated with fire and sword. The fires were burning for more than thirty years, from 1400 to 1431, and priest and artisan, nobleman and peasant, went to the stake. Even the bones of Wyclif, which had been laid to rest in the church, were exhumed and burnt to ashes. The ashes were thrown into the nearby river: but the river flowed down to the oceans of the world, " a symbol of Wyclif's teaching which spread far and wide."

This comforting image does not apply to England herself. When Hus was burnt at the stake in Constance, the flames set the Bohemian movement ablaze but the reformation in England was choked by the ashes of the fires kindled there. The centre shifted to Bohemia and the Czech people fed the fires until the greater conflagration was kindled in Germany.

First only the philosophic writings of Wyclif reached Prague, but even this was an event for the younger generation. The curriculum of the University, adhering to the same books for centuries, was so rigid that the introduction of a new author was in itself exciting. From the beginning Hus was in favour of the books of Wyclif. In 1398 he completed the copying of five treatises and took them as a basis for his lectures. These treatises had nothing to do with reformation. Nevertheless, Hus's annotations to them show that he was beginning to awake. He could not conceal his joy and wrote in the margin, " Dear Wyclif, God grant you eternal bliss," or " That is worth a gulden, what you have heard." Finally, prophetically, but certainly still unconsciously, he wrote: " Wyclif, Wyclif, you will turn many a head." From this year onwards there are records of remarks made by Hus which show that his allegiance to the Church was no longer absolute.

In other respects, too, this year was decisive. Jerome, bound to Hus by a friendship which not even death could sever, took his Bachelor's examination, which he passed with distinction as the second among twenty-seven candidates. According to the regulations of the University he had now to remain two years in Prague, in order to continue learning and to begin teaching. But his restless nature drove him far afield. As often happened later, he felt he could bear Prague no longer. It was his luck that in this year Hus obtained his first influential position and was elected to the board of examiners. He used his influence in 1399 to obtain leave of absence for Jerome. Jerome began his long journey through the world which was soon to take him to England. From there he was to bring back to Prague copies of the writings of Wyclif in the cause of reform.

BOOK TWO

THE SUMMONS

HESITANT BEGINNING

JOHN HUS has survived in history as a rigid and uncompromising fanatic. His enemies picture him as vain, dogmatic and cantankerous, his admirers as an enlightened and progressive leader. But both agree in making him, for good or ill, a fanatic, striving vehemently towards his goal and carrying people forward with him. Only such a man, surely, would have hastened to embrace death at the stake when a slight compromise could have saved him : only such a man, surely, could have inspired the unyielding and militant movement set ablaze by the fire in which he was burnt. To Hus is attributed the fervent fanaticism of the Hussites who bore his name.

This traditional picture is as false as are the heroic legends of his little-known youth. The development of his personality was slow. His awakening was certainly not before 1398, and even so full consciousness of his mission was reached only after long years. The man of thirty gradually began to realise his vocation. This alone precludes unalloyed fanaticism.

Hus's mind, too, moved slowly : he clung to tradition and to the scholastic apparatus of thought. He was not readily receptive of the new, and even when some fresh truth forced itself upon him or, as rarely happened, he reached conclusions of his own, he was always open to correction. In his treatise, "On the Trinity," he said : "From the earliest days of my studies I have abided by this rule, that as soon as I learn to know a sounder opinion, with joy and in all humility I abandon the earlier one." He was in earnest when in debate he used the conventional formula, "I declare, in accordance with the usual academic custom, that neither by this present act nor by any future one do I intend to assert obstinately nor so to defend aught which is against the Holy Scriptures or is in any wise false, and that when any cleric of the Church through Holy Scriptures or on other sufficient grounds shows me to be wrong, I am quite willing to submit to him."

This was not the language of a fanatic. And this was the language that he would speak at the Council of Constance. When Hus believed, however, that he had recognised a truth, it was for him a deep emotional experience which merged with his enthusiastic surrender to Christ and his fervent concord with the

Holy Scriptures ; and then, as a result of these feelings, he clung firmly to it, ready to face any suffering for it. No practical advantage, no threat, no danger, could turn him. Only a fresh conviction, the possibility of which with a total absence of fanaticism he always admitted, could change him : only a fresh interpretation of Holy Scriptures or a new experience of Christ could make him withdraw. As there are many tenets that arouse no vital emotional response, there always remained in him a surface uncertainty and hesitation. But what fanatic does not hold fast to the most superficial detail ! Hus was guided not by his fighting-spirit but by the fervour of his feelings, not by the energy of the man of action but by the fixity of the faith firm within him. Spiritual experience was for him the source of strength and decision, and only to such experience did he accord complete expression.

Even when convinced of a truth he hesitated to give the call to action to his faithful followers, the Czech people, and to the generality of mankind. He was a realist and therefore conservative. Knowing the value of the vast organisation of the Church he did not wish to destroy it : he respected the state too, since the Kingdom of Christ is not of this world. He hesitated to ask others to make the sacrifices for which he himself was so joyfully prepared. The outward campaigning was all started by others. The struggle about Wyclif was introduced by Stanislav of Znojmo, who vainly besought Hus to define more radically his attitude : the struggle about the University by Jerome, who had to act almost single-handed since Hus was seriously ill in the decisive weeks : the struggle about communion in both kinds by Jacobellus the unyielding, who gained his point although this greatly increased the danger for Hus, then in Constance. Only when the struggle was unavoidable or had already broken out did Hus intervene. Then, however, he threw himself in unreservedly and all eyes were focussed on him, since his strong personality, his emotional certitude and his powerful oratory made him leader at once. But the victories he helped to win swept over him and left him not a victor but a martyr. The national victory in the University compelled his decisive turn from the national to the purely religious struggle. The flames which kindled the Hussite movement were his grave. The inexorability of the times alone made Hus inexorable in defiance of his own nature. Hus lived after Petrarch, and was the contemporary of the first humanists. His age saw the rediscovery of the antique, the beginning of the Renaissance. But he belonged to the early Middle Ages and was almost a reactionary, but the times made a revolutionary of him.

His personality was such as to offer the Church the possibility of peaceful reform without the Reformation having to take place; only after this great wealth of feeling, which could not be suppressed, was rejected by the Church for constructive purposes did extreme elements step in and make of Hus a symbol of radicalism. The true Christian, utterly without fanaticism, had the effect of a revolutionary in an age which confessed Christianity and its decisive power in life without, in reality, putting this doctrine into practice.

Hus, the hardheaded peasant, is perhaps to be seen only in his rapid rise once he had taken the first steps. In 1401 he was elected Dean of the Faculty of Arts and in 1402 was already Rector. In the same year he became preacher at the Bethlehem Chapel, although he could not have been ordained before 1400. He was suddenly a respected and influential man and, thanks to his many offices, no doubt also a prosperous one. The dreams of the peasant lad had been completely realised. But in this rise, force of personality must have played as substantial a role as ambition: there were many famous Czech names in the University at this time and that one of the youngest was chosen as Rector and preacher speaks for his achievement. Ambition, at any rate, must have been completely satisfied. The once nameless poor boy had scaled the heights: established in high offices and moving among the most respected of the age, he had finally left far behind the dangers and humiliations of poverty. If he now confessed beliefs that endangered once more all he had won, inner compulsion alone could have moved him.

It seems almost symbolic that according to tradition his first utterance against the Church was in a dispute about John of Pomuk. Protiva, predecessor of Hus at the Bethlehem Chapel, one of his most convinced opponents and a witness against him in Constance, had declared after the drowning of Pomuk that services must be held for him throughout the whole of Bohemia. Hus energetically opposed this as concealing within it the seeds of adoration of the saints. "It is nowhere written in the Scriptures that for me as a priest or for any other who might be taken prisoner or killed, services should be read throughout the whole of Bohemia. Tell me the passage in the Scriptures that authorises it." Protiva answered that such was the teaching of the Church of Rome. "Oh, the Roman Church! There the Antichrist has gained so firm a foothold that it would be a hard task to shake him!"

Hus was early to see the misery of his nation. In 1401 when the Bavarians and troops from Meissen, off to besiege Prague, senselessly ravaged the countryside, robbing, torturing and killing the peasants, Hus in a moving speech cried, " The Bohemians are herein more wretched than dogs and snakes, for the dog defends the lair in which he lies and fights for it when another dog seeks to drive him away; thus do snakes, too. But the Germans oppress us and take up office in Bohemia and we are silent. According to law, according to both divine command and natural impulse, the Czechs should be first in the kingdom of Bohemia, like the French in France, and the Germans in their own lands, so that the Czechs may rule their subjects and the Germans theirs. What good is it to anyone if a Czech who cannot speak German becomes a priest or a bishop in Germany? It is about as useful as a dumb dog, that cannot bark, to a herd. And a German is worth as much to us Czechs."

Hus must, however, by no means be regarded as nationalistic at this time. Such expressions escape from him often in the heat of the moment but in general he is anxious to suppress them. His first sermons, preached in the cause of pure Christianity, were far from aggressive; he seemed purposely to conjure up Christ the peacemaker in order to assuage the general resentment. His appointment to the Bethlehem Chapel was confirmed without any dissent by the Archbishop; he was elected Rector, in spite of his speech, by the votes of the Germans as well. There was no clash of opinion about him. Violent attacks on the Church were not unusual in this time of schism, faithful members often making bitter reproaches. And, too, the national grievances of the Czechs met with great understanding from some of the Germans. The general problem was first and foremost not a national but a social one and a question of justice. True most of the Germans belonged to the higher bourgeoisie and the Czechs were straining upwards from below in their discontent: on the other hand, a part of the nobility belonged to the Czech nation. The national consciousness was at first by no means nationalistic and the demands made had a practical basis. Only the intensification of the religious struggles led to a temporary sharp cleavage between the nations. Even then the religious questions proved the stronger and the struggle about them soon continued within the victorious Czech nation.

The appointment to the Bethlehem Chapel prepared Hus for his later activities. This chapel was a proof of the harmony between the nations; it was founded in 1391 by the German citizens to provide a worthy place for Czech sermons to be preached in; but later indeed it served to intensify the strife.

" In the towns of Prague," ran the foundation charter, drawn up by John of Muhlheim, who, unlike the Church in general, highly valued the sermon, " there are indeed many buildings devoted to church services, but most of these are so claimed by other Church activities that the finest of all offices, the announcing of the word of God, has no place specially and exclusively devoted to it, and the preachers, above all those using the vernacular, are for the most part compelled to use out-of-the-way corners and houses, which is not meet." In the same charter precautions were taken that the preacher did not fall into the evil habits of the priests : his office was endowed with twenty-one groschens a year, which ensured him a moderate income ; he for his part had to give up any surplus from gifts and new presentations and lay it out for a second preacher and the support of poor Czech students. Residence near the Chapel was rigorously commanded, that the preacher " may not do as the others do who seek not what is Christ's but what is theirs, drawing the salary and the benefits and caring least of all for their calling and work." Hus was thus called to a place where the traditions of Milic and Janov and the other champions of the Czech reformation were alive and consciously fostered and as a Czech preacher he came into immediate contact with the national struggle, here bringing to fruition what Waldhauser and Milic had begun.

The greatest experience for him was to find a congregation which brought him into intimate touch with his own people. Thereby were reawakened memories of all the long-forgotten experiences of his youth which made him so familiar with the daily lives of these people and gave him living contact with them. The springs of his soul began to well afresh. In this Bethlehem, which Hus soon loved above everything, he was met with living love, so different from the overcharged scholastic atmosphere of the University divided into so many parties. People thronged to listen to him and ask his counsel in all the needs of their conscience. Their craving for church services that were not pure formalities and sermons in a tongue they could understand, a thirst no longer quenched by the time-serving and greedy clergy, found here such sustenance as brought them into ecstasies. Devout women settled near the church to lead a life pleasing to God outside the degenerate conventual orders. Once again it was they who, zealous and self-sacrificing, prepared the way and disseminated the new message. Such must have been the effect of Christ on the first congregations. Hus, enveloped in an atmosphere of trust, was raised above himself in piety, love and submission. Here at last he had found a task which made demands on all his forces, especially his feelings, strengthening and satisfying them. Now, with all the dross purged from him, he resembled the mild form of the Saviour, and the clear simple words of the Holy Scriptures, all learned interpretations forgotten, became the very breath of his life. He lived in the bosom of the Christian congregation, and for it, and from it he derived the strength to live according to the ideal he saw ever more clearly before his eyes; to show through suffering that he adhered unswervingly to the teaching of Christ and was worthy to be a disciple of the Saviour. His needy and oppressed Czech congregation was for him somehow merged into the congregations of the early Christians and separated from the surrounding world which, although it called itself Christian, was as far from Christ as were the Jewish and the Roman communities in the time of our Lord. His words, the words of the Scriptures, rang forth like a revelation through the Chapel, summoning the elect who were to raise this Word again in all its splendour before the world and attest its holy truth with their life's blood. Here was the band which was to resist the Antichrist and in the last apocalyptic hour wrest his domination from him. And Hus was to lead this fight and win it.

Freed from the fetters of scholastic pedantry he sought the most vivid and popular images to make Christianity real once more. Like Christ he drove the money changers from the Temple. "Robbers, usurers and receivers of stolen goods deceive themselves vastly if they imagine they please God when, having gathered much together by evil means, they give a little to the poor or build altars or set up chaplains." Not after death but in this life Christianity must be proved. "To give a farthing to God while one is alive and well avails one's soul far more than giving all the gold in heaven and earth after one's death." True humility alone and not any outward habit counts with God. "He who bears patiently a cross word does more for his soul than if he beat his back with all the rods that might grow in the largest forest." Not the proud and the haughty, even when they obey the Church, are pleasing in the eyes of God, but only those who humble themselves. "He who abases himself before the lowest does more good to his soul than he who makes a pilgrimage to the farthest corners of the earth." Penitence and not absolution brings forgiveness. "He who sheds a tear for the sake of his sins does more good to his soul than if he wept so much after death that two rivers flowed from his eyes." God helps, not the saints. "He who holds God above all creation helps his soul more than if the Mother of God and all the saints prayed for him." The words have a prophetic ring: "He will conquer who has learnt to accept defeat."

And at this moment when Hus was ready and receptive, Jerome brought back from Oxford copies of the theological books of Wyclif. He concealed the fact that in England the fires were alight : he concealed the fact that the followers of these books must live in hiding and continually flee from place to place like cruelly hunted animals. He did not explain that the heavily-chained clasps on the books were a warning of the decision of the English Parliament that every follower of Wyclif should be dragged to the place of execution in chains. Jerome avoided any mention of that dangerous and cruel word " heretic " and turned back the clock for Bohemia. In order not to endanger the effects of the books he described Wyclif as a respected and recognised teacher of the University of Oxford. Even so Hus first cast only a fleeting glance into them and begged his friend to cast the books into the Vltava to all eternity since they contained a poison to the soul. Once again Hus hesitated : these writings seemed to him too daring and provocative, too remote from his own road ; perhaps even at this first encounter he had some premonition of how fateful for him would be the " sweet poison of the evangelical doctor."

Jerome would give Hus no peace : he compelled him to consider the books seriously ; he spurred him on. Now Hus could no longer ward off the vast and overwhelming impression and soon he confessed : " I am moved by his writings, which reinforce every effort to lead back to the laws of Christ all mankind, especially the priests, who should abandon all sumptuous living and worldly dominion and with the Apostles of Christ lead a pure Christian life. I am moved by his love of the laws of Christ, of whose truth he asserts that they cannot err in one jot or tittle. I would that my soul were there where that of Master John Wyclif is." His Bethlehem Chapel, loved above all things, was merged in his heart with the Master whom he honoured above all. He would not for the Bethlehem Chapel full of gold deviate from the truth he had found in the teachings of Wyclif.

With incredible rapidity the quarrel about Wyclif developed. The canons of the Prague Cathedral transcribed the twenty-four articles which had been rejected in London in 1382, and a further twenty-one chosen from the two hundred and eighty articles denounced by the University of Oxford. These forty-five articles, henceforth to play an important role in Prague, were declared false or heretical. As long as Hus was Rector his antagonists did not trust themselves to act ; hardly had he resigned, however, when the whole University was summoned to meet and condemn these articles. The meeting took place on May 28,

1403. There was unprecedented excitement. The Rector, once again a German, Master Walther Harrasser of the Bavarian "nation," had the articles read out one by one so that the Doctors and Masters could discuss them in turn. Nicholas of Litomysl interrupted to attack Doctor Hubner, the man who had prepared the copy. "Thou hast extracted the articles falsely, imperfectly and inaccurately from the books, which do not run so." Hus seconded him. "Such falsifiers of books more justly deserve to die at the stake than did the two adulteraters of saffron who were recently burnt." (Saffron was an important commodity in the Middle Ages and any adulteration of it, brought from so far, was a serious offence. As for the bonfire, it was always in the background of any debate in those days.) In spite of this invocation of death, Hus still took a moderate attitude. He defended only a few articles "which are true in a good sense if people only examine them with good thoughts." Of these articles alone did he declare : "I cannot agree that they are damned lest I bring down upon myself the pains due to those who call good evil and evil good." He declared that the most dangerous articles were falsifications. Much more sweepingly, Stanislav of Znojmo defended all the articles. According to a later report he spoke so fervently and keenly that "some of the older Masters could no longer bear to listen and left the meeting." Palec, a pupil of Stanislav, threw one of the books of Wyclif on the table crying out : "Stand up, who will, and speak a word against this book ; I will defend it !"

Through the influence of Wyclif the two opposing camps emerged clearly for the first time. Hitherto there had been sympathy for the reform of the Church in all circles of the University. Now that the matter became serious the conservative, the vacillating, the cautious and almost all the Germans were afraid to entertain the idea any longer and were driven back into the Church camp. On the other side there now stood only the followers of Wyclif, the Wyclifites as they were soon named, almost all of them Czechs. Their leader was Stanislav of Znojmo and not Hus, who remained in the background. His division of the articles into true and false was probably an unconscious evasion : Hubner's copy was certainly careless and the articles thereby made more extreme, but they were almost free of misrepresentation. That their exaggerated formulation did not disgust most Wyclifites shows how far the anti-clerical tendency had progressed since Janov. "The Roman Church is a meeting of Satan," said one of the articles. Or, "It is foolish to believe in the remission of sins by the Pope or the bishops." It was no longer necessary to adduce reasons. Tithes were described as alms: no more Popes were to be elected. In one year Bohemia had caught up with England. In the other camp were the opponents of Wyclif, mostly Germans. As the voting was by "nations," the Germans had a clear majority; the Bavarian and Saxon "nations" were completely German, the Polish predominantly so; when they stood together the Bohemian "nation" was always outvoted. And thus the resolution was passed: "that no one may teach, preach or assert the articles mentioned, either publicly or secretly, under punishment of his sworn oath."

But the movement could no longer be held up. The resolution of the University remained ineffectual in practice and the teaching of Wyclif spread.

Yet once again Hus hesitated for years to take up a decisive stand and thus the movement remained moderate. From the time of the return of Wenceslas to Bohemia in 1403, the Archbishop was Zbynek Zajic of Hasenburg, a militant young member of the Bohemian nobility who honestly and energetically strove to improve conditions in Bohemia and the Church. He welcomed such a pure zealot as Hus. He begged him, "if he sees an abuse of the Church to point it out personally to him or to apply to him in writing if he is not present in Prague." He cooperated with him more and more and even appointed him preacher to the Prague Synod. Hus could thus work within the Church for its reform. The court too was mainly Czech and honoured and respected Hus. In 1406 he was appointed Court Chaplain to the Queen, whose confessor he was made. For four years, from 1403 to 1407, the aims of the Court, of the Archbishop and of Hus, could be reconciled. In four years of quiet Hus gathered the strength that he would later need. Not until then were the differences, in reality irreconcilable, no longer to be bridged. Not until then was Hus, almost forty years old, finally involved in the struggle that he had never sought.

THE long war had destroyed law and order in Bohemia. Large robber bands made life insecure. Prague had fortunately scattered the gang of the hatter Trinkaus. But in his place the nobleman Zul with his followers made a bloody expedition into the very neighbourhood of Prague. Archbishop Zbynek went out with an army to overcome the robber-knight. He succeeded in capturing Zul and fifty robbers, who were condemned to be hanged. Zul stubbornly resisted all the efforts of the priests to bring him to a state of penitence. Only when Hus was accompanying him on the way to the gallows on July 9, 1404, did he suddenly melt. " Holy congregation," he cried aloud, " I beseech you to pray to our Lord God for me ! " Exulting, the crowd greeted this fresh evidence of the irresistable influence of their beloved Master on all hearts. Repentance did not help Zul much longer in this life : with his fifty robbers he was executed. But in death he still remained their chief ; his body hung highest and was to be left hanging for seven years as a terrible warning. A crazed person who used to bury the corpses of the hanged ignored this order and attempted to loosen Zul's corpse from the gallows. It hung too high, however, for him to be able to grasp it properly and he only succeeded in tearing off a leg. And so the one-legged corpse hung there before the gates of Prague for seven years.

Under the influence of Wyclif, Hus's line of development was now straight and undeviating. It was thanks to the Archbishop's efforts and not to himself that he could still remain in the Church. As preacher of the Synod he could promulgate what the Church was elsewhere inexorably fighting ; he was praised and encouraged by the Archbishop when he preached to the assembled clergy the very things which the clergy opposed in others.

His accusing words rang through the assembly. " Among the clergy a monstrous prodigy has arisen upon earth : high in rank, low in spirit ; a proud office, an abased life ; a busy tongue and a lazy hand ; much talk and little fruit ; a severe face and light conduct ; vast respect, little constancy ; a blind watcher, a dumb herald, a crippled warrior, a doctor ignorant of medicine ; stupid, dirty tipplers, priestly vessels full of rotten morals which are an abomination to God. There are among you, prelates, canons, and priests, many who live with women whom they idolise, burning with lust and love. And you, unholy vessels of priests, who first have smirched yourselves with whores and still have adulterous thoughts, do you dare thus to take into you the sacrament which has all deliciousness and all sweetness ? Do you not fear that the wrath of God may smite you ? There are many among you who besmirch themselves with intoxication and drunkenness far more scandalously than the laity ; they go, stick in hand, to the ale house, like the laity to the threshold of the saints, and when they return home they can hardly walk, still less speak, and least of all know what their priestly dignity demands. The richer among you visit each other for entertainment at the expense of the alms, and food and drink are richer and more abundant, costlier and more delicate, than among the wealthy citizens and noblemen. Not even while celebrating the Mass can they drop their unseemly, arrogant, immoral and greedy conversations. Verily, they, more than dogs, should be driven forth from services."

Nobody was spared from his forthright attacks. " Because like clings to like, the highest spiritual offices are filled by those who understand much of worldly matters, nothing of wisdom, and whose morals are completely ruined." Even the Archbishop must have felt a breeze as Hus exclaimed, " Say, you clerics, where do we see in practice the rule that the greatest among you must be as the youngest, and the most exalted as the lowest servant ? Perhaps because you love to have the most honourable seats in the School, the most distinguished place at table ? Perhaps because you love to be greeted by the people and the civic fathers, to be called Lord and Master ? Perhaps because you would rather see at your heels a crowd of vassals with blood-bespattered swords than the lower clergy with their breviaries ? Perhaps because you do not care so much for the spiritual goods of the Church but cling with all your thoughts and cares to temporal goods ? Perhaps because you seek benefices and church offices, not that you may thereby truly serve but that you may thereby have power and live well ? Perhaps because you despise a small church office entrusted to you and aspire to worldly mastery that is unbecoming for you ? Or is it that you glory in flowing, costly slashed garments, raiment magnificent from head to foot, a dignified train of followers, a concourse of horses, palaces in superfluity and precious furnishings, collections of treasures, with taxation and contempt of the poor, reverence of the rich and proud, scorn of sincerity and approval of flattery, in a word, every kind of earthly glory and greatness ? Oh, in such insult and vexation of Christ, the sun, the higher clergy, is changed into darkness, and the moon, the lower clergy, in blood ! " He appealed to them all to repent and the Archbishop to intervene. " Therefore must our Archbishop work and strive, to the top of his bent, and in every wise, even when it endangers his life, that all his vessels dedicated to God may be purified of the stain of concubinage, and as he has the fire of prison and of cleansing and servants enough, he must let such unclean vessels as will not cleanse themselves be purified effectively in the fire of prison."

In this speech we see in its fullness one side of Hus's development. Hard and clear, attacking without fear and unsparingly when the honour of Christ is concerned, frank to the powerful, lovingly inclined to the low. But another Hus remained living in him to the end, a schoolman, cautious, self-contained, delving into subtleties. This Hus came to the fore when the Archbishop put into his hands the investigation of the miracles of Wilsnack.

The church of Wilsnack, a little town on the Elbe near Wittenberg, was destroyed by some knight or other in the fourteenth century. Only the ruins of the stone altar remained. Among the stones, wafers were said to have been found with Christ's blood oozing from them. The news of the miracle spread rapidly and more and more pilgrims came to Wilsnack where business boomed for the local monks. Pilgrims came even from Poland, Scandinavia, Hungary and Transylvania. Gradually reports spread of miracles performed by the wafers. A certain knight Henry vowed before a single combat with the knight Frederick to offer his armour to the Holy Blood of Wilsnack, and he succeeded in overcoming Frederick. A lay-brother, Peter, imprisoned for murder and theft, made a vow to the sacred blood, and lo, his fetters broke asunder and he succeeded in escaping. Other communities profited by the discovery of the Wilsnack monks and bleeding wafers appeared on all sides : in Chrudim in Bohemia monks were arrested and confessed their fraud : in Cracow the blood turned out to be rust and rosin, in Bratislava twelve monks who manufactured bleeding wafers were thrown into prison. But still the pilgrims thronged to Wilsnack.

Much that had seemed a matter of course to the mediæval Church seemed intolerable to the progressive Church party in Bohemia. The Archbishop appointed Hus and two Masters to examine the pilgrims returning from Wilsnack. Remarkable things came to light. Peter of Ach had a paralysed hand. He offered a silver hand to the Blood, but was not cured. Raging, he waited to see what the monks would preach. On the third day, the priest, who did not know of his presence, announced : " Listen,

Children, take note of the new miracle : a citizen of Prague has been cured of a paralysed hand by the blood of Christ, and as a sign thereof he has offered this silver hand." But Peter called out to him : " Priest, what lies are you telling ! You see that my hand is still paralysed ! " It was related that two blind women had had their sight restored, but they confessed that they merely suffered from sore eyes from time to time. A boy was supposed to have had a diseased leg cured. The commission examined him and found the leg worse than ever. None of the miracles stood the test. The Prague Synod forbade pilgrimages to Wilsnack. This indeed did little harm to the monks of Wilsnack. Another full seven years were to pass before the Magdeburg Synod passed a similar resolution.

Hus made use of this opportunity to broach the whole subject of belief in miracles. He composed a treatise entitled, "Whether Christ in the hour of His resurrection transfigured all the blood that had flowed from His body." In this treatise he did not attack the obvious fraud. With great circumstantial learnedness Hus proved that Christ had offered up His whole body for man and therefore must have risen again with His whole body. No blood and no relics of Christ were thus left upon earth ; the hairs of His beard and suchlike were frauds, because His whole body with all its blood had risen again. Where there were objects stained with blood, such as parts of the cross which were to be found everywhere, only a trace of colour was there but no blood. And suddenly from the scholastic wilderness there arose a thought that revealed what Hus was striving for, the intensification of faith. Miracles had only been for the unbelieving, and the Church did not need miracles any longer, for now it would be a sign of lack of faith if belief came only through them. But Hus quickly dropped this living thought : he did not deny that there were still miracles but they were the work not of God but of the devil, for the strengthening of the power of Antichrist. Such ideas and methods are repeatedly to be found in Hus, and they often seem an evasion of a vital decision or even a surrender. This treatise, too, was particularly cautious and avoided any attack on those who now cultivated and defended miracles. In the same spirit Hus, reproached with having pronounced his errors before all the people, will later defend himself in the same hairsplitting fashion by saying that the charge is false because all the people had not been in Prague at the time, some being in Rome and others travelling. Or, caught in the narrow cleft between Wyclif, with whom he did not agree in his explanation of communion, and the Church, which he was opposing, he would take refuge in the subtlety that the bread remained bread in the sense that Christ said, " I am your Bread ! " At the Council of Constance, when life was at stake, such questions played far too important a part, according to our way of thinking.

But these hairsplittings were not evasions ; this second Hus was merely to a higher degree than the first the child of his times. That it disturbs us only shows how completely we are now estranged from the scholastic spirit. It was the essence of scholasticism that every question was driven to the last logical absurdity. Hus certainly had an immoderate respect for scholastic forms ; his arguments were already old-fashioned in his own times, for under nominalism thought had progressed beyond this type of proof, and Hus was ridiculed for it in Constance.

How keenly even the people were interested in such abstract arguments is shown by the reception given to a later Czech sermon of Hus's, a sermon definitely intended for the people in general. In it he discusses the question " whether it can be ascertained from the writings of the Doctors that some of the people of the army of Pharaoh that was drowned in the Red Sea or some of the inhabitants of Sodom enjoy salvation." This question seemed so important that an attested document was drawn up on the sermon because, as Hus said, " such a document commands greater belief." It was for all a great consolation and reassurance when question and answer were drawn up in writing even though the answer was never unambiguous, and this sermon only stated that without divine revelation it cannot be asserted of anyone that he is damned. And this happened in the year 1412, one of the most decisive and stirring years of the struggle. We are very far from our own times. But if we examine these writings of Hus within the framework of their own period, the first Hus who is near and familiar to us emerges ever more clearly. Through all the strange forms of expression we are aware of a human heart that lives and loves and suffers like every human heart in all ages. Only when we judge the contents as modern thought, with modern logic, they seem meaningless and dry and their passion is lost. Obviously these writings are reflective and cautious since they are scientific works but of their kind they are as courageous as the real fighting treatises. The mind that followed every argument to the last ramifications of scholastic hairsplitting was the counterpart of the character that would allow Hus to follow his line of action to the last consequence and go to the stake unbroken.

The Archbishop's protection guaranteed the utmost scope for Hus's intellectual and reforming activities. But his opponents could not rest, and unable to reach him, they turned to the other Wyclifites.

In 1405 they succeeded in persuading the Pope to issue the first of the bulls which called on the Archbishop to combat the false teachings spreading ever more rapidly in Bohemia. Stanislav of Znojmo was summoned to appear and forced to recant. The Church, with a sure touch, had once again chosen apparently the most radical but in reality the weakest of its enemies. This recantation prepared the complete downfall of Stanislav who later became one of the keenest and most dangerous antagonists of Hus. But Hus himself was hardly touched by the blow, for the point of issue was Wyclif's doctrine of communion which he had never accepted. He could therefore concur in the decisions of the two Synods of the year 1406 and 1407 which threatened to curse as heretics all those progagating this doctrine. For the Wyclifites this defeat was balanced by a triumph ; in the year 1406 Nicholas Faulfisch and George of Knehnice, two students, arrived in Prague with a letter from the University of Oxford stating that Wyclif's teaching had not been condemned and that Wyclif himself was a respected and God-fearing man, of such distinction that the University did not know his equal. The Wyclifites were jubilant. None suspected that the letter was a forgery and that England in reality was the scene of a bloody struggle that would soon begin in Prague.

Hus himself scarcely needed this encouragement. Unflinchingly he continued his outspoken sermons ; unflinchingly he still castigated at the Synod and before the people the loose morals of the clergy. In July 1407 a magnificent funeral wended its way through Prague. Master Peter of Vserub, one of the richest pluralists, was being buried with all the pomp and honours that the Catholic Church of the Middle Ages could bestow. The whole of Prague was on its knees in admiration of the spectacle. Hus, too, preached at the open grave. But his words were not those expected of him by those who had invited him. "Lo, Master Vserub too is dead," he stated ironically, "so pray to God for his soul ! I hope indeed that God's grace has redeemed him, but at the same time I fear that he may be damned : both rest in God. But I would not for the whole world die holding so many rich benefices." And then his voice was raised in a shattering condemnation. "Whoever demands money for the sacraments and will not abandon such exploitation, all those who shamelessly oppress poor people, compelling them to give, all those who act thus and all those who are thus, are false prophets. They are guilty of simony and are indeed heretics !"

This sermon at the open grave, this public answer to veiled attacks, aroused an outcry. Hus did not allow this to deter him. Shortly afterwards he once more levelled the customary charges against the assembled Synod. This time, however, the words that the Archbishop had hitherto approved led to a breach. The words alone were not the only cause ; the political situation had changed in the meantime. The power of King Rupert was dwindling and Wenceslas was beginning to hope that he might once again seize royal power in Germany. To achieve this, however, he had to free Bohemia from its reputation of being a home of heresy. Only when he ruled an orthodox country could he hope to gain the support of the Pope and be recognised in Germany. The Archbishop was weary of the continual reproaches and the papal bulls. Superficial order had been restored in the land and in the Church. Hus's zeal could now only harm the Archbishop, and so he yielded when the Pope and the king joined to urge him. Hus's sermon in the Synod on October 18, 1407, was to be his last.

A dreary winter set in. It was the coldest for fifty years and the frosts lasted for five months. The Danube was frozen, and wolves ravaged the country around Prague. Hardly was this over when the fight against the Wyclifites was taken up with redoubled vigour. Even their first successes did not make his opponents feel ready to tackle Hus himself. They merely attempted to prove the foundation of the Bethlehem Chapel illegal. This attack, however, failed. The merchant Kreutz, the second of the founders, at great expense purchased in Rome a new papal bull which protected the Chapel. Then Matthew of Knin, one of the younger Wyclifite Masters, was summoned to appear before the Synod. Knin had shortly before been elected to a high university office in opposition to the vote of the Germans—the voting had not been by " nations " and it was seen that the Czechs won when it was a question of a straight majority.

This victory was to be cancelled out. Knin defended himself energetically against all the charges, demanding that his errors should be proved. A vain demand ! The Vicar Kbel, the moving spirit of the Church party, shouted at him, " You must abjure heresy even if you are not guilty of it ! " And the Archbishop threatened him, " Cease all talking, Master. Either you abjure or you remain here in my court." With the departure of Hus might had triumphed over right. Knin suddenly complied and recanted. But the Church records left the case unclarified ; the usual attested report of the proceedings was not drawn up and thus it is not clear what was aimed at. Knin remained a courageous follower of Hus and no further steps were taken against him. In May, 1408, a meeting of the Bohemian "nation" was summoned to define its attitude, but here too all took care not further to increase the general tension. A resolution representing a compromise was agreed to and Hus supported it. The students were forbidden to read the theological books of Wyclif, and no member of the Bohemian " nation " was permitted to defend the condemned forty-five articles " in their false or heretical or objectionable sense." The Archbishop was dissatisfied, however, because this reservation robbed the prohibition of any practical meaning. For the Bohemian Masters, however, it represented the utmost limit they were prepared to go to.

The line-up was now quite clear, but the leaders on both sides hesitated to open hostilities, knowing the serious consequences for the people and the kingdom. The priests, however, exploited the situation to the full and their long-suppressed spite sought new outlets. The tension increased from day to day and in spite of all attempts to prevent it the year 1408 saw the crisis. On June 16 at the suit of the Prague parish priests, the Synod, without naming Hus, prohibited public preaching against the immoralities of the clergy. There was no sign of the prohibition being put into force. But the Archbishop under pressure from the clergy decreed that all the books of Wyclif should be handed over to him for examination. Hus obeyed this order ; perhaps he hoped for a just examination which would prove the emptiness of the charges, or perhaps he had to travel all roads to their logical end. He handed over his books with the words, " See, reverend father, I here give up my books and wherever you find false doctrine let the passage be marked that I may acknowledge it for false before the whole congregation." Other Wyclifites did not obey but lodged a protest with the Pope, who had, however, long ago condemned Wyclif. This protest shewed that they did not see the situation as it really was and this in its turn intensified the struggle, the hopes they entertained of the Pope carrying many Wyclifites much further than they would otherwise have gone.

On July 30 more Wyclifites were cited. Sigismund of Jistebnice and Nicholas of Velemovice, called Abraham, were singled out. This time the attack was on Czech sermons which were not desired by the Church. The accused refused to submit. Abraham defended himself with the words of the Gospels. What was the use of such a defence ! Only submission could help. Thus for the first time Wyclifites were thrown into prison and handed over to the Inquisitor. The proceedings before the Inquisitor took place on July 5. Abraham swore by God and refused to swear by the crucifix and Bible. Thereupon he was accused of the Waldensian heresy, one of the severest charges of the times. Then Hus, in indignation, intervened and proved how unjust this charge was, " as though it were greater to swear by a creature than by God." Vicar Kbel now shouted at Hus in turn, " Master, you have come here to listen and not to prove." Hus would not be thus silenced. " Lo, you wanted to prove this priest guilty of the Waldensian heresy although he swore by God. Is that just ? " But Hus's defence did not help. Both the Wyclifites were expelled from Prague and forbidden to preach.

Hus, however, was concerned with the injustice of it. He had been smitten at the heart of his belief ; external considerations no longer counted, hesitation was done with. No danger could be so great as to outweigh a threat to justice, a threat to true faith. Hus now availed himself of the former demand of the Archbishop's that he should write to him, and he sent him a letter after which there could be no going back. " What is this," he wrote, " that the incestuous and those guilty of other crimes move about without severe punishment, while humble priests who draw out the thorn of sin, who discharge with worthy zeal the offices entrusted to them by you, not indulging greed but offering God's services freely and working to spread the Gospels, have been thrown into prison as heretics and must suffer exile for preaching the Gospels ?" The same day, July 14, he preached a public sermon, soon regarded as a manifesto, in which he took up all the nameless accusations made against the Wyclifites and refuted them. Unworthy priests must be publicly attacked, he proclaimed, for one increased the dignity of the whole order when error was chastised. The tacit condonement of their sins that the parish priests demanded could only injure the priesthood as a whole since people then charged it generally with wrongdoing.

Since the ultimate and most important issue had now been raised, the right of freely preaching the truth, Hus for the first time unreservedly obeyed his own principle, " In matters of the soul, God must be obeyed before man." Now he had burnt his bridges. The Church had put God far into the background and was not concerned with the godless life of its priests. It demanded first and foremost unconditional obedience. Hus sought God and refused obedience. The revolt had begun.

The history of the Hussite movement is rich in dramatic turns. All too new and daring were the demands it made; all too many were the cross currents in Bohemia's struggle for power in Germany; and all too vacillating was King Wenceslas, one of the protagonists in the drama. At one moment Wenceslas stood with the Archbishop against Hus; a change in international politics, and he was with Hus against the Archbishop. Through this the beginning of the revolt once more gained an appearance of legality.

The rebellion which threatened the Church began within the Church in Italy and France. The longer the schism lasted the more intolerable did it become. Gregory XII, the Roman Pope since 1406, had to swear that he was prepared to retire at any time if the duality of Popes could be abolished. He had as little intention of honouring his vow as had Benedict XIII in Avignon. However, in 1408 both Popes had to yield to the pressure of the cardinals: the general grievance was so apparent that there remained nothing but to agree to a meeting in Savona. There, finally, the healing of the schism would be discussed. But from this a new comedy developed. Benedict XIII went as far as Spezia and Gregory XII to Lucca, and then they skilfully played into each others hands to make the short distance still separating them an impassable barrier. With one accord they sought new excuses. Finally the cardinals lost their patience and secretly the Romans left Lucca, the French Spezia; their quarrels at any rate were settled. They met under the protection of the Florentine Republic in Pisa.

For the first time for many years the opposing parties met to restore the unity of the Church. From this sprang the first revolutionary act. The French cardinals refused to obey Benedict and the Romans Gregory and they called upon Christendom to follow their example. At the same time, an event without precedent, they formed a Forum to stand above the highest authority of the Catholic world. They summoned the longed-for Council for March 25, 1409, in Pisa to judge between the two Popes.

The general confusion was at first merely heightened. France seized the opportunity for which it had so long striven and declared Benedict deposed. He had to flee to Perpignan where he still held out for long. Gregory placed himself under the protection of King Ladislas of Naples. He was in reality his worst enemy since he had conquered Rome, but Gregory immediately sacrificed Rome for the chance of remaining Pope. King Rupert too remained loyal to him for Gregory had long supported him. Rupert's power was already so slight that any change was to be feared. All the vacillating and insecure attached themselves to Gregory, and thus formed a considerable power. On the other hand the Luxembourgs were forced into the camp of the cardinals. Wenceslas saw in the cardinals the only hope of regaining the German crown and Sigismund supported the decision of Wenceslas since Ladislas had a claim to the Hungarian throne. In this way the voice of the Luxembourgs gained a weight that for years it had not had on account of their fratricidal strife. They once more took up their positions in the great struggle for might.

Wenceslas, however, encountered great difficulties in his own country. The Archbishop considered himself bound by the oath he had sworn to Gregory. Probably in view of the external threats to the Church he hesitated to join the internal revolution. The University, where the Germans had the upper hand, supported the Archbishop because he was against Hus, and perhaps too because they were for Rupert. They did not change their attitude even when John of Mainz won over the German electors to the cardinals. For in Prague in the meantime the whole question had become bound up with the national one. The Germans were for the maintenance of the existing social and national order which could only change to their disadvantage. They were therefore against Hus and for Gregory. Hus and the Czechs were for any reform and therefore for the cardinals. What was the use of Wenceslas's support, however, when he could not even prevail in his own country? He must at least have the powerful University on his side, and for the sake of gaining power in Germany he must help the Czechs to recognition of their point of view. Thus Wenceslas was stimulated to new and decisive activity in Prague.

In December 1408 a meeting of the University was called to declare neutrality towards the two Popes, which in effect meant declaring for the cardinals. But only the Bohemian " nation " under the leadership of Hus was for neutrality : it was out-voted by the three German " nations." The excitement was so great that the Rector did not dare announce the result of the voting. Then the Archbishop intervened ; he suspended all supporters of neutrality from their offices as priests. This time Hus was mentioned by name in the first place. The Archbishop too had burnt his bridges. His decree was hung on all the church doors in Latin and Czech. Hus was indignant at the shame thus heaped upon him. He did not comply and continued to preach. In great excitement he wrote again, and for the last time, to the Archbishop. It seemed, however, that in the thick of the fight Hus had lost his perspective, for though the letter was indeed sharp and excited, he still thought mediation possible.

He had not seen that the hour had struck. He held fast to logic. When father and mother quarrel, he wrote, a son cannot take sides, and therefore he was for neutrality. In all that was good and lawful, on the other hand, he must continue to obey his parents and in this sense he followed Gregory. He had not released himself from his oath nor repudiated him, and had expressly announced this in his last sermon. It is to Hus's honour that he still considered mediation, but by this time all attempts at it were already meaningless. The political situation demanded a clear-cut decision. It seemed the moment for putting into effect the demand made long previously that the German majority in the University should be broken by doing away with voting by " nations." Hus did not at this time suspect that even victory could be fraught with fateful consequences and was wholeheartedly for this demand ; but equally not realising that out of the daily struggle had now developed the decisive battle he did not at once press the point. However, another champion was found who had retained his perspective since he had been abroad during the previous struggles. This was Jerome who had now returned to Prague.

Jerome intervened but rarely in the fight, for his insatiable love of travel repeatedly took him from Prague. But in moments of crisis he was there and then his intervention was of the utmost significance. He had brought the books of Wyclif to Prague and forced Hus to study them. Now he carried on the struggle until Hus, his hesitation abandoned, had awakened to his task. Jerome fanned the flames among the people ; he saw the goal, described the way to it, and carried others forward on the wings of his enthusiasm. Although he rarely took part in these fights, his contribution was hardly less than that of Hus himself. His spirit rent the old, spurred after the new, and gave form and direction to the activities of Hus, whose strength was deeply rooted in feeling.

For with Jerome, the intellectual *par excellence* took up his stand at Hus's side. Jerome was no mediæval figure ; he was no longer at peace within himself. He was akin to the first humanists, on whom he made the impression of a philosopher of classical times. His restless modern spirit drove him incessantly through the world, from Oxford to Palestine, from Paris to Lithuania, from Cologne to Hungary ; it drove him, as the great discoverers decades later were driven, to seek a comprehensive vision of the world. Modern times were in his blood although his longings were purely intellectual and not scientific. On his journeys, which were exceptionally extensive for the age, he shone everywhere by reason of his outstanding intellect, his fiery eloquence and his wide knowledge. He was a Master of four universities—Paris, Cologne, Heidelberg and Prague—and he was first in all his examinations. Unlike Hus, he had escaped the spell of scholasticism.

He had also the urge to put his stamp upon the world, to spread his views and gather disciples around him. Wherever he went, rebellion flared up. He sought to fan the flames of a revolution which went far beyond the comprehension of his contemporaries. " Although he stayed here only a few days," the Bishop of Cracow reported, " he caused such a stir among the clergy and the people as has not been seen in the diocese within living memory." Again and again he was denounced as a heretic and thrown into prison. He did not work from one small point in ever widening circles like Wyclif, Hus and all the teachers of the Middle Ages ; he sought the international community which later developed among the humanists.

He rather than Hus could be described as a fanatic, but the term hardly fits even him. For his character was not equal to his intellect. As long as he was in the midst of a fight he waged it fanatically and with gusto. He knew no bounds and rejected no weapon, from an appeal to the lowest instincts of the people to scorn and mockery so lashing that his own followers must have been bewildered. Thus he himself provoked counter-measures from his enemies, but when he was in danger he showed an utter lack of endurance and character. He recanted what he had just proclaimed, he promised whatever was demanded of him, only to regain his liberty. Hardly had he succeeded than he mocked at those who had believed him and proclaimed once more what he had just abjured.

These instabilities did not touch the inner kernel of his being. He was faithful to his convictions in spite of all recantations, but his loyalty was purely intellectual, shackled by no conventions and no moral standards, and conditioned by expediency and

B. Picart Inv. 1712.

effect. The noble kernel of his being he revealed directly to his friends. When, in spite of all warnings, he followed Hus to Constance, it was almost conscious suicide, a valid proof of friendship. When he made an enemy, however, any weapon was good enough, whether lies and treachery, hypocrisy and violence, or the complete violation of his own nature. He would pay any price for his personal freedom. When he could no longer help Hus, he besmirched even his memory and that of Wyclif; he spurned all that he held sacred, only to regain freedom. When this attempt proved vain he accepted death at the stake with admirable fortitude and an unshakable spiritual superiority. For his evasions, his retreats, his compliances, never sprang from cowardice: escaped from the greatest danger, he would again plunge consciously into the same danger; he bore all for the sake of his convictions. His apparent disloyalty was only a manœuvre.

Beside the clear-cut stability of character of Hus, rooted in his feelings, the figure of Jerome appears changeable and uncertain; beside the simple way of Hus his path appears tortuous and confused. But above all superficial inconsistency, irresolution and lack of character there was always a last deep consistency, an intellectual integrity, which was of the future. In Jerome the intellectual man took his stand beside the religious man, and this figure was far too new to be able to prevail at once in a straight fight; he had to make evasions and yield, he had to flee and deny himself if he was not to go under in the first clash with the mediæval world.

But the struggle for the reform of the Church gained its human character through the intervention of this philosopher who made it a fight for freedom of thought and conscience. More plainly than Hus, Jerome voiced an ardent demand for individual responsibility and a new vision of the world in the teeth of the Church's demand for unconditional obedience and recognition of tradition.

Hus's wealth of feeling was the compellingly Christian element in the Bohemian reformation. Jerome tapped a new and not specifically Christian motive force which was to play a fateful role in the later reformations and revolutions. There was apparent in Jerome the danger threatening the man who no longer found his stability in religion. To make his ideas prevail he would use any means, even though they debased man and undermined his faith. He was great only in the shadow of Hus and at his side. As soon as he was left alone he was betrayed into that instability to which the whole world would be exposed once it had lost its mainstay in Christianity.

There are today only a few indications left of the significance of Jerome. His writings have not survived and scant traces remain of his effect on his world. Only from time to time in many of his traditional sayings and in the charges made against him, probably maliciously, there flash forth like lightning those modern touches that he alone possessed. But these few signs bear eloquent witness to his achievement.

Again and again his courage, his audacity and his lucidity of mind, which were never obscured even in his shameful surrenders, betray themselves. When he was copying the books of Wyclif in England, the fires were already ablaze and he risked his life to perform his task. In Prague he did not boast of the danger he had faced but passed it over in silence. He was the leader who directed others ; he made the writings out more harmless than they were, his own performances smaller, to secure his end.

Then he went to Palestine and got into touch with the Orthodox Church whose teachings often were in harmony with those of Wyclif ; on his own initiative he engaged in far-reaching political schemes in order to find support against Rome. He attempted too to pave the way for the Czechs to join the Eastern Slavs, a move which could have changed the face of Europe.

In 1405, he received the degree of Master in Paris. Little is known of his activities there, but the charge against him at Constance gives some indication of the position he gained. Gerson, the great opponent of the Hussites, witnessing against him made the reproach, " When you were in Paris you considered yourself an angel with your eloquence." Jerome answered him, " What I asserted in Paris in the public schools and what I replied to the Masters' arguments, that I asserted in philosophic fashion as a philosopher and Master of that University. If I asserted anything that I should not have done, I accept correction and in humility I will amend myself and accept instruction in what is right. At that time I was not plucked for this evil-doing but accepted as a Master." This was not the answer of any Tom, Dick or Harry of a Master. The accused heretic took up his stand as a recognised philosopher and insisted on his right to think and dispute. In 1407 Jerome went once again to Oxford, although he had already been denounced there as a heretic ; he was able to escape only with the greatest difficulty. But he dared it, although only shortly before he had had to flee from Cologne and Heidelberg.

He arrived in Prague in the nick of time to intervene in the quarrel in the University. In England, France and Germany he had seen the characteristic life of each nation developing unimpeded, and he wanted the same freedom for his own people. As he was on the offensive, the split nature of Jerome came into evidence. He mixed nationalist arguments and attacks on the aberrations of scholasticism in a demagogic hotch-potch and adduced strange modern arguments to heighten the excitement. He poured ridicule on such questions as whether the devil could baptise or whether Adam spoke Hebrew. So much fine money must not be poured down German gullets to get these problems solved, he said, as if Czech Masters were not concerned with the same futile problems too ! He dragged down to a lower level the conflict from which Hus shrank. He harangued indefatigably, gained recruits among the nobility, and incited the people until there were street riots and German Masters and students were beaten. Any weapon was good enough for him. But he waged this war with a consciously directed and untiring energy that brought him success.

In the meantime Wenceslas was being urged on all sides to enforce his policy of neutrality in Bohemia. A French delegation arrived to end his eternal shilly-shallying. When the Germans won their victory for Gregory in the University, he summoned a German and a Czech delegation to him in Kutna Hora to insist on his policy of neutrality. Everything seemed to be decided : the Czechs, headed by Hus and Jerome, came with high hopes. The king in the meantime, however, had heard of street rioting. There was nothing he hated more. The Germans were thus able, to everyone's surprise, to win him round completely. Jerome's campaign seemed to have been a failure.

When the Czechs appeared before Wenceslas, who was probably feeling sore about his own weakness, the king, beside himself with anger, roared out at Hus, " You are always stirring up trouble for me with your comrade Jerome. When they whose duty it is do not bestir themselves, I myself will light the bonfire for you ! "

Hus was so deeply affected by the bitter disappointment and the dangerous threat of the estranged king that he fell sick and for a time the fight had to go on without him. Jerome, on the other hand, in spite of the blame due to him, did not allow himself to be intimidated. The leadership now devolved completely upon him, and unflinchingly and untiringly he worked on for the Czech cause. He found support in the queen, in the influential Nicholas of Lobkovice, the chief court copyist, and in the French, who pointed out to the king that in the University of Paris the French " nation " had three votes and the foreign nations only one. They all urged the weak king to reconsider his decision.

On January 19, 1409, Andrew of Brod and John Eliae, the most important of the older Czech Masters, visited Hus. He was still in bed and was very weak and depressed. The two Masters were in despair. Andrew of Brod cried sadly, "O, Hus, is there no saviour for us in our cause?" John Eliae believed no longer in a solution of the problem. "If only God would grant it," he answered despondently, "but we shall never succeed." Only Hus, sustained by Jerome, still cherished hopes. "I believe we shall find somebody." But the tone of his voice betrayed how slight was his hope. At this moment a messenger arrived. He brought to them the celebrated decree of Kutna Hora, which ran, "As the German nation, which is however foreign in Bohemia, has in all matters in the University of Prague arrogated to itself three votes, while the native Bohemian nation has only one vote, We, convinced that this is inequitable and disproportionate, do decree that the Bohemian nation shall, on the example of the Paris and Italian Universities, have three votes in all decisions, examinations, elections, voting and similar acts, while the foreign nations together have one vote." Victory had been achieved.

It seemed as though everything would now go smoothly. The king issued a further decree on January 22 whereby in his realm obedience was withdrawn from Gregory. With Cardinal Landulf, the envoy of the cardinals, Wenceslas concluded a treaty which assured his claims to the royal power, for he could now promise that representatives of the University would be sent to the Council. These representatives would be received, those of Rupert not.

Hus was soon on his feet again and spoke jubilantly in the Bethlehem Chapel. "Children, praise be to Almighty God that we have excluded the Germans and have gained the ends we fought for and are the victors. And especially let us thank Master Nicholas who brought it about that our petitions were heard by the king." Jerome, above himself as usual, went to one of the great Quodlibets, the public debates, approached Matthew of Knin who was presiding, and tenderly stroked his beard. "See, dear boy," he gloated, "they were after your life and wanted to kill you for Wyclif although you were innocent; look where they are now, those who have dishonoured you." The Germans did not wish to comply, preferring a split into two universities. They referred to the foundation charter of Charles IV to which they had taken their oath. But as they would not yield them voluntarily, the seals and keys, the registers and offices were taken from them by force. The University was finally in the hands of the Czechs.

At the same time the Council was meeting in Pisa. Each of the two Popes had also convened a council. For so long none had been called, and suddenly, three met, but only the Council of the cardinals was of any importance. It was a glorious assembly which represented the real power of the catholic world and this assembly completed the revolution which had begun ; it obtained recognition for the principle of Gerson, the great Master of Paris University, that the Council personified the Church and was above the Pope. With this new principle, a decided break with tradition, a new era seemed to have started in the Church : regeneration and reform seemed assured. The long period of eclipse was followed by a memorable day which overshadowed anything that had previously happened in the history of the Church. On June 5, 1409, the Council declared both Popes as deposed and pronounced a ban on them as schismatics and heretics. Then it proceeded to elect a new Pope. On June 17 Alexander V was proclaimed Pope and recognised by all the cardinals.

This great success of the party of reform in its turn strengthened the Czech party in Prague. Here the Archbishop was waging a desperate struggle on behalf of Gregory ; in Lent he excommunicated Hus and all his friends. For the first time Hus and all Wyclifites were pronounced heretics and cast out of the Church. The Archbishop damned all realists who "postulate a common man and a common ass." But his first blow at Hus was a failure ; the king forbade the reading of the ban from the chancels. When a few clerics defied him the king took action against them and seized their goods. Then Zbynek resorted to his strongest weapon ; he placed Prague under an interdict. But this interdict, pronounced in the name of a deposed Pope, rebounded on himself. Once again street riots broke out, notorious clergy were dragged from their beds and put in the pillory and it was only with difficulty that the palace of the Archbishop was saved. Speeches by Hus and Jerome set Prague in such an uproar that the Archbishop had to flee to Roudnice. He took with him the treasures of St. Wenceslas. Thereupon, Wenceslas, with eager speed, confiscated more church property. By the summer of 1409 the power of Archbishop Zbynek in Prague was completely broken.

None of the victors, however, could long enjoy the fruits of victory, for even greater setbacks followed on the heels of these intoxicating successes. They sprang once more from the Church. The Council had vowed not to separate until the reform of the

Church was complete. The new Pope disregarded their vow and dissolved the Council as soon as he was crowned. Alexander V was a weak, spineless old man but behind him was Cardinal Balthasar Cossa, who well deserved his nickname of "diavolo cardinale." He, ambitious to be Pope, was concerned not with purity and clarity but simply and solely with power, and he prevented any reform which could undermine the absoluteness of the papacy. The cardinals, having fought two Popes, could not now resist the third, for by their election of him they had surrendered their power and they had no option but to obey the decree of dissolution.

Their work, grandly begun, had the most fateful consequences: exuberant hope gave way to utter despair. As reform was not carried out the new Pope could not completely assert himself and so instead of two Popes Christendom now had three. The schism was even more intolerable, the general chaos worse than ever. The Council that might have saved the catholic world had plunged it still further into the depths.

In Prague the Germans did not yield to force. They swore to leave Prague if the Kutna Hora decree came into operation. If one of them broke his oath he was to be exiled, stripped of all honours and made to pay three hundred score groschens, a vast amount for a teacher or a student and attesting to the seriousness of the decision. They did indeed keep their oath. When all their efforts proved vain, they withdrew to Leipzig and founded a new university there.

On May 16, 1409, a long train of riders and waggons, Masters, students and servants, left Prague. Reports varyingly place their numbers at from one to forty thousand. It is probable that, including servants, about two thousand people left Prague. This figure was high enough; the other grotesquely high figures show what an impression this trek made. None shrank from the great sacrifices involved; they went without protection, and robbers took their toll of life and goods. What was to the Czechs an act of justice, setting right decades of wrong, seemed to the Germans a cruel injustice. Whether just or unjust, their departure was a severe blow to Prague, for with them went the greatness and the glory. Prague University, till then one of the biggest and most important centres of mediæval learning and thus an important power, sank to the status of a provincial university. The whole town felt the loss: trade and crafts were paralysed. For years to come Prague was a storm-centre. Could anyone preserve order when three Popes were reigning? Fresh resistance to the successful Masters was brewing.

When, in the same year, on October 17, Hus was solemnly elected first Rector of the Czech University, this dearly bought victory could no longer bring him satisfaction. For shortly before there had been a change pregnant with trouble for the Wyclifites. The Archbishop, realising that Wenceslas could not return to Gregory, had transferred his allegiance to Alexander and thus had regained power in Prague. The rejoicing that greeted his decision showed that the major battles still lay ahead.

NATION AND FAITH

THE national struggle which Hus and Jerome had led was at once just and unjust. The Germans, who had been invited to the country by all the Bohemian kings, had brought culture and civilisation to Bohemia. Important concessions were made to them in return for their developing the country and educating the Czechs in the spirit of western progress. The foundation of the University in particular had only been possible with German help, the original number of Czech Masters being very small. But the Czechs learnt rapidly and were soon ready to take management into their own hands. Then they found all the important and lucrative professions and offices filled by Germans, all privileges worth having in German hands.

Were the Germans to leave, having fulfilled their task? That would mean that they had to abandon what they had themselves built up with sacrifice and hard work. Prague and Bohemia had become native to them, they were members of this state which also played an important role for the whole of Germany. Why should they therefore leave?

But the Czechs, on the other hand, had to seek elbow-room on their own soil. Where in the whole world should they develop and rule if not in the land of their birth which they naturally regarded as theirs? The people were mainly Czech, which meant that the lucrative offices were paid with Czech taxes. Should not Czechs therefore reap the benefit?

These were rival claims that could never be satisfied as long as nationality was the decisive factor. In this case the situation was aggravated by social considerations. Any higher class resists encroachment by the class below, and here the higher class was mainly German, the lower mainly Czech. It is true that German citizens, for these very social reasons, understood the needs of the Czech people. This is attested by the foundation of the Bethlehem Chapel. In the course of the religious struggle it will be seen that the Czechs had the highest respect for devout Germans. But this does not alter the fact that economically the country was too small for the two nations once the Czechs claimed equal rights with the Germans. The Czechs could advance only at the expense of the Germans. The standards of simple justice cannot decide such a case.

Similar conditions to those in the country in general also prevailed in the University. Must the Germans suddenly leave Prague University because the Czechs had proved apt scholars? They had built up their position laboriously enough, resigning their prospects elsewhere. Or must the Czechs, because the Germans were good teachers, renounce the leading position in the University of Prague, maintained and financed by their own country? This was after all the one university in the world where they could be masters. The voting by "nations" may have been unjust; the Bohemian "nation" had grown continually while the German "nation" had been weakened by the founding of new universities in the Empire. But the simple reversal of the proportion of the votes was in its turn unjust. The more so as the Germans of Bohemia, coming with the Bohemian "nation," were always outvoted and thus remained without influence.

Hus attempted to keep this national struggle within reasonable limits. He once again used the image of the dog that cannot bark and is therefore useless to the herd, but it broke down as soon as he applied it to the University where Latin was used. He likened the Czechs to heirs growing up: sons who inherit a farm are at first servants of their father, but as soon as they are grown up they take over the inheritance. In the same way the Czechs, while learning, were the servants of the Germans, but now that they have learnt their lesson they must enter into the inheritance of the Germans. But this likeness too was not quite correct. For the Germans did not die like the father but in turn had their own heirs; although this was no reason why the Czechs should go on serving the Germans. Hus defended himself by saying that he had not driven out the Germans but that they drove themselves out by swearing not to obey the king; but the king had yielded to Czech pressure. However the problem was regarded, there was no just solution. And thus it was decided by a plain resort to force.

At this time, however, the emergence of the national problem was exceptional and shortlived. Hus was in earnest in his efforts to keep the struggle just and within moderate limits. It was not his fault that he had touched on a problem that knew no bounds. He and his age did not think nationally; as soon as their immediate aim had been reached, religious problems once more came to the fore. In Hus himself national and religious motives were for a while mingled; when he triumphed over the liberation of the University he was perhaps thinking nationally. This success itself, however, resulted in his turning from the purely national issue and brought to light the clear predominance of religious feeling in him.

National aims were from the beginning a means of paving the way for true Christian teaching. The departure of the Germans cleared the ground for the Wyclifites, but Hus had to recognise that the religious struggle had not been won by this victory. To his bitter disappointment those Czechs who only thought nationally went over to the enemy in religious questions; the national victory alone seemed to them adequate. This led to Hus's shedding all national ideas and fighting only for the religious cause. The nation was for him never an aim and an end in itself but a means and a preliminary to higher goals. And that led, it seemed to outside observers, to a united revolt of the Czech nation since the Czech people for the most part stood behind Hus. Yet this revolt was no national revolt: some of the Masters and Czech members of the Church still fought against Hus, and this hostile detachment of Czechs on the side of the enemy played an important role. Both sides fought without consideration of the nation; the aim was purely religious. The apparent national aim was due to the fact that on the other side the majority was German. But for this national reasons were not responsible but social conditions, as already described. The lack of a clear-cut national factor is typified by the royal family. The Luxembourgs were considered national Czech kings, although on their father's side they were French and at the same time were German princes; that might be passed over lightly as they were of Czech origin on their mother's side. Sophia, the wife of Wenceslas, who is regarded as a true Czech queen however, was a Bavarian princess of pure German ancestry. She was only reckoned as Czech because she followed and protected Hus.

After the victory of the Czechs it became rapidly very clear that religious issues were stronger than national ones. In the fight for the upper hand in the University all Czech Masters stood behind Hus and Jerome; when Hus became Rector he was still greeted by John Eliae with a solemn triumphal speech which praised him as the father of the nation. He may have been disappointed when Hus, far from exultingly, replied with Christian humility in a modest speech. Hus had already changed. He saw the new difficulties looming. And indeed, when the power of the Archbishop was once more established in Prague and the struggle about Wyclif started afresh, the older Czech Masters took up their stand against Hus under the leadership of John Eliae and Andrew of Brod, who had played such an active part in the national struggle.

At the same time the party also received a dangerous and considerable reinforcement through two renegades. Stanislav of Znojmo and Stephen Palec had led the first delegation of the King's to the cardinals. They were denounced to the " diavolo cardinale " as Wyclifites and thrown into prison by him. This confinement, about which they would report nothing, broke their conviction, and these two extreme Wyclifites, who had tried to convert Hus to Wyclif's doctrine of communion, returned as fanatical defenders of the Church. Palec in particular was dangerous and in Constance he was Hus's most active enemy. " Bowing his knee and baring his head he made every effort to attest his reverence for those whose behaviour had previously shocked him and who are still the same people ; " thus Hus described the transformation which for him was particularly painful since he lost in Palec one of his most loved friends. But in spite of the pain there was no doubt in his mind about his decision. " Palec is my friend, truth is my friend, and of these two I must choose the truth." Sadly he renounced all those fellow fighters who had only fought for national rights and not for true faith. He took up the fight against them too.

The decline of the University and the town through the withdrawal of the foreigners was for Hus a further spur in this fight for the faith. Whether the national fight had been just or unjust, the damage it had done could not be denied ; the clamours of those who had suffered could not be silenced. The idea of nation was too weak to justify such a sacrifice. Thus there took place in the spirit of Hus and of his followers a complete revaluation of this fight; the Czech people had been persecuted, poor and humiliated for the sake of its faith ; now that it was victorious and the national agitation was dying down it had to prove that it had been justified in waging this fight. It had to prove that Bohemia really was a pure nation which confessed the true faith. Hus adopted an old and probably wrong but haunting etymological interpretation of the name Bohemus ; he connected it with the Czech word " boh," God, and Bohemia became for him " the elect of God." The whole nation had to prove itself worthy of the name. And now that the fight was free of national alloy, of the struggle for power, he at last waged it with undivided energy and assumed leadership himself. He gloried in having been the stumbling block in the fight, for " Christ was a stumbling block and a rock of vexation." The temporary national occasion of the fight had vanished and ever more frequently he proclaimed, " Christ knows that I love a good German better than a bad Czech even if he be my blood-brother."

Hus had soon to stake his all in the fight. When the Archbishop announced on October 2, 1409, that he vowed obedience to Alexander V, there was an unexpected outburst of rejoicing in Prague. Solemn masses were read, the bell of the town hall in the Old Town, only rung on solemn occasions, pealed forth thrice, and bonfires were lit on every side, and all the six hundred alleys of Prague were illuminated. The German Mayor of the Old Town, together with the aldermen, went in procession through the streets of Prague with music until far into the night. All believed that the split in the Church was now at an end.

This belief soon proved false. Hus now faced a united Church front in Prague and this front was supported by Pope Alexander, the most important of the Popes for Prague since he supported Wenceslas and had, in the meantime, reconquered Rome. In October Zbynek was still out of favour with the Pope. A delegation of the Wyclifites, led by Marcus of Hradec, managed to persuade the Pope to summon him to Rome. But the Archbishop sent to Rome a much more magnificent delegation which took with it valuable horses, golden chalices and large sums of money as presents for the Pope. How could Alexander, no different from the other Popes, resist such arguments, even if he were not in any case glad enough to be able to dispense with his Wyclifite allies? The summons to the Archbishop was quashed. Instead the Pope sent to Prague a bull which fulfilled all the hopes of the Archbishop. It forbade under penalty of excommunication any preaching in private places, including certain chapels, by which the Bethlehem Chapel above all was meant. It ordered that the books of Wyclif were to be called in and condemned by a commission. And, as special concession to Zbynek, any appeal against the bull was forbidden. By a strange accident it took some months for this bull to reach Prague, but without it the fight had already entered a new phase.

One incident followed another. Hus's old enemy Protiva slunk into the Bethlehem Chapel, shrouded in a cloak and hood, and took down the sermon as Hus preached. Before the assembled congregation Hus called to him, "You there in the hood, take it along to the other side!" For he knew that the Archbishop was collecting evidence against him. On January 10, 1410, Zdenek of Laboun was arrested through the agency of the Town Council of the Old Town, which was completely in German hands, and taken to the Archbishop's palace and tortured. Zdenek had temporarily discharged the duties of Rector when the University offices were forcibly taken from the Germans. The Wyclifites must be made to fear vengeance. Hus soon succeeded in getting him freed, however. But the old enemies of any reform were rising up against Hus. The Prague parish priests raised a fresh charge against him. All heads were co-ordinated; the utterances that Protiva had written down, the charge that Hus openly preached against the clergy, that he "defamed, insulted and injured" them, that he attacked the Archbishop, that he incited the Czechs against the Germans, that he had driven the Germans out of Prague; and for the first time he was accused of a heretical attachment to Wyclif. Hus defended himself with the arguments already known: he could point out above all that his activity as preacher of the Synod, which did not differ from his later activities, had been approved by the Archbishop. It seemed most important for him to refute the charge of having driven out the Germans. He sent his answer to all the universities and had it stuck up in the streets of Prague. He succeeded too in convincing the Court of the Inquisition. On March 9, 1410, however, the papal bull arrived in Prague.

The Archbishop believed that he could now settle the whole opposition at one blow. He immediately set up a commission, which included John Eliae and Andrew of Brod, who were becoming more and more active against Hus. On June 18, eighteen books of Wyclif's were declared to be heretical and their burning was ordered. The University was ordered to hand over the rest of his writings within six days. Simultaneously it was decreed that the chapels were to be closed and any preaching outside the walls of the churches forbidden under pain of excommunication.

This reacted against the Archbishop, however. Till now all the Czech reformers had in the last resort complied: Milic had made a pilgrimage to the Pope, Janov had recanted; but Hus and the Wyclifites went over to the attack. In spite of the express prohibition Hus appealed from the "misinformed Pope to the Pope who might be better informed"; the University proclaimed a resolution that it was not satisfied with the measures of the Archbishop and openly lodged a protest with the king. It proved impossible to close the chapels and prevent Hus preaching. The king had not forgotten how little he could rely on the Archbishop and thus was the first to take his stand with Hus and the Wyclifites. But quite apart from all this the general indignation was far too great for the Church authorities to be able to implement their decisions.

On June 22, defying the ban, Hus preached a sermon that marked a turning point. From the whole of Prague the Czechs streamed together to the Bethlehem Chapel till the last seat was filled. (The name "chapel" only showed the status of this building in the Church; it was a large Gothic structure with its vaultings supported by fifteen columns and could hold several thousand people.) When Hus entered the pulpit his glance rested lovingly on the vast congregation. The breathless silence greeted him like a benediction, for he was boundlessly excited. The reception of this sermon, in which he bared his heart, would determine his whole future attitude. He consulted his people in order to explore the will of God.

Loudly and clearly he began with some words in memory of Alexander V who had died on May 3. This speech resembled his previous funeral oration which had had such dangerous consequences. Emphatically he castigated this Pope of whom he could not assert "whether he is in Heaven or Hell," this Pope who had risen "to persecute the Gospels and the Epistles and faith in Christ when he wrote to the Archbishop on his asses' skins that the Archbishop should burn the books of Wyclif."

These words rained down on his listeners. Then again he appealed to them mildly, gently, and from his heart—would he have to choose between his beloved congregation and his revered teacher? "See, they write in their bulls with which they seek to root out the false doctrine of Wyclif that the hearts of many of the people of Prague are infected with heresy." These words at last brought the silence to an end. "They lie, they lie," came echoing back to Hus. He felt once more the trust which enveloped him. "Yes, they lie," he said, taking up the words of his congregation, "for I tell you, and I thank God for it, that I have never seen a Bohemian heretic." And in the growing excitement he proclaimed: "I have appealed against the decision of the Archbishop and will appeal again." Then he put the question on which everything depended. "But will you, too, stand by me?" For a moment there reigned again that eerie silence—was his congregation going to abandon him? Then, like a chorus, the words greeted him: "We shall, we do, stand by you." Then he spoke the all-important words, long meditated, for which the moment was ripe: "The time has come for us, as Moses in the Old Testament commanded, to gird on our swords to defend the Word of God." He solemnly vowed that he would not submit and that he would endure to the end, even if they drove him into exile, even if it meant that he must die in prison.

The support that he found in his congregation gave him the strength to proclaim to the University, "In order that I may not by my silence lay myself open to the reproach that for a piece of bread or for fear of man I have abandoned the truth, I will defend to the death the truth that God has vouchsafed me, especially the truth of the Holy Scriptures. I know that truth remains and is strong and will retain victory to all eternity. If the dread of death makes me afraid, I hope in my God with the help of the Holy Spirit that the Lord Himself may give me steadfastness. If I have found grace in His eyes He will crown me with martyrdom. And that is a splendid victory."

He lodged with the Pope a fresh protest against the bull. It was wrong, he said, to accuse Bohemia of heresy since the same Archbishop had announced on July 17, 1408, that "after an investigation as careful as thorough, he had found no believer in false doctrine or heretic, nor could any have been found." This statement had been issued by Zbynek on the insistence of Wenceslas to support his claims to the kingship, although he was convinced of the contrary; and he had not been ashamed to confess he lied almost at once. Further, the books of Wyclif should not be burnt, Hus continued, for they contained much good and Hus and those like him had defended only the good. "The Church itself has ordained that books by heathens and heretics may be read according to need and occasion, not in order to obey them but that the false doctrines and heresy in them may be rejected and cursed and the useful things in them made serviceable in holy instruction. At the Universities there exists the regulation, approved by the Apostolic See, that the scholars and students may know, read, study and discuss the books of Aristotle, Averroes and other heathen philosophers although they call in question the foundations of faith and contain patent heresies." How then could Wyclif's books be condemned, as they had been, by a prejudiced commission within a period of time far too short for them to be studied seriously and thoroughly? In conclusion, the closing of the Bethlehem Chapel must not be allowed since Christ Himself had till his death preached "in the schools, in the streets and alleys, on the highways, on the lake, on the mount, in the fields and the wilderness," and at His resurrection had proclaimed that preaching, the bringing of God's word to all, everywhere and at all times, was the most important duty of all.

Readiness to die for his conviction had still further heightened Hus's fervour, inner fortitude and faith. "Must I obey the Archbishop when he gives commands that contradict the commands of God? Far be it from me. Am I greater than Christ and his Apostles that I should not suffer for the Gospel?" he wrote in a letter. His decision to accept a martyr's death slowly changed to a deep longing for it that he might prove his loyalty to Christ to the last. Martyrdom became for him a longed-for proof that he had not only been called but also chosen. This transformation increased the clarity and forthrightness of his language. The appeal to the Pope, for all its scholastic reserves and reservations, showed no fear of plain speaking. " Because God must be obeyed more than man in all things which are necessary for salvation," he concluded, " we demand for the first, the second and the third time, emphatically, more emphatically and most emphatically, and with all the rights that are ours, that a just answer and messengers be sent us, be they who they may, who will establish justice and administer it to us." He demanded that " as long as this appeal is not answered. Nothing new shall be attempted or introduced, be it by whom," and he demanded this without making concessions, " whereby we do not bind ourselves to bring superfluous proofs, but only such as seem suitable to us to the support of our ends." In the face of Christ differences of rank among men vanish ; Hus spoke to the Pope on equal terms. He who had given himself to Christ need fear no human power.

This appeal too made no impression on the Archbishop, for the new Pope was Balthasar Cossa, the " diavolo cardinale." He had ascended the papal throne as John XXIII, after, it was said, poisoning Alexander V. The Archbishop need not fear that the unimpassioned arguments of Hus could call forth a sudden change of outlook in the Pope. The protection given Hus by the king did not restrain the Archbishop either, for the power of the king was once more in the balance. On May 15 Rupert had died and a fresh quarrel broke out for the German kingship. Sigismund wanted to be king, Wenceslas wanted to prevent him : and as he felt too weak alone he joined with Jost who promised to recognise him as " elder King of Rome and Emperor to be." Jost undertook to get Wenceslas crowned in Rome on condition that he was allowed to exercise the real authority. Sigismund was supported by three electors, Jost by the remainder. So there were now not only three Popes but also three Kings of Germany. The great powers that had safeguarded order in the mediæval world were sinking ever lower.

If the Czech people were striving for national independence they could have made use of the general chaos to strike for their liberation. But the Archbishop led one side and Hus and Jerome the other, and all followed these religious leaders. As long as Wenceslas lived and, be it never so inadequately, guaranteed the preaching of the faith, all struggles remained internal. The influence of the anti-reform Germans within the country was further reduced. The impotence of the kingdom and of the empire was obvious, but even so neither had as yet been encroached upon.

The only person exploiting the chaos was the Archbishop. The king demanded the postponement of any decision until the arrival of Jost, whom he expected for consultation. The Archbishop attempted to forestall him. On July 17 of that same eventful year of 1410, a strong guard was mounted around the episcopal palace to prevent the entrance of any strangers; none of the opposing party was to learn prematurely what was afoot. In the meantime in the courtyard of the palace a huge bonfire was feverishly erected and on it the books of Wyclif which had been handed over were laid. There were about two hundred volumes, including many splendid ones which in those days of hand copying were exceedingly costly. The Archbishop himself hastily lit the fire; a loud, monotonously chanted Te Deum lent solemnity to the precipitate step. Bells were tolled as if for a funeral. Were they ringing for the sacrifices that would soon be made on account of these books? At the same time the condemnation of these books was proclaimed again and preaching in chapels finally forbidden. The Archbishop wanted to confront the king and the Wyclifites with an accomplished fact. He held his victory for assured. In view of the bonfire nobody would dare resist.

But the Archbishop had once again miscalculated. Instead of defeating his enemy he provoked a counter-attack that drove him from Prague. The excitement aroused by the burning of the books was so great that the Archbishop had to flee to his strong castle of Roudnice two days later. From there he proclaimed the excommunication of Hus and all those who had supported the appeal to the Pope. Bloody street rioting ensued in the seething town. The people prevented the proclaiming of the ban, bursting into the churches and driving out the priests who would obey the Archbishop. At St. Vitus's forty priests were driven from the altar. Heedless of the sanctity of the place six men with drawn swords forced their way into St. Stephen's and the preacher hardly escaped with his life. The courtiers, with Voksa of Waldstein at their head, took the side of the insurgents. When they happened to find themselves in the majority many of the priests and monks took their revenge on the followers of Hus, dragging them into their refectories and beating them half dead with newly-cut switches. But even the chance of this petty revenge was rare. They could not hold their own against the people, and the ban was not proclaimed. Instead, lampoons on the semi-literate Archbishop were sung in the streets and rumours spread that the costliest books had not been burnt but only confiscated.

Under cover of this unrest the University began a grand and thorough defence of the books of Wyclif on July 27. For fourteen days on end every separate work was cleared of the shameful allegations made against it by all the weapons of scholasticism. It was a mighty demonstration by the defenders of spiritual freedom, of freedom of thought and instruction, against coercion backed by stupidity and appealing to the fire and the stake to enforce it. There was a severe castigation of priests who exploited superstition instead of combating it, like the priest who was spreading the tale among the people that he had been to Hell and there seen the English Master roasting. The motive of the condemnation was rejected, since it credited Masters and students with no powers of discrimination, no intellectual standards. The decision to burn the whole world could equally well be justified since, as in Wyclif's writings, so in the world too, false doctrine and heresy occurred. " It is an ignominious logic when these bonfire theologists say that the bad must be burnt with the good, for it would be equally logical to say that the good people must be burnt with the stubborn heretics and cursed with the accursed." Thus Hus summed up his charges. Later he added that Christ had forbidden that the tares should be torn up from the harvest field lest the wheat should be trampled and torn up with the tares. At this meeting Hus declared that he was ready to face martyrdom for the truth. He trusted that the truth would triumph even though might had the upper hand for the moment ; he knew that even victorious might was impotent before the spirit.

Hus had looked death in the face ; the flames could not frighten him even though they were already consuming his books.

On the eve of the burning of the books in Prague the battle of Tannenberg took place. Far from Bohemia, in a corner of Europe, Poland and Lithuania together smashed the army of the dreaded Teutonic Knights. It was proved once again that heavily armed knights could not stand up to the latest forms of warfare. They were utterly helpless if their first assault failed and the foot soldiers could close in on them. Flight was impossible. Even the numerous mercenary troops supporting the Knights at Tannenberg could not keep open their retreat for them and thus they suffered losses which were huge for the comparatively small armies of those days. Two thousand Teutonic Knights and six hundred foreign knights assisting them were left on the field, and fifteen thousand prisoners were taken. The main strength of the Order was destroyed and its fate seemed sealed.

Prague had its stake in this far-off battle. King Wenceslas had been called on to arbitrate but Poland had refused to recognise his award. Enraged, he assisted the Teutonic Knights. This made little practical difference. When they did not appeal for his mediation in the peace negotiations he was again vexed and turned to Poland, so often his ally. It carried more weight that Bohemian sympathies in general were with Poland ; two of the fifty battalions of the Polish army were Czech. The bond of sympathy between the Slavs was so great that the king's anger could not prevent help being given. This sympathy, however, was as ineffectual as national feeling at that time. The bond with Poland, to whom Jerome would soon be turning, had no practical results. Hus, on hearing of the victory, congratulated the King of Poland in a joyful letter " from the depth of his heart," expressing his hope at seeing the king with " his bodily eyes." This wish, which if fulfilled might have changed events so much in his favour, remained ungratified. Czech help at Tannenberg, however, did mean that Zizka, the unconquered Hussite general,took part in a decisive victory and learnt a lesson he was never to forget.

It taught him more than good generalship. The great victory was never pressed home ; when Marienburg and several other fortresses still resisted, the Lithuanians dropped out of the fight. Then the Hungarians penetrated into Poland and the Poles had to patch up a hurried peace with the Knights. This left the situation substantially unchanged. Thus one of the most overwhelming victories in world history was inconclusive because a unifying idea was lacking. On the other hand, since the north-eastern territories, the militant conversion of which to Christianity was the *raison d'être* of the Knights, had in the meantime become Christian of their own accord, the Knights too, having outlived their inspiration, failed to exploit this favourable peace. An idea alone can give a consistent direction to clashes of power and use them for pressing forward with closed ranks towards a goal. The consciousness expressed in the words of Hus, " I know that truth remains and is strong and will retain victory to all eternity," this consciousness alone lent Zizka the strength to resist the assault of the whole world with a weak army based on a small nation.

The idea and the consciousness were emerging ever more rapidly in Prague. The two great powers whose quarrels had constantly dominated the Middle Ages were now in spite of their internal decomposition forced back into the picture by Hus's clear cut challenge. King and Church must contend once more for mastery. The struggle for the separation of secular and spiritual rule emerged once more from the confused clash of powers.

The king, away from Prague all this while, now returned to play the mediator. He forbade the singing of satirical songs under pain of death, and took a cautious stand on the side of Hus. The Archbishop was to pay compensation for the books he had burnt and Hus was allowed to continue preaching. Wenceslas thus sought to lead the quarrel into harmless channels : the burning of the books was reduced to simple damage of property, and the decision about Hus postponed until after the appeal. If the Archbishop were really the weaker he could still honourably withdraw. But he did not comply for he knew that a greater power stood behind him ; he counted on the help of the Pope. His trust was not disappointed. John XXIII, the keenest enemy of any reform, handed over the appeal to Cardinal Colonna, who would be Pope in Constance and would again frustrate any reform of the Church. This cardinal blindly pursued the Church policy and decided against Hus ; the appeal was rejected, the bull of Alexander V was confirmed and Hus was summoned to appear in Bologna, the seat of the Pope, on October 1, 1410. The Archbishop immediately enforced the ban which was to operate until Hus had cleared himself in

Bologna. Now, however, the king took up the gauntlet. With the energy shown once against Archbishop Jenstejn and Pomuk he abandoned any further attempt at mediation and intervened in the fight.

There were still three kings and three Popes. But as big issues were at stake the king ceased playing off one Pope against another, and the Pope one king against another. King Wenceslas and Pope John XXIII stood face to face.

The king wrote to the Pope. He enclosed letters from the queen, a number of nobles, and the town councils of the Old Town, the New Town, and Small Side. The last two speak for the energy of Wenceslas, for the Old Town and Small Side, predominantly German, would never have written voluntarily. As the first letters arrived too late, a fresh letter was sent by a solemn delegation richly supplied with gold. In this second letter, in which he tried to help his " faithful, saintly and beloved chaplain," Wenceslas took up the demands of Hus in a forthright fashion : he insisted " that the dispute about the books be completely settled, that our kingdom may see an end of discord which we will not tolerate, since with the help of God nobody in our realm, as far as we know, has fallen into error or heresy on account of the books. We also wish that the Bethlehem Chapel, provided by us for the free preaching of the Gospels to the honour of God and the salvation of our people, shall continue to discharge its task, and that the Master John Hus, confirmed in his appointment to this chapel, shall preach the word of God in peace. We further desire that the summoning of this Master to Bologna shall be quashed, most blessed Father ; should anyone have any charge to make against him, however, let him do it in our land before the University of Prague or another competent court, for it would not be salutary for our land for a man preaching so beneficially for all to be handed over to his enemies and a whole nation thereby brought into disquiet." Such plain and energetic language was seldom used by Wenceslas. He proposed in addition that at the king's cost the Pope should send a legate to Prague to arbitrate in the dispute.

The Pope, however, was no less firm. This was particularly clear when Hus himself sent a delegation to Bologna. It was led by his courageous and skilful disciple John of Jesenice, who consciously risked his life. He first arranged for a defence of the books of Wyclif by the University of Bologna, which was prepared to do this, having lived on uneasy terms with the Pope since he had become a close neighbour. Then he obtained from the lawyers of the Curia Romana a certificate that Hus was genuinely unable to come to Bologna : this was only a matter of money. Finally he offered himself as surety. He was ready to go to the stake if his case could be refuted on biblical grounds, provided that a representative of the opposing side also declared himself ready for trial by fire. But why should the Church thus place one of its own in danger ? The skill of John of Jesenice was vain. Explanations meant nothing even when they complied with the formal demands of the Church : the Church did not want to listen but to rule. The delegation was not given a hearing. Without examining their arguments, without considering the letters of the king and the court Cardinal Colonna in February 1411 excommunicated Hus for not obeying the summons of the Church. The people of Prague this time dared not oppose the proclamation and on March 15 it was read from all the chancels in Prague, except where followers of Hus officiated.

This apparent success, however, revealed how powerless the Church had already become in Bohemia. The papal ban proved completely ineffective. Instead, one of the basic demands of Wyclif and Hus seemed fulfilled. The secular power became conscious of its spiritual rights and set about purging the Church, curtailing its excessive wealth and making necessary reforms.

Royal power had in the meantime been consolidated : Jost died on January 17, and Wenceslas thereupon made up his quarrel with Sigismund and satisfied himself with the mere title of emperor-elect while Sigismund was sole and undisputed German king. This agreement proved its worth. Wenceslas inherited Moravia and Lusatia ; this secured and satisfied his thirst for power. Sigismund on the other hand, now clearly in possession of Brandenburg, leased this eternal bone of contention to the Hohenzollerns, in whose possession Brandenburg remained henceforth. He thereby created for himself strong and reliable backing in the Empire. Brotherly quarrels between the last two surviving Luxembourgs did not entirely cease, but they had lost their sting.

As always, the limitation of his scope increased the energy of Wenceslas and he threw himself into the cause of Hus against the Church. The Archbishop, attempting to enforce the ineffectual papal ban, had his goods and properties confiscated by the king. Enraged, Zbynek replied from the security of Roudnice with the excommunication of fifty court officials. When this proved unavailing he placed Prague and its surroundings for a radius of two miles under an interdict. But even interdict had lost its force by now. Instead unprecedented scenes testified to the power of the king and a new spirit in the country. On May 6,

1411 the king rode into the Cathedral and confiscated all its treasures to prevent the Church from removing them. They included the costly reliquary and the coffin of St. Wenceslas, both infinitely precious to this devout country. Henceforth they were to be guarded in the royal castle of Karluv Tyn : the secular power would watch over the Church. On May 25 the clergy reported to the Pope that the secular power prevented the interdict from being carried out. The confiscation of Church property continued ; the greater part of Bohemia was in the hands of the reformers, who almost seemed to turn the country into an island of reformation.

Engaged in a struggle with the highest clergy in the country, excommunicated by the Pope, summoned to appear at Bologna, Hus quietly carried on his work under the protection of the king as though oblivious of the storm he had raised. The king protected him so ably that nothing changed for him during the whole dispute. He could carry on his work, continue his activities at the University, and preach in the Bethlehem Chapel. For his sake Prague bore the interdict ; the Czech people stood by him with touching love, the court and some of the nobility were with him. The queen herself quoted his words and defended them in a letter to the Pope : " The word of God shall not be fettered but shall be proclaimed in the streets and squares and from the housetops, yea, wherever the need of the people demands it." She often listened among the congregation to the sermons in the Bethlehem Chapel.

The fame of Bohemia as a hearth of the faith reached England. This shows how confident was the voice of Hus and how near the Bohemian Wyclifites thought themselves to their goal. English Lollards, with death at the stake before them, were fired with fresh hopes and wrote to Prague enthusiastically. Hus answered them, relating what joy the letter had caused when he read it during a sermon which " almost ten thousand " people had come to hear. His congregation begged him to translate the letter into Czech. For, " already the people that wandered in darkness have seen the great light of Jesus Christ : those who dwelt in the shadow of death have seen the light of His truth which now, with the help of our Saviour, is seized by our people, by the peasants, the knights, the counts and the ordinary citizens. Our King and his whole court, the Queen and the common people, have been won for the word of Jesus Christ. Know, dearest brother, that the people have ears for nothing but the Holy Scriptures, above all for the Gospels and the Epistles ; whenever a preacher of the Holy Scriptures appears in town or village, on a farm or in a castle, the people stream to him, disdaining the clergy who would not preach to them." Hus concluded this letter, through which his readiness for martyrdom shone forth, with greetings from the "Church of Christ in Bohemia" to the "Church of Christ in England."

The king's ride into the Cathedral must have seemed an important success to Hus. Enthusiastically he supported the king in his writings and his sermons, quoting the words of St. Augustine. "Say not, What have I to do with the king? For what have you to do with earthly possessions? Earthly possessions are only held through the right of the king." Then he added, "It is therefore presumption to assert that our princes, however fallible they may be, cannot take away the incomes of the clergy. For by such correction the intentions of the founders are not violated but in very truth fulfilled. It would be strange if a priest could go forth and rob, and rape virgins and honourable women without his weapons, horses, guns and swords being legally taken from him. Yet may churchmen undermine whole empires and their peoples, swear to betray the king to his enemies or to depose and even kill him, and yet the crown not be permitted to oppose the clergy and take away the goods which it had given them?" He described the right of confiscation of goods as "the easiest and meetest way of bringing the clergy back to the way of the Gospel."

Temporal goods were "a burden holding back the clergy from their offices, and to relieve them of this would be a great help for the clergy, leading them back by the easiest way to the life of Christ and the Apostles." "Kings must do this," Hus said, "in accord with the Word of God and not in obedience to human statutes." The faithful must themselves "take heed and with a lively mind discuss whether the orders of the Pope and the princes in any way are contrary to the law of God. If they come to this conclusion, then they must resist to the death and in no wise obey."

In the case of the interdict, Hus asserted, it was clear that the king was right and the Church wrong. "It is clear that our King Wenceslas, by withholding the incomes of the priests and thus compelling them to preach and perform the offices due, is exercising the power entrusted to him by God. It is further clear that the Archbishop in imposing an interdict on Prague and the district for two miles around is fighting against the power of God, and that all priests who thus resist God with him are, unless they repent it, heading for damnation. For it is the king who demands the good works of preaching and praising God." And how was the Church behaving? "They scorn and excommunicate, pronounce interdicts and rob God of His honours: without reason they excommunicate those who are their friends and do them good in that they wish to bring them back to bondage to Christ. For if they respected the example of their Master they would not murmur against the withholding of their income—I do not even say the taking of it away. The Founder of the faith bore patiently the taking away of His very clothing, and when men sacrificed His Body He did not command any suspension of services or pronounce an interdict." The priests, "cohabiters, greedy, adulterous, venal, and burdened with other crimes," had simply "ceased to perform their duties at the frivolous command of an Archbishop, given without any just reason."

It is striking that after such preachings Hus still held back from the final struggle with the Church. The temperamental Jerome, who would have rushed pell-mell into battle, was once again away from Prague. For his preachings he was now in flight from Hungary. Shortly afterwards, he would flee from Vienna. He was the "problem-child" of the University, continually in need of rescue as he brought one hornet's nest after another about his ears. Hus, on the other hand, did not force the pace of developments and intervened only by his writings or words. For another question of conscience loomed up before him.

The papal ban was a relief in comparison with the Archbishop's for it excommunicated him for disobedience and not for heresy. The Pope had not yet confirmed the Archbishop's course. Once Hus decided to go to Bologna the ban would be lifted. But in this very improvement in the situation lay the problem that weighed upon him so heavily. Hus did not obey the summons to Bologna; instead he called upon the secular power and under its protection remained in Prague. This secular intervention was in harmony with his doctrine of Church reform: but had he the right to shield himself thus? He had often declared his readiness to suffer martyrdom for his faith: he believed he felt no fear and would accept death cheerfully for Christ. Was he not therefore in duty bound to go to Bologna, whatever the risk? The king and his friends did not wish him to go and the conduct of the Pope betrayed clearly enough how justified were their warnings. John of Jesenice was not only still refused audience but had also been imprisoned. Hus might meet his death in Bologna: and this would throw Bohemia into confusion and demand sacrifices that Hus could not but hesitate to take repon sibility for. Had not Christ, however, accepted death knowing full well what terrors he would thereby unleash? Feeling held Hus back from this step, but in the scholastic world reason alone carried weight. How should he defend his conduct?

The accusations of his enemies must have touched Hus very deeply at this time. Above all those of the Prior of Dola, one of the wisest of his antagonists, seemed to proclaim the secret thoughts of Hus himself. The Prior reproached him, "You have heard of no wars or rumours of wars, and yet you are already miserably frightened despite the admonitions of Christ! You call yourself a fearless preacher for the defence of truth, which is Christ, and yet where no danger is you are frightened of death! Is then the word of God dead within you, 'Fear not those who slay your body but cannot slay your soul?' Have you not read, 'Who will accuse the elect of God?' Justice is of God. Who will condemn? Summoned by the Curia you should have appeared in all humility and said with the apostles, 'If God is with us, who is against us'? Lo, God did not spare His own Son who for us all gave Himself up to the court of Pilate, the godless judge: are you then greater than Christ? Christ did not evade this but for us all was judged by an unjust judge, and you scorn, nay, damn, the sentence of the highest Pontifex, Christ's Vicar, for the purging of your sins!"

It seems like mockery when the degenerate Church produced such arguments, quoting the example of Christ only as a weapon against their opponent. Hus, however, ruled his life by this example and for years had examined all his deeds in its light, hoping ultimately to lose himself in Christ. He felt, though, that his hour had not yet come. Christ did not go to Jerusalem at the first summons: He had exhorted his disciples to avoid danger, He had carefully chosen the hour of His death. But what were the signs for rejecting this present hour? When he was once more cited by the Pope, Hus set out his reasons for not obeying. Some of these reasons already applied: but the decisive sign granted him at the second summons was still lacking. He obeyed the clear dictate of his feelings but yet some doubts remained because he could not explain them by the Scriptures.

This hour in which Hus contested the summons to Bologna marked the beginning of his way to Constance. The problem remained henceforth for him a thorn in his flesh, at once driving him forward and dragging him back. Even the later sign could calm him only for a short time. He could from this moment evoke his own martyrdom at any hour. This had an immeasurable significance for him, for he truly longed for it and with his longing there was now mingled the perpetual doubt as to whether he had not absented himself from martyrdom too long already. Hardly a day passed in which he was not tormented by this question. At the same time this longing also began to appear to him as a seduction. The feeling holding him back was a wonderful feeling breaking across the whole tradition of the Middle Ages, a new respect for human life. He was suddenly aware of his life as a unique and precious gift which he would not and must not throw away : his death was truly a great sacrifice not to be made meaninglessly. "Because within and without Bohemia persecution threatened me, especially from the Germans, I held more to the counsel that it is tempting God to expose one's life except when the good of the Church demands it." This was the first reason he later gave for his conduct. Simply because he longed for death he was frightened to embrace it too soon. This reason, however, appeared inadequate in an age which contemptuously squandered human life and he continually examined himself to find a clearer and more convincing one. Only then, did he believe, would he be able to say when his hour had come.

His new uncertainties were, for a time, so great that they even seemed to endanger his way. For he had also to confess to a mistake : he had trusted too much in the secular power. The ride into the Cathedral was only an episode. The opposing powers were already far too weak to be able to fight out an ideological battle : they were much more inclined to treat with each other. The real fight for the faith had to be carried out on a different level. The religious fervour of the court was only apparent : lust for power and greed were more and more the motive of the attack on the Church, and enthusiasm for Hus veiled selfish ends. The sudden energy of Wenceslas could as suddenly die down : many signs indicated that his will might soon be paralysed again. Hus, however, although he began to perceive his false position, found himself inextricably involved in this struggle. As he believed his hour had not yet come he used the king's protection. He must reach inner clarity before giving himself up to death. This explains why he joined in a new attempt at mediation by the king almost to the extent of jeopardising his convictions.

Now that the power of the rebellious Archbishop seemed broken, the king was concerned with restoring quiet to his country. He therefore called on the Archbishop and Hus to submit to arbitration by himself and three advisers. This time the Archbishop complied, as in the meantime he had become only too aware of his lack of power. He hoped in this way to regain influence. And, at Hus's behest, the University too complied. On July 3, 1411 both parties solemnly accepted in advance the award of the tribunal. The Archbishop was ordered to write to the Pope that in " Bohemia, Prague and Moravia " he had been unable to find any false doctrine or heresy and that all dissension between him and Hus and the University had been settled by the king and that he therefore begged the Pope to raise " all punitive measures and to absolve worthy Master Hus from any personal summons and for his not yet having appeared, let the benevolence of an absolution be granted him." In return, the goods of the Church would be returned. Hus on his side had to make a public confession of faith that would clear him of all the charges made against him by the Church.

This confession of faith by Hus, which plainly betrayed his incertitude, was made on September 1. " Paying due obedience to the Church of Christ and its Supreme Head," he began, and it was not clear whether he meant the invisible Church and its head, Christ, or the visible Church and its head, the Pope. This ambiguity ran through the whole confession : the separate sentences appeared loyal to the Church if they were interpreted in the sense of the Church : they seemed Wyclifite if they were interpreted in the sense which Hus and Wyclif had given them. Hus spoke before a scholastic audience who all knew the purpose of his confession : they, enjoying subtle explanations, may have seen and welcomed in it a saving solution. Hus simply enumerated the charges made against him and described them as baseless, as in most cases they were, especially the Wyclifite interpretation of communion ascribed to him. Then, however, there followed such sentences as, " It is not true that I have taught the people that the secular lords should take away their incomes from the clergy, not true that I have advised them to strike at the clergy with the secular sword, not true, that indulgences are worthless." What was the position with regard to these assertions ? Had Hus regretted his alliance with the secular sword ? This would explain some of these sentences : but was he not here steering dangerously near the recantation he had always refused to make ? He concluded proudly, " I offered to answer to all and sundry, without distinction, and if anyone could prove anything against me to suffer death at the stake if I did not desist. And I am still ready to render an account before the University of Prague and all the Prelates if anyone has aught against me. But up till now none has appeared who was prepared to accept the law of retaliation, one, that is, who, should he be proved wrong, would suffer death at the stake." Was Hus still justified in this pride ?

This question cannot be clearly and finally answered. A cruel-kind fate allowed this dubious confession of faith, wrested from a tormented soul, to be swallowed up in the confusion of the times. The moment of weakness, which descends on every religious genius in an hour of decision—for religious genius lies in responsibility and not in action—remained without consequences. By degrees alliance with the inadequate secular power dissolved and both king and Pope, each in his own way, forced Hus to pursue his path even more consistently than hitherto. Hus himself, freed from all false considerations, trusted now only in his faith and his friends.

Shortly after his confession of faith, nevertheless, Hus betrayed that he was not ready to give up the fight. In the same month of September envoys to Sigismund from the King of England arrived in Prague: among them was John Stokes, Master of the University of Cambridge. The Prague Masters invited him to a banquet at the Prague University. Stokes, however, was opposed to the Wyclifites and brusquely refused the invitation, saying, "He who reads Wyclif's books or studies them must necessarily fall into heresy in the course of time, however well disposed he may be and steadfast in his faith." The Masters were rightly indignant over such language, unheard of in the friendly intercourse between the universities of those days: thereupon Stokes modified his statement somewhat, without, however, altering the gist of it, and thus he fanned the quarrel once again. Hus entered the lists in defence of his beloved Master: on a public placard he challenged Stokes to a debate. Yet this renewed outburst of Hus failed. Stokes did not put in an appearance, maintaining that as an envoy he was not obliged to accept such a challenge. Stokes was later in Constance to make common cause with the most inveterate opponents of Hus when protected by the Council. Hus went through with the debate in the absence of Stokes and disproved the contentions of his antagonist. As, however, there was no reply, Hus's speech caused no repercussions and did not efface the impression of his strange confession of faith.

It almost seemed as though one moment's weakness on the part of Hus has sufficed to resolve the whole struggle into nothingness. The Archbishop, disappointed in his hopes, did not hesitate to break his solemn undertaking. He fled to Litomysl to John "the Iron Bishop," the keenest opponent of the Wyclifites and later of the Hussites. This Bishop, whose strong personality overshadowed that of the Archbishop, had consistently supported Sigismund. Wenceslas had therefore twice prevented his being nominated Archbishop. His bitter energy lent Zbynek the strength for the last resistance. From Litomysl Zbynek raised the interdict but not the ban on Hus and the fifty court officials: instead he complained to the king that in Prague he had held a splendid five weeks' court and yet had only once been received in audience with the king while "my adversaries have received audience by your grace as often as they begged it." False doctrines were still being preached, spiritual offenders were not summoned to the Church courts and the incomes of parish priests and prelates were still being withheld, he alleged. He therefore refused to send the Pope the letter which was to be the preliminary to any change. He threatened the king to enlist the help of Sigismund against him. This threat compelled him, in fact, to continue his flight to Sigismund, but he died on September 28, 1411 in Bratislava.

Hus's position was much improved by this. But this also condemned him to further inactivity. The more so as the appointment of the king's personal physician, Albik, as Archbishop was confirmed by the Pope after some protest: this Archbishop wanted nothing but peace and quiet. This appointment was indeed a scandal. Albik was a layman, even a widower, and only when he became Archbishop was he ordained to the lowest order of priesthood. But how could Hus oppose the trusted man of the king who had been appointed simply on his account? Even the Pope seemed tired of the quarrel. He passed on the Hus case from one commission to another, obviously with a view to postponing indefinitely a final verdict. Thus, after Hus, the Church, too, betrayed its weakness. The Archbishop's ineffectual measures were neither confirmed nor abolished.

At this moment, however, Jerome returned to Prague. He was the man who for good or ill knew no weariness and no second thoughts. He had escaped from custody in Vienna. He had dared to go to Vienna although in Buda, "in the royal Chapel, clad as a layman and with a long beard, he had in the presence of the king and many reverend fathers, bishops and other prelates and men of various degrees, preached many vexatious, false and heretical principles of faith, and other things offending the order of the Church and offending pious ears, whereby rebellious motions against the clergy by the secular lords might easily have followed." The Viennese had quickly taken him into protective custody: but now he was writing from the safety of Moravia to the official Grillenperg to whom he had pledged himself not to leave Vienna and who had therefore, apart from being ensnared by his charm and learning, guarded him all too laxly.

In this letter, as in hardly another document, Jerome's mocking, confident, winning personality, conscious of its aims, comes to life. He wrote, " Know that I find myself sound and well, and ready with many friends to serve you and yours at any time. Of the promise extorted from me I hold myself relieved when the worth of such a promise is well weighed. For I have not by any means evaded the law, which, on the condition of just bail, I am ready to face. But to stand alone among so many hundreds of enemies, you yourself if you loved me truly would by no means advise me to do. For behind my back my enemies have set intrigues afoot and spread the nets of their injustice. But my soul is now saved like a sparrow from the snares of the hunter : the snare is torn and I am free. I thank you, however, and will always thank you. And as for all my adversaries, send them to me in Prague together with all the witnesses and there I will conduct my case. Know moreover that I was in your Church in Laa and that I entertained there the schoolmaster and town copyist in thanks for the hospitality you showed me : and wherever I may be at any time I shall serve you and yours."

Shortly afterwards Jerome arrived in Prague. Here he soon had a chance of intervening, aflame himself and kindling fire in others. For the opposition between Hus and the Church was too deep to be removed by petty politics. It did not arise from political differences but from an inward faith. In actual fact the very essence of the Church was the issue, and a new manifestation of it soon inspired Hus and Jerome to conduct this their most bitter fight.

STORM OVER INDULGENCES

WHEN Sigismund was finally elected Roman King on July 21, 1411 and received general recognition, he on his side hastened to recognise Pope John XXIII as the only legitimate Pope. The years of turmoil had taught him that he could only hope to re-establish the royal power if he succeeded in healing the fateful schism. John XXIII was supported by those cardinals who at the Council of Pisa had wanted at least to begin the reform of the Church : he was at that moment also the most powerful of the Popes. Sigismund could thus hope most speedily to reach his goal with the help of this Pope. Selfish considerations also played their part. John was engaged in a struggle with Ladislas of Naples, who claimed the Hungarian throne and thus was an opponent of Sigismund. Yet it seemed as though this reason carried less weight and that with the years Sigismund had developed a greater seriousness and a consciousness of his task. For he did not satisfy himself with the recognition of the Pope : he also urged him to call the second council, promised in Pisa, to begin the work of reform that had so oft been postponed.

In the meantime in Italy this Pope elected by the Council was making war on the Roman Pope Gregory XII who still held office and honours. This struggle was little concerned with the healing of the schism. It was simply a fight for power carried on with the weapons of the Church. In spite of his promises to resign, Gregory still clung to his papal office. To save himself, he even delivered over Rome to Ladislas of Naples. Ladislas had, however, lost Rome again, and Pope Alexander V, the predecessor of John, could in the meantime have returned there. John, however, still the "diavolo cardinale" at that time, grudged him this triumph. He constantly postponed the re-entry. This was probably the reason for his finally poisoning Alexander. On April 12, 1411 John himself re-entered the Holy City with great pomp.

On May 19 Ladislas suffered a new defeat. On this occasion John's dreams of himself as Cæsar were very clearly revealed. The captured flags were first hung high from St. Peter's, then lowered before the crowd and then dragged in the dust in a triumphal procession. But the triumph was premature. The victory was so badly followed up that the fortunes of battle changed. " On the first day after my defeat the enemy had me in his hands, on the second day my realm, and on the third neither me nor my realm," said Ladislas later. In August he was once more before Rome. The war entered a long and indecisive phase with John entrenched in the Vatican, Ladislas encamped before Rome, and Gregory residing in Gaeta. The opponents were all too exhausted to gather their strength for the decisive blow.

In spite of all setbacks, this war was welcome to John, for more than Ladislas he feared the new council which might undermine his power. His dissolute rule, justifying all the reproaches levelled against the Church, made his fear seem well-founded. As long as the war with Ladislas continued he had a reason for postponing the meeting of the council, for, he argued, only when the Antipope was defeated and Rome saved could he re-unite the Church. He therefore paid no heed to the urgings of Sigismund, instead summoning Christendom to a crusade against Ladislas. To get the money for this campaign he issued two new bulls on September 7 and December 12 in which he excommunicated Ladislas as a perjurer, renegade, blasphemer, heretic and a supporter of heretics, and promised a plenary remission of sins to those who in person or by sending armed forces or by money supported the new crusade. A new wholesale business in indulgences was about to begin.

At this time the dangerous path of Hus was becoming ever straiter and narrower. He had largely renounced the national struggle and taken up the fight for a pure faith without consideration of his Czech opponents, and thus of national unity. He had lost his illusions about alliance with the secular power and was about to renounce its protection. He simply offered himself as a sacrifice to his convictions. Even the importance of friends was gradually dwindling in spite of the recent intervention of Jerome. On his way to the true sacrificial death for which he strove nobody could support him. But as his way grew straiter, the more broadly flowed the stream of his creative force.

It was as though the premonition of death spurred Hus on to his highest achievement. In the last three years of his life, which were overflowing with difficulties, struggles and dangerous distractions, the writings he produced would have sufficed to fill many a long life. His turning from many of the Masters and the deceits of worldly powers, the disappointments that lay in store for him from court and nobility, served to free his creative spirit from its last shackles. Hitherto he had preached in Czech but written almost exclusively in Latin : now in his writings, too,

B. Picart del.

GREGOIRE XII.

he turned to the true faithful, the people. This use of Czech for the first time made his writings of great importance. The Latin works were to a large extent bound by the conventions of scholasticism, but now the vital proximity to life of his sermons permeated too his written style.

The Czech people owe their literary language to Hus. He began at the beginning: he formed a new alphabet which is substantially still in use. He based on this a systematic orthography which was repeatedly referred back to after periods of disuse. He sedulously waged war on an excessive use of half-assimilated German words and replaced them by Czech expressions. Untiringly, he spurred on teachers and parents to learn and teach correctly the mother-tongue which up till then had been half despised and picked up only in daily life. Czech literature could look back over a century, but it was Hus who forged the clumsy language, saturated with foreign terms, to a pliable, expressive, easily-handled and beautiful instrument.

Hus composed several hymns, polished others and gave them a form which made them popular. For the sake of these hymns, too, people streamed to the Bethlehem Chapel. Hus made them, next to the sermon, the central point of the service. The hymn sung together caused a general uplifting of the heart that welded the congregation. He began to collect and edit his sermons, which in turn gave rise to some clear expositions and explanations of the faith, and a treatise against simony. The works which resulted give an insight into his world of ideas and an impression of his mastery of language and his great effect on the people. At the same time he collected the crude fourteenth-century translations of the Bible, worked through them, supplemented and collated them. He did for the Czech people what Wyclif did for the English and Luther for the Germans. In spite of the short time he had still to live and work, he left behind him a complete translation of the Bible. Like Wyclif and Luther he did not only defend God's word but also made it immediately accessible to the people.

At the beginning of the fateful year of 1412 Hus was so deep in his work that he did not even take part in the great Quodlibet which as always was held in January. His place was taken by Jacobellus, who was also to be his successor in the Bethlehem Chapel. He proclaimed that Christ's words had been fulfilled in that the Antichrist had gained the highest place in Christendom. The name John XXIII was not mentioned, but who could doubt that John was meant when Jacobellus said, " When such a sinner and son of damnation reaches among the Christian peoples the highest rank and place reserved for virtue, truth and justice, then there can be no further doubt that he is the highest, the dreaded Antichrist." This speech introduced the new year symbolically enough. It unleashed no storm because the storm was to break later for other reasons. Hus was torn from the work he had just started when at the beginning of May 1412 the new papal bull of indulgence reached Prague.

Wenceslas Tiem, Canon of Passau, brought the bull together with the confirmation of the appointment of Albik as Archbishop. The king and the Archbishop did not approve this bull and they knew the danger attending its proclamation in Prague, still seething with excitement over the excommunications and the appeal : but as at the same time their request had been granted after initial opposition, they saw no chance of attacking the bull. They only stipulated that when indulgences were dispensed the Gospel should be read and no charge made at confession. Tiem did not even keep to this. As he had a very large district to administer, including not only Bohemia but also Salzburg and Magdeburg, he divided it up into regions and farmed them out to agents who wanted not merely to get back what they had paid but also to make a profit. Thus the dispensation of indulgences in this case assumed a particularly scandalous form. There was individual bargaining and prices were driven up as high as possible : it was simply a question of wringing as much money as possible out of the people of Bohemia. "The sale of indulgences," said Hus in Constance, "seemed to me completely unworthy and scandalous because Master Wenceslas trafficked in them with the archdeaconate, the deaconates and the parishes, for fixed sums of money, just as though houses, inns and taverns were being leased to inn and tavern keepers. In addition he trafficked with sluggish, coarse, adulterous and unbelieving men who had done many an evil deed and taxed the people miserably in their faith only in order to increase the selling price and make still more profit. Many thereby made large sums of money and thus stained their souls with simony and avarice."

Tiem kept rich Prague for himself : but he too was a business man and above all wanted to get a profit. The usual pilgrimage was commuted to a payment. Indulgences were simply sold in the three largest churches, St. Vitus's Cathedral, the Tyn Church and in the Vysehrad. Faith in the efficacy of the indulgence only served to drive the prices up extortionately. Once again the bells rang out over the town of a hundred towers to promise remission of sins, but their solemn pealing this time contained a false note. Louder, more piercingly and more convincingly, rang out the voices of Hus and his followers, who denounced indulgences. The hope of a union in pure faith which nineteen years previously had silenced all criticism had long since been dissipated. The Popes themselves, dragging out the schism endlessly, had destroyed it. The younger generation, still too immature and uncertain at that time, had in the meantime learnt how to fight. Today, too, they had a leader who was frightened by no outcry and no danger. Hus, filled with fresh strength, left his writing for the pulpit. He could no longer keep silent. " I was driven by the anxiety, not that the people were being plundered against all right, but especially that they should not, seduced by the pedlars of indulgence, abandon true penitence, and that I should not myself be made an accomplice in this sin."

The true believers did not throng to the large churches but to the Bethlehem Chapel in their thousands. The inner steadfastness of the congregation grew to a passionate fervour. Breathless, as only in the days of the greatest perils, they listened to the words of their beloved Master.

Could they not believe his words? Could any objection be raised against his clear proofs? Hus explained to them, " They preach that whoever gives money receives forgiveness of his sins and salvation from eternal torment. That is not right, that the one gives money and by such barren repentance of his sins reaches Heaven immediately after his death while another who does not pay must suffer the greatest torment for his sins, even though he has committed fewer than the other. Let us make it still more obvious. Let us suppose that there are two men, one of whom for fifty years has sinned mortally with all the lusts of his fleshly will and has never repented his sins : the other lives virtuously and has not yielded to any mortal sin. Let us further suppose : the first dies without the deep repentance which could wipe out his sins, soon after he has given the Pope money : the other dies too, with far greater repentance of his little daily sins, but has not bought his salvation from the Pope. And see, the one goes straight to Heaven, according to the teachings of these wretched cheats, because he has given money : the other must suffer the torments of Hell simply because he has not bought his exemption from the Pope. Whence has the Pope such iniquitous power? Is not God's justice completely overthrown by such a doctrine? With such godless words the greedy teachers of Antichrist canvass the people of Christ and are to blame that men leave the paths of truth and set their hopes on indulgences and money, whereby they are cheated of eternal happiness. And if one confronts their false teaching with the Holy Scriptures, one is a heretic ! "

All simple and unsophisticated people were on the side of Hus when he plainly stated, " Let anyone, whoever it may be, Pope, bishop or any other priest, cry, ' Man, I forgive you your sins, I free you from your sins and all the pains of Hell,' it is empty clamour and it is vain : it avails nothing unless God forgives the sinner who heartily rues his sins."

Hus opened the fight in the University too. He called a great debate for June 7 on the question, " Whether it be to the honour of God and the salvation of Christian people, as well as to the service and piety of this kingdom, and permissible and advisible according to the laws of Christ, to approve the papal bull on the launching of a crusade against King Ladislas of Naples and his allies and to commend it to the faithful ? " The form of the question betrayed that here the bull of indulgence was to be contested in principle and in detail. This intention was stressed by the unusually large number of invitations to the debate plastered on the walls of the town. Indeed this brought to a head the indignation which had been silently fermenting among the people of Prague.

The mere announcement of the debate aroused the opposition of those Masters who were hostile to the Wyclifites. Palec, who had hitherto held his hand and had tried to conciliate Hus, finally went over to the enemy camp and himself lodged a protest with the Archbishop. He had little to say in defence of the bulls ; he merely contested the right to criticise papal decrees and demanded the forbidding of the debate. Thereupon Hus was summoned to appear ; he stood face to face once more with one of those small clerical assemblies which were schooling him for the Council. The papal legate asked him whether he would obey the papal orders. He replied, " With all my heart I will carry out the apostolic orders." The legate remarked to the Archbishop, " Lo, he will obey the orders of our Master." Promptly, however, Hus shattered this premature joy. " You must understand me rightly," he interrupted, " I call apostolic orders the teachings of Christ's apostles and in so far as the papal orders coincide with those I will obey most readily. But if I find something contrary to them I will not obey them even if you conjure up before my eyes the stake at which I shall burn."

Hus had in the past disobeyed the Church but he had shown by his protests, by his appeals, and by the despatch of a delegation to Bologna that he wanted to remain within the Church. His disobedience had only been to individual decrees which he held to be wrong and which he wanted the Church to redress. The judgment of the highest tribunal had not been finally given then and Hus seemed ready to accept the rulings of this authority. It was for the first time that he now defied even papal orders to the face of a representative of the Pope. He was obviously aware of the gravity of the step he had taken. To mention the stake was no empty phrase and he thus entered deliberately upon the road which needs must lead to the stake. He did not obey the legate. The debate took place and in it Hus outspokenly opposed the Pope.

On June 7 a disturbingly large number of students and simple folk crowded to the Charles College, the Carolinum of today, where, in the largest hall of the University, the debate was held. Marcus of Hradec, who presided, tried to keep the ordinary people away, at any rate, but he did not succeed for all wanted to hear Hus and to protect him should this prove necessary. All the Masters appeared : Jerome, impressive with his piercing eyes and long black beard, at the side of the simple Hus, who, with his broad peasant face, hardly betrayed his inner agitation : Palec, the renegade, keeping with the older Masters, John Eliae and Andrew of Brod, whose lustre as national champions was to be dimmed on that day. The crowd respectfully made room for little Jacobellus. The great hall was dangerously overfilled. People overflowed into the street. The loud talk betrayed the general excitement. Gradually the noise subsided and when Hus began to speak rapt attention produced a breathless silence which for many hours was broken only by interjections and applause.

With this great speech Hus entered upon the road which led through the Bohemian brothers, through Chelcicky and Komensky, to Tolstoy : he spoke against violence. Although he did not question the right of the " secular arm," the state, to wage war, yet even such wars, which in those days were a matter of course and daily occurrence, did not seem to him unquestioningly to be accepted by a Christian nation. Wicked and damnable were they if they were for the sake of " earthly dross," for power, riches and domination : they might be waged only in defence of the faith and only with the intention of restoring unity. The spiritual power, however, the Pope, might never resort to the sword. " For can the killing of men, the devastation of land, spring from the love of our Lord Jesus Christ ? Can it be a genuine good cause for which to suffer martyrdom ? Does the Pope order this ever for any other reason but that they do not recognise him ?" If you deprived the Pope of his wrong worldly domination, there would be no war. The bull itself showed how un-Christian this call to war was. It damned not only Ladislas but also his subjects who had nevertheless to obey him, and damned even posterity to the third generation although the Scriptures explicity said that the children should not suffer for the sins of their fathers. And the bull called Christians to war against Christians : Christians must slay as many Christians as possible ; and " the more people you have killed, the more you have sinned against God and man, and yet the more easily you will be absolved by dint of this bull." Christ, however, forbade Peter to draw the sword : He forbade James and John to call down fire upon the city of the Samaritans from Heaven. " Either Christ acted without good sense and papal dignity is to be preferred to the life of Christ, or the Pope has struck a road in the opposite direction from that of Christ." He should ask the Lord Himself whether the bull was just, and now Hus raised his voice : he felt that he was filled with the spirit of the Lord and he gave them the reply that alone was in accord with the Scriptures, " You do not know of whose spirit you are the children that you should want to ruin so many human souls by excommunicating them, cursing them and slaying them. Why do you depart from My example although I have forbidden My disciples to vie in cruelty with those who have rejected Me ; I, who prayed for those who crucified Me : 'Father forgive them for they know not what they do'." Hus emphasised the very kernel of the Holy Scriptures : the true Christian did not fight with violence but spiritual weapons. " If the Pope wants to conquer his enemies let him follow Christ whose vicar he calls himself, let him pray for the enemies of the Church, let him say, 'My kingdom is not of this world', bless those who curse him, do good to those who hate him, and then the Lord will give him the words and the wisdom, which none of his enemies will be able to withstand."

Still more wicked seemed to Hus indulgences and the power which the Pope thereby arrogated to himself. What could one think of an indulgence which was good for " more than a hundred thousand years " : in that case God might have to postpone the final judgment or else the indulgence would have to hold good " even in eternal damnation after the Day of Judgment." And what was one to think of an indulgence that invalidated all the earlier ones—one good can only be the complement of another good and not the destruction of it. " For the sake of the so-called fullness of papal power, however exalted it might be, God will not injure His own justice," Hus insisted. The only explanation of all these contradictions was that fresh money was needed. This combination of money and forgiveness of sins was unequivocally mortal sin : it was simony. " Freely have ye received : freely give." The true essence of repentance was completely falsified through indulgences. " By such indulgences the foolish rich are led to cherish vain hopes, the laws of God are held in contempt, the unschooled populace more readily become sinners, heavy sins are accounted but light, and the people in general are plundered." Only the truly penitent could have forgiveness of their sins : but of sorrow and penance there was no mention in the bull, only of money. It was culpable presumption to grant remission of sins simply for the sake of money and " the Pope cannot possess such a power."

Hus grew more and more fervent as he spoke : he marshalled more and more arguments against the possibility of indulgence of sins, they flowed from him, he could hardly put them into words quickly enough. " If it is the rule in trade in unimportant material things that the purchaser shall at least know that he really receives what he has bought, how do matters stand with the trade in indulgences, since the Pope cannot assure anyone that either before or after death he will truly receive such a forgiveness of his sins ? " Without divine revelation no Pope could know what man was really chosen for salvation. Indulgence was extolled as a great and unique grace that the Pope might dispense only for " sufficient reason," that was, " when he was made war upon or was in need of money." " The faithful, therefore, had only to pray that the Pope might have war made upon him or need monies so that he might open to the faithful the treasure of the Church for their salvation." Each act of authority by the Pope, however, should not be conditioned by necessity, but by the example of Christ : if the Pope were as kindly as Christ and could forgive sins, he would long ago have wrought the salvation of all mankind. No one need adduce it as an argument that the majority of people approved of indulgences : one might as well say that four hundred priests of Baal were more right than one Elijah. Even Peter had erred after the Holy Ghost had descended upon him. " Therefore a disciple of Christ must examine well the papal bulls and if they are in agreement with the laws of Christ not oppose them in any way. But if they are against Christ's laws he must join with Christ Himself to oppose them." The Pope, Hus declared, was not the highest authority. " Holy Writ is the law of Christ and therefore nothing must be added to it and nothing taken away. For the law of Christ is sufficient, and alone it is enough to lead and rule the militant Church."

Hus called for resistance to the papal bulls. He concluded, " Thus, the faithful must keep far aloof, yea, very far, from such indulgences." At these words the general tension was suddenly discharged : the excitement could no longer be held in check. Hus's opponents were howled down. And then, after Hus's speech, which for all its severity was moderate and unimpassioned, there followed a speech by Jerome which unrestrainedly fanned the passions. Jerome would go with the students to the Council of the Old Town to convince them of the wickedness of indulgences. Marcus only restrained him with difficulty from this open rebellion. The students, however, insisted on solemnly accompanying Jerome to his house. Hus, too, was accompanied by his followers, but the crowd following Jerome was much larger.

Consequences were not slow to follow. In the indulgence box of St. Vitus there was found a defamatory letter beginning with verses which were soon in every mouth :

Believe rather Hus, who announces the truth,
Than the Prelates who're out to deceive you.

On June 24 the courtier Voksa of Waldstein, a friend of Jerome and probably in league with him, organised a strange procession through Prague. On a waggon drawn by students there stood two well-known prostitutes with the papal bulls dangling round their necks. They were covered with little silver bells which rang at every movement like the bells at Mass. The waggon was accompanied by several hundred students with sticks and daggers, some of them dressed up as executioners and torturers. They shouted out, " We are taking the bulls and writings of a certain heretic to the stake. Make way ! We are taking the bulls and writings of a heretic to the stake ! " The procession passed the palace of the Archbishop, went over the main bridge, and through the whole of the Old and the New Towns as far as the Charles Square. The way was lined by a crowd agog with excitement, controlled by students and courtiers but also incited by them. Before the pillory of the New Town a bonfire was lit and there the bulls were burnt, a contemptuous revenge for the burning of the books of Wyclif. Beside the fire stood an iron chest, like those used for indulgences, and lampoons and libellous compositions and songs were thrown into it. The rule of the street had begun.

Hus held aloof from these demonstrations but he preached untiringly against indulgences. Jerome and his followers on the other hand came ever more frequently to blows with priests and monks in the streets and churches. In the meantime, however, the other side had lodged a complaint with the king. As so often happened when he ought to intervene, he was not in Prague but away hunting. Frightened by the street brawls which he hated as much as ever, he fixed the death penalty for any who opposed the papal bulls. This order was probably not very seriously meant as Voksa of Waldstein remained his favourite in spite of the procession but the adherents of the Church made good use of it and it rapidly had dangerous consequences.

The unrest in Prague continued. There were serious clashes on July 10. In a Church in the New Town a priest was preaching one of the appointed sermons for the period of the indulgence when suddenly an artisan's apprentice shouted out, "You lie. We heard something quite different from Master Hus. It's all fraud and lies!" Outraged, the priests fell upon him and beat him: then they took him along to the Town Hall of the Old Town, for they knew that the German Old Town was loyal to the Church. In the meantime two other artisans had been brought there: the same thing had happened in two other churches. Probably these interruptions had been staged by Jerome. The three artisans, Martin, John and Stanislav, were tortured and called on to recant. But the severest torture had no effect. The Council decided, in accordance with the King's orders, on execution.

When Hus heard of this, he went with several Masters and two thousand students to the Town Hall to prevent the execution. He gained admittance with difficulty. "They are innocent although they have been convicted!" he cried. "If they are guilty, so am I. I have done it and I will bear it. I and all those who are with me are prepared to accept the same punishment." Two thousand people stood at Hus's back: an assault on the Town Hall and the prisoners would soon be free. Hus, however, was against violence and wanted to suffer in the cause of justice. The Council attempted to appease him, and promised that nothing should happen to the three prisoners if Hus would only calm the general excitement and send the people away. Hus believed this promise and the crowd dispersed at his words, for they too were filled with the Christian teaching of their master who knew no violence.

The Council, however, chose force. They gave no second thought to this promise, anxious to seize this opportunity of making an example. Hardly had the crowd dispersed before the executioners with a strong guard of soldiers led the prisoners towards the place of execution. But they did not get far. More and more people thronged together to prevent them. Then the executioners stopped in the public street, the soldiers with great difficulty cleared a space, and quickly, before anyone could interfere, the three artisans were beheaded with swords. In accordance with their orders the executioners cried out as they did it, " Anyone doing the same will have the same punishment to look forward to." Tremendous excitement swept through the crowd but still they did not think of violence. " We are all ready to do the same and to suffer the same ! " they cried, seized with mystical enthusiasm. Without resisting many of them suffered themselves to be arrested and led to the Town Hall. Only the bodies were snatched from the executioners and many women dipped their handkerchiefs in the flowing blood while others shrouded the bodies in linen cloths. Master John of Jicin came with many students from the University, a vast funeral procession was formed and a hymn used only for martyrs was chanted. " They are holy, for God's testament they have offered their bodies to death." Slowly the procession wended its way to the Bethlehem Chapel, with more and more people joining in and no one daring to oppose it. There the bodies were solemnly buried. The other side then contemptuously named the chapel " the three saints," but the people seized on this as a title of honour which kept alive the memory of the three who had given their life's blood.

The movement had thus its first martyrs. The next day Hus celebrated the Office for Martyrs and Jerome stated emphatically that this was " in honour of the three saints over whose spilt blood the angels rejoiced." On July 17 more people than ever thronged to the chapel, expecting that Hus would preach on the executions. But Hus still refrained. The general excitement seemed to him too fraught with danger. He sought to pacify the people by silence so that they might not allow themselves to be moved to rash acts. As blood had flowed he could no longer soothe them with reason. His silence, however, only increased the general agitation. Everybody grew still more excited, believing that the executioners had muzzled Hus and fearing that their Master might really allow himself to be muzzled. Under these circumstances his very silence threatened to call forth an outbreak of violence. He therefore let his last caution drop. On July 24 he preached a great sermon for the three martyrs. This too still showed great restraint although it almost amounted to a canonisation of them.

Hus employed an old figure of speech : he would not accept the chapel full of gold for those three bodies. Then he continued, " The merciful Saviour let many Masters, priests and laymen see through the sham of the bull of indulgence. Some have even staked their lives in contradicting the priests who publicly spoke for the bull. For this those true confessors of divine truth, Martin, John and Stanislav, were executed and buried, in the holy name of God, in the Bethlehem Chapel. Others were arrested, tortured and imprisoned. This I report as a true chronicler so that our descendants may, when need arises, know that others before them sacrificed themselves for Christ's sake without fear of death." He appealed to his congregation not to be frightened from the truth by any martyrdom.

The congregation obeyed Hus. For weeks on end people streamed to the Town Hall of the Old Town to offer themselves for arrest, torture and death. At first the Council imprisoned them, but when severe torture did not break the ecstasy of the prisoners and people were unafraid, they tried to release them. King Wenceslas indeed raged once more, "If there are a thousand of them, the same shall happen to them as to the others, and if there are not enough hangmen in the kingdom I will get them from other countries." But the Council found something uncanny in this unequal fight. Violence could be met with violence: but all power failed in the face of this joyful determination to suffer and meet death. The prisoners were discharged : but they did not want their freedom and remained in prison with the doors open. Subterfuges had to be used to lure them out of jail. Executioners pretended to lead them to a hearing, and then as soon as they were clear of the Town Hall the doors were shut on them and the executioners fled as if danger threatened. The will to suffer had overcome naked violence. Spilt blood unites any movement and gives it fresh inspiration. The martyrdom of John, Martin and Stanislav liberated that stream of fervent enthusiasm that inspired Bohemia to fight for the faith through decades : and it received its last impetus through the death at the stake of Hus and Jerome. In the mystical frenzy that now seized Prague the whole kingdom would soon be plunged. The fight against indulgences was soon merged into it. The chance cause of the rebellion was early lost sight of : the real issues, true faith and the purification of the Church, were once more paramount. Hus was soon absorbed in his work again. Simultaneously with his Czech exposition of the faith he was writing a Latin defence of the writings of Wyclif. For ever again it was necessary to protect those principles of the faith which alone seemed to guarantee a way out of the general chaos.

In Italy a number of acts of treachery changed the unsettled state of affairs to the advantage of Pope John. The first of the traitors was Sforza, the father of the future Duke of Milan. He went over from the Pope to Ladislas. This desertion of the most capable of his military leaders forced John to negotiate with Ladislas. Thereby he cut his losses and even profited. John declared that he was ready to betray his ally Louis of Anjou, who had conquered Rome for him, if Ladislas would betray Gregory. Anjou had old claims to Naples and thus there was the constant danger that Sigismund might intervene on his behalf since Ladislas as long as he ruled in Naples also claimed the throne of Hungary. The proposal must, therefore, have seemed attractive enough to console him for the loss of his old ally Gregory. Ladislas pronounced Gregory a heretic and banished him with such suddenness that he succeeded only by chance in escaping to Rimini by devious routes with two wretched Venetian barques. John and Ladislas made peace in July 1412, the very month in which Sforza had deserted. Ladislas recognised John as Pope and ruler of the papal state, in return for which he was recognised as King of Naples. Peace was secured in Italy till the next betrayal, a bare year hence.

Such a papacy naturally had little understanding of the high seriousness of the war of faith in Bohemia. In the confusion John of Jesenice had succeeded in escaping from imprisonment in Rome. The Pope and his commission had never given him a hearing. They had nothing but violence to offer this adversary who wanted to discuss the salvation of the Church, and resorted to excommunication when he escaped them. By the time he reached Prague John was under the ban of the Church. Thus the fate of Hus's unsuccessful envoy was the fate of Hus in his efforts to reform the Church : the Church had nothing for him but excommunication, curse and damnation.

This policy of blind violence of the Church, which in its own interests should rather have tackled the problems of reform itself, was reflected in the mentality of Hus's opponents in Prague. Palec, too, made a memorial speech for the three martyrs but to him their deaths and heresy appeared to be linked in a strangely distorted way. " So sugared appear many of Wyclif's writings," he preached, " that it seems sweet to them to go to the death for them. You have seen how foolhardily some of them bent their heads beneath the sword. That is a sign of heresy. Among us there is none who would die for his faith." And he betrayed his own recognition of nothing but power when he mocked the Wyclifites. " See how fearful is their doctrine: they dare go nowhere with it. If they went to Rome or elsewhere, perchance to Germany, and would not forswear it, they would be burnt as heretics. But we with our belief dare go where we will." Did it seem to him so shameful that he had once suffered for his faith? He would at any rate try and obliterate this memory. " As there were no scriptural grounds on which he and his colleagues could prove us in error," Hus reported, " and seeking safety in numbers, he thought over how he could best ally himself with those who had once been the arch-enemies of him and of Stanislav. And as he had no case against us, he seized upon the articles which the prelates detested and they were not a little overjoyed to see the retrogression of him and Stanislav." All Hus's opponents had this in common that they did not make their stand on reason but on numbers and power.

The dispute was nevertheless taken more seriously in Prague than in Rome: Hus's success showed that the issues were vital. King Wenceslas continued to aim at a solution or at least some measure of agreement. After the three executions he charged the theological faculty with the task of working out a draft for an agreement. The " eight Doctors," as they were called to distinguish them from the " Masters " of the Wyclifites, embodied the Church party. Among these doctors were the four chief former friends of Hus: the old Masters Andrew of Brod and John Eliae, and the renegades Palec and Stanislav of Znojmo. Perhaps for that very reason their proposal was far from conciliatory. They did not want to reach an agreement but to force a decision in the favour of the Church. The famous forty-five articles of Wyclif together with six new articles of Hus were declared heretical and to be condemned at a solemn assembly of the University and the clergy: anyone preaching them was to be banned from Bohemia. The king, angered by the increasing street rioting, agreed to the proposal. When things had gone so far that the three young men were executed, he called a synod for July 16 in the Town Hall of the Old Town, where the Church found its main supporter in the German Town Council.

The " Town Hall Synod " took place as the people were streaming to the Town Hall to demand martyrdom for their faith. The University did not attend but sent a delegation to protest against

B. Picart del. 1713.

IEAN XXIII.

decisions being taken in the Town Hall that were within the province of the Forum of the University. This protest received as little attention as did the revolt raging throughout Prague. The Synod passed a resolution that under pain of excommunication, loss of property and exile, the fifty-one articles must not be defended. This decision did not prevent Hus from defending all the articles once more before the University. His defence was also published as a treatise. Once again he proclaimed that the Antichrist was reigning, that the secular arm had the right to chastise the Church, that priests alone could not forgive sins and that the sale of indulgences was a criminal fraud. He reproached Palec with the words, "You simply cut the knot that you cannot untie," while he himself studded his speech with quotations from the Scriptures and the Fathers of the Church. Palec thereupon called on the secular arm to act against Hus, but Hus preached on unmolested. The dispute in Prague could no longer be settled by a unilateral decision.

The king sought once more to bring about an agreement. He invited Hus and the eight Doctors to meet his Privy Council in his hunting lodge. Hus was asked to hand over his writings for examination, but this time he refused. "I have publicly spoken and taught in the schools and the Temple of Bethlehem, where the Masters, bachelors, scholars and all the people met together, and I have never in private said anything whereby men might be led from the truth. Do but ask! And if I have spoken ill, let an ill report be given of me. I do not feel bound to deliver up all the writings that I have into the hands of my enemies."

This speech revealed that Hus was ready to face anything, as he plainly showed to the King's Council. Palec had at last worked out a long and thorough defence of the papal bulls, but Hus would no longer be drawn into an argument on them. He had already said what he had to say: now he threw into the scale his readiness to face death. He said he was ready to defend his case alone to the eight Doctors and he would face death at the stake if he were proved wrong. His opponents must, however, firmly declare themselves willing to abide by the same conditions. Was he not challenging fate? Eight against one, they must surely be able to defeat him or at least to talk him down: were the councillors sufficiently impartial to prevent this? Certainly, up till now none on either side had been subjected to death at the stake: but could they avoid it now that Prague was in an uproar and the king clamoured for a decision? Hus dared—and won. His opponents were simply not prepared to suffer for their faith. Their faith must give them security but not demand sacrifices.

Embarrassed they consulted together. In order not to retreat completely they finally tremblingly declared themselves ready to let one of their number meet Hus. Hus, however, answered, "You stand there united against me who am alone, and I have none other with me nor will take none: thus the penalty must fall either on me alone or on all of you!" For the time being Hus had won. The inner uncertainty of the enemy who appeared so dictatorial was clearly betrayed. The king dared not carry out their proposal. "Forbear ye one with another": with these tragi-comic words the King's Council concluded the meeting. The fight went on.

In the meantime, however, Hus's position in Rome had deteriorated. The Pope offered no more protection to the opponent of indulgences. Cardinal Brancas, who presided over the last commission, finally confirmed the sentence of Cardinal Colonna. The ban on Hus was to be proclaimed with all due formalities. Hus and his followers were no longer to be admitted to divine services: and those who ate and drank with him, bought from or sold to him, talked or went about with him, gave him shelter or handed him fire or water, also came under the ban. If Hus did not submit within twenty days measures would be intensified. Then divine services must be suspended in town or village, hamlet or castle, if he were there. Throughout the kingdom, on every Sunday and holiday he was to be solemnly cursed from the chancel. The altars were to be set with lighted candles, and at the mention of his name the candles were to be put out by sweeping them from the altar as a sign that his name had been wiped out from the congregation of believers. If within a further twelve days he had not submitted, any place in which he stayed was under an interdict for three days after his departure. No services must be held there and no sacraments administered except extreme unction. Mass could only be read behind the closed doors of the church. If he died while under the ban he could not be given burial by the Church. And if he was nevertheless buried in a church, his body must be dug up again and burnt. This sentence was also to be read in all churches: the priests must be fully vested, all the bells must be rung, and with a raised crucifix the priest must sweep the candles down from the altar: and while hymns were chanted three stones were to be thrown in the direction in which Hus was, as a sign of his eternal damnation.

Still heavier sentence was to be passed. Michael of Nemecky Brod arrived in Rome—and his own countrymen were always the most malicious opponents of Hus. Once again the measures of the Church reached their final severity through the intervention of the Czechs. What did it matter that Michael had had to flee from Bohemia because he had embezzled money entrusted him by the King for the restoration of a gold mine: any enemy of Hus was welcome to the Church. The Pope appointed Michael Procurator de Causis Fidei, and his name has gone down to history as Michael de Causis. Michael complained to the Pope of the courtiers who protected Hus, he demanded the arrest and punishment of Hus, he demanded that the works of Wyclif should be burnt afresh, he demanded the arrest of Hus's followers. The Pope did not grant the requests against the court and the books of Wyclif, but Hus and five of his followers were excommunicated and summoned to appear in Rome. In addition to this, Hus, wherever he was arrested and by whomsoever, was to be handed over to the Archbishop or to John the Iron Bishop, judged and burnt. The Bethlehem Chapel moreover was specifically condemned to be razed to the ground. This rightly aroused the anger of the other side.

The messages from Rome reached Prague in August. This time the king remained neutral. He interfered neither with the Church nor with Hus and his followers. Thus Prague witnessed the ghastly ceremony of the pronouncing of the ban. The priests swept the candles from the altars and violently trod out the flames, as if they had underfoot the hated enemy whose destruction was thus symbolised.

When the due period had elapsed the interdict came into operation. No services were held in Prague. There were no weddings, baptisms or burials. Only a few of the people of the court who were loyal to Hus hastily buried the dead at night. The people, eager for faith, were aghast as they saw themselves deprived of all the blessings of the Church: Hus and his followers indeed redoubled their efforts, but could their hasty attempts really replace the time-honoured customs, the forms and formulas that had so long commanded belief? The people of Prague had been able to fight against the last interdict and the king had compelled the priests to perform their duties: then it had been easy to exult with Hus who had been fighting these priests. Now a sinister silence hovered over the town; the bells had been silent ever since they rang to pronounce Hus accursed. The church doors were shut and it seemed to the people as though the doors of Heaven were thereby shut.

With every day that the interdict lasted the burden grew doubly hard to bear. Here there was a child to baptise, there a dead person to bury, there someone desiring communion or confession and absolution: was it sufficient to have the one Bethlehem Chapel where God was extolled and his Church rejected? The priests and monks went about among the people frightening them with dreadful pictures of the torments of Hell, and how else could end a life without the sacraments of God? Hus's congregation appeared large if one looked at the overcrowded Bethlehem Chapel but small in comparison with the population of the three towns forming Prague, which included the Germans, whose words now fell on open ears when they attacked the Czech enemies of the Church in an effort to restore the Church to the whole community. Once again national differences were sunk in a religious issue.

This clash of opinion was particularly dangerous as Prague was now the scene of constant disturbances and disquiet. At any moment the real struggle might start. Jerome above all raged with all his old unrestrained passion. Shortly before the interdict came into force there was almost bloodshed once again. On St. Wenceslas' Day Jerome forced his way into the Carmelite monastery. Relics were on show and the monk attending them was begging for offerings for the extension of the Church. "You lie when you say that these are relics of saints," Jerome called out to him. "They are simply bones from any old body. You are cheating Christians with your begging!" On the same day, according to the charge made against him in Constance, Jerome "laid violent and sacriligious hands upon a brother of this monastery who was preaching to the people that the doctrine of Wyclif was heretical and rejected by the Church of God, and led him forth captive with two other brothers. The two other brothers he handed over to the secular authority but he kept Nicholas for several days in his house and inflicted many hardships upon him, and not content with that but heaping evil upon evil he threw him, bound, from a ship into the Vltava saying unto him, 'Now tell me, monk, was not Master Wyclif a holy and an evangelical preacher?' And he would have drowned the brother had he not been freed from this danger by the intervention of a nobleman and his servant." The later charge against Jerome was maliciously distorted at many points but here it must have been more or less correct for Jerome attempted to correct only the beginning. "While I was talking peacefully with him several monks armed with swords threw themselves upon me. As I had nothing in my hand I seized a sword from a layman and defended myself against them as far as I could." That this armed clash in a church was possible, no matter whether it had been begun by the monks or Jerome, and did not seem out of the ordinary, affords eloquent proof of the excitement in Prague at the time.

Full of tormenting cares, Hus saw that the clash of opinion developing from the interdict might soon find an outlet in fresh bloodshed. For the second time he was summoned to appear before the Pope. Should he obey now since by staying he plunged Prague into need and discord? He had only to turn his back on Prague and three days later the interdict would be raised. The Pope was indeed the Antichrist and he need not expect to find justice with him. But even the three simple artisans had accepted death and thereby given fresh strength to the true faith. Would he not put an end to all this hateful vacillation and help truth to prevail by dying for Christ? Or would his death only increase the chaos: would his followers be sacrificed, and the leaderless people abandon true belief? It was more difficult now, with Prague under the interdict, to decide this question than it had been on the previous occasion. Had his hour come or must he again restrain his longing for a martyr's death?

Events answered this question. It seemed to Hus that God gave him the sign he longed for. On October 2, after the pronouncing of the interdict, the Germans assembled to arrest Hus in accordance with the Pope's orders and to tear down the Bethlehem Chapel. "Under their leader Bernard Chotek they came for me with missiles, lances and swords," said Hus, "to the Bethlehem Chapel where I was preaching." The Czech congregation was unarmed, but they crowded round Hus with such determination and enthusiasm that the Germans abandoned their intention and withdrew. "The Lord led them astray, that they knew not what they should do. They came at an unseasonable time. Thus did the bishops send out their servants against our dear Saviour that they might take him while He was preaching, but His hour was not yet come, and therefore they rather listened to Him and did not take Him, and thus the hour of my death was not yet come and therefore they let me preach in peace until such time as God saw fit."

Hus solemnly felt that his way was merging into the way of Christ. God had therefore given him a sign that he was on the right path, the path of his dearly beloved and revered example.

He therefore did not go to Rome. In a great sermon Hus surveyed his reasons for refusing a second time to obey the Pope although he did not fear death. He valued the opinion of his congregation above all and they must learn why he thus avoided death and whether he had done rightly.

In this sermon Hus emerges vividly. Arguments in accordance with the teaching of Wyclif are strangely mixed with scholastic subtleties and a pure and beautiful exposition of his human reasons for not making the journey to Rome. He began with a simple statement of fact. " First of all, for three years I have myself appointed my defenders in Rome. They were, however, never admitted to a hearing, nay, they were even held and thrown into prison because they begged for a just court and sentence." But the second reason led deep into the scholastic maze. " From Prague to Rome is incomparably further than from Jerusalem to the Sea of Tiberias, whence Jesus went from Jerusalem," and the third reason was similar : nowhere is it commanded in Holy Scripture that men should be hounded to Rome and vain proceedings taken against them. But these very scholastic excesses which today seem senselessly naive and anachronistic once again go to prove that Hus had dissected his problem to the last jot and tittle.

A beautiful earnestness rang through his whole sermon. " The struggle which I wage is directed against the usages of the Pope," he exclaimed, " against his might, which is not granted him by God but is arrogated by him in diabolical ways." Was there any sense in leaving that one all-important thing, the preaching of the Gospel, and using for the journey money given as alms to the poor? "What good could I do on my journey? At the papal court I should find no holiness but only strife and dispute and the best opportunity for simony. At the papal court there is little truth in accordance with the teachings of Holy Scripture." What had such a court of justice for him? " The Pope, my enemy and my judge, and the cardinals too my enemies, as can be seen in their letters in which they call me a heretic, although they have never seen me or heard me yet. To preach against avarice and above all simony is to be immediately their enemy. I should fare before such a court as did our Lord Jesus Christ, above all now when so many false witnesses rise up against me and send to Rome the testimony that they have given against me in Prague." These testimonies of witnesses, which were later made the base of the charge in Constance, were piling up against him in Rome. Hus knew that his enemies in Prague reported that " daily I preach heresy and false doctrine in the Bethlehem Chapel and that I am the chief of all heretics, an arch-heretic." These false charges did not frighten him. He need not defend himself against them. " That does not harm me in the hope that I have in my Saviour nor trouble me. I know what the priests did against His holy grace and what they did to Him."

Hus here touched, however, upon what was for him the most important of the reproaches of his enemies, the only one that really touched him. Had not Christ appeared before the unjust judge? "I still hear them saying, 'If he will really answer for his teaching with his life, let him go to Rome as Christ did to Jerusalem.' To this I answer, if I knew it to be God's will that I die in Rome, then I would go there, nay, even if I merely knew that thereby I might serve some useful purpose, as Christ by going to Jerusalem prepared salvation and blessings for the people after Him and the saints before Him." God Himself, however, had given him the sign that this was not so. He explained to his congregation the meaning of the vain attack of the Germans which they themselves had repelled. And afterwards, when he wrote down his sermon, he could add still another powerful sign. "Shortly afterwards the Pope's men wanted to pull down the Bethelehem Chapel and were consulting together about it in the Town Hall in the German language. Thereupon the Bohemian Holubar spoke to the Bohemians, whether they agreed to this, but the true Bohemians would by no means consent." Thus the second attack failed for "God was not with them in it."

But more plainly than any of the other reasons this attack itself spoke against Hus's placing himself in the hands of the Pope. "Behold and admire the papal temerity. Without the King's orders none may tear down the stove or the stall of his neighbour, but here they had the audacity to consult together about tearing down a house of God." How did this agree with the word of Christ that man should spread His teaching on all sides? "Usually bishops have erected chapels that sermons might be preached in them, and not destroyed chapels!" Hus could not submit to such a diabolical power. He appealed instead to Christ. "To Him, the crucified, have I handed over and entrusted the whole of my dispute, that He may end it according to His counsel, even though it be with my shame and my death: only may He vouchsafe that I do not depart from His holy truth."

This sermon revealed in Hus an inner calm and certainty such as he felt seldom and only momentarily, since at each step he took his sense of responsibility always tormented him. This time too he was not long left to enjoy this inner quiet. Ahead of him was a new disappointment which made his path ever straiter, narrower and more dangerous.

Daily it became clearer that the interdict was having the desired effect. More and more of the timid turned from Hus and went back to the Church. Hus emphasised in his sermons the differences between the Germans and the Czechs. He did not thereby aim at fanning the flames of a new national struggle ; he was only conjuring up the unity of the Bohemian people who for him were the chosen people of God. These simple people enjoyed his utter confidence. He saw in them the true believers on whom he could lean. But this last external support he had now to do without : only the kernel of his congregation stood unshakably behind him. The people as a whole had not courage enough to resist the Church. It no longer mattered that this Church still appeared to the Bohemian people as " the German church." Their fear of hell was stronger than their weak national consciousness or their certainly stronger love of their revered Master. " I dearly wished to resist the interdict," Hus said, filled with sorrow, " but what mainly held me back was that the people did not show much courage in the defence of divine truth by remaining without the Pope's services, burying their dead as they might and in an emergency baptising their children themselves until God the Lord had destroyed the snares of the Antichrist." Hus had dreamed of a strong and splendid revival. The interdict was to be the call to the last fight for Christ and the Holy Scriptures. Through inner steadfastness alone his people could have proved to the world on which side true faith stood. Then indeed would Bohemia have become the land of God. Instead Hus was forced to recognise that this land and this people were not yet ripe for the great test. A still harder convulsion was needed before maturity was reached. Hus had to tread his road to the end.

In addition the ever vacillating king, upsetting all calculations, was again more openly on the side of Hus. He at last returned to Prague and from now on he remained there, but he begged Hus to leave the city for a short time. On this condition the king would protect him. He still hoped to bring about an agreement once quiet was restored through the raising of the interdict. Hus was once more involved in an internal struggle by this. He had only just recognised that he must not go to Rome and now another question of conscience, still more naked and threatening, confronted him. Ought he to leave his congregation at all ? Ought he to flee from his enemies who were after his life or must he face them ? By his mere flight Prague would be freed from the interdict : but would not this flight be a falling away from God ?

At the end of October Hus yielded to the urgings of the king and his friends and left Prague. In many letters to his friends and to the people of the city he defended his step. He showed how often Christ had evaded the officers of justice and had ordered His disciples not to allow themselves to be seized : he himself wanted still further to fulfil his task and serve the word of God. Moreover he was frightened by the great effect of the interdict, the " fast net of the Antichrist," on the people of Prague. " I do not wish to be the cause thereof, that my enemies on my account should suffer eternal damnation : I will not be the cause that the just on my account should have to suffer and bear affliction, I will not be the cause that on my account the foolish hinder the work of God : I will not that my presence, through the evilly-conceived interdict, should be a cause for the withholding of the holy communion and the other sacraments which aim at salvation." He himself, however, was not soothed by these reasons. " I am oppressed by the consciousness that my absence is a vexation even if my herd do not lack the necessary nourishment of the word of God." Again and again he begged his friends to pray to God that he might find the right path.

Hus was rent by tormenting doubts. At first it was not known where he was. He was hiding not only from the officers of the Church, but still more from himself. He was unaccustomed to being powerless to defend his decisions publicly with all his personal ardour. Hardly had he left Prague than it seemed to him that he had taken a false step and he returned there and continued to preach. Once again, however, his position was impossible. The agreement the king desired seemed to be in sight if only he would comply, and so he once more turned his back on Prague. Hardly had the talks broken down, however, before he was there again. It was a constant coming and going that betrayed the torments of the hunted. He did not fear death. Whenever he was in Prague he preached in the Bethlehem Chapel. But all his sermons betrayed his fear as to whether he was doing right when he left again.

Ever afresh he asked his congregation whether they approved his conduct, whether they advised him to avoid Prague. His congregation, full of fear for the life of their beloved Master, one moment wanted to have him with them to protect him, and the next would have him go to secure for him the more powerful protection of the king. But even this approval of his flight could not calm Hus : was he not a cowardly traitor ? Passionately and restlessly he searched the Scriptures and the writings of the Fathers in order to find an answer to this most terrible of all questions. As in the days of his first awakening he clung to every letter in order to wring from it the truth, the truth upon which he could rely. Holy Scriptures were adequate and sufficient to shape human life : Christ must tell him too what he had to do in this case. But for the first time the Scriptures seemed unclear and contradictory.

In the writings of the Fathers he came across a question completely attuned to his own state of doubt. Bishop Honoratus asked Saint Augustine, " They seek my death : what shall I do ? I know not what to do. Once Christ says, ' If they persecute you in one town, flee to another ' : and another time our Lord says, ' A hireling who is not a shepherd, whose sheep they are not, sees the wolf come and leaves the sheep and flees.' What shall I do that I may fulfill the first words and yet be no hireling ?" The answer, however, was not as clear as the question since Augustine wrote a whole book on its solution. The following answer appeared most important to Hus : if the shepherd were alone so that the sheep would remain without a shepherd, then the shepherd should stay, but if several priests were there, some should flee that the doctrine might be preserved, either those especially persecuted or some chosen lot. Hus clung fast to this answer during his tormenting flight and return. " And thus I relied on the counsel of God and of many men the latchet of whose shoes I am not worthy to unlace, and on these words of Saint Augustine, and betook myself off when men sought my life : for the people were well supplied with the word of God and cared for in my absence and their other spiritual needs were satisfied. Then I returned and again preached. And when at the king's orders a meeting was to be held to aim at an agreement, then I once more departed after my people had approved it during a sermon. But when nothing was attained at this meeting, I resumed my preaching although I had been forbidden to preach. Then when the interdict stirred the people deeply since none could be baptised and no dead buried, and therefore great disorders were to be feared, I left once more." Hus did not conceal from himself that the problem of conscience had not thereby been solved. " I hardly know whether I did right or wrong, and whether all these reasons are sufficient that I am not a hireling." What else could he do since he felt in spite of all that his hour had not come. " I console myself with the thought that hoping in God I would gladly give up my life if I were aware that by my actions I was sinning."

This feeling that he could not do other than save his life for it hour slowly overcame doubts in his mind. Hus decided to go into exile consciously and voluntarily. But before making this act of submission he gave splendid expression to his feelings so that there could be no misinterpretation of his yielding. In the December of the eventful year 1412, when the University declared the papal bulls illegal, he protested in his own way against the ban and interdict. He appealed from the Pope to that " highest and justest of judges who was not swayed by fear or moved by gifts and not deceived by false witnesses " : he now appealed expressly in writing to the true head of the invisible Church, Jesus Christ. " He who because He is almighty God, a unity in essence and a trinity in person, the first and last refuge of all oppressed persons ; He who is the Lord who protects truth to all eternity, setting right wrongs suffered unjustly, who is nigh to all who truly call Him, who looses the bond and does the will of those who fear Him and protects those who love Him, but destroys the sinner who will not redress his ways : Jesus Christ, true God and true man, who in His need, hemmed in by high priests and scribes and pharisees and priests and unjust judges and witnesses, gave by His shameful and bitter death a splendid example as a memorial to His followers, that they should commend their affairs to the almighty, omniscient and omnipotent Lord ; to Him do I now appeal, following this holy and fruitful example, turning from heavy oppression, unjust sentences and vain excommunication at the hands of the high priests, scribes, pharisees and judges who sit in the seat of Moses, and commending my case into the hands of God." And once again he set forth all the reasons that spoke against Rome, and solemnly handed over, in a sermon in the Bethlehem Chapel and in writing to the University, this appeal to " Jesus Christ, the judge who knows the shortcomings of all men's disputes, who protects and judges, brings the truth to light and rewards."

This appeal to Christ brought no outward change in Hus's cause and practically and rationally made no difference. Nevertheless it was of great significance. For in it Hus gave expression to feelings that went further than he was aware. In this appeal, although he might once again repeat all his complaints against the Church, reform was no longer the issue but immediate contact between man and Christ. The appeal was to play a prominent part in Constance where it aroused nothing but scorn and loathing. His opponents understood more clearly than Hus himself the way he had trodden. For Hus rejected the traditional role of the Church as mediator between man and Christ. The direct and personal appeal to the Bible was a violation of the teaching of the Roman Catholic Church to which Hus thought he remained faithful and wanted indeed to remain faithful.

Hus himself remained unconscious of this chasm between him and the Church. This was clear in his letters to the people of Prague. In hem he spoke with extreme modesty of his own achievements. Playing upon his own name which resembled the Czech word for " goose " he wrote, " The goose is a tame creature, a domestic bird, which cannot reach the heights in its flight." But there are " other birds with stronger pinions which can rise to the heights of God's words and rend all snares." He spoke of falcons and eagles which could achieve what was beyond the weak and uncourageous goose. But wherever it was a question of his own path and trial, he admitted of no limitations and no excuses: here he betrayed that unyielding pride which made it possible for him to turn immediately to Christ, sweeping aside all men and all human institutions. For he felt that here was a responsibility that he alone and he personally had to bear and which could be lifted from him by no Pope and Church. But though that contradicted the very essence of the faith of the Middle Ages, Hus still felt one with the Church in general and he still attempted to adapt and submit himself; he therefore made little of his achievements and referred to others who would perfect his work: but emotionally he was an individualist whom none could relieve of his own personal task and responsibility.

The fact that this duality was not consciously realised by Hus made his fight against the Church hopeless. Hus always believed that he was fighting only for the purity of the Church and of the faith. More severely and exclusively than the Church he took up his stand on the Holy Scriptures, that is on the original word of God, and on those first Fathers of the Church whose interpretations of the Scriptures were still so near the source. Only so far did he follow Wyclif. He believed he was leading the way back to the early severity of the Church. He did not grasp that in reality he was blazing the trail to a new freedom by emotionally acclaiming this freedom. For the explanation of the Scriptures that the Church recognised might be never so false or arbitrary: the Church, nevertheless, was right when it forbade any other interpretation, and did not allow the people to read the Bible themselves. If the Church interpretation might be rejected, the way was opened to individual interpretation and all that this implied.

Hus as an adherent of scholasticism believed severely in reason; he believed that with her help it must be possible to find one single all-compelling interpretation. The Church, which was beginning to leave scholasticism behind it, saw through the glorification of reason. Must not the general compulsion break down if only one new interpretation were admitted? Hus fought with arguments; he wanted to be refuted or to prove his case. The Church had to make an appearance of being drawn into these discussions, which accorded with the scholastic custom of the time, but in reality the Church was concerned exclusively with obedience. Hus's proofs might be never so convincing: since he refused obedience and must refuse it in the light of his feelings, his fight was forlorn in spite of all his proofs.

For both parties the fight for reform was paramount. Hus consciously wanted reform, and he fought the Church's demand for unconditional obedience above all because it hindered reform. Here Hus was unquestionably right. It was infinitely better for the Church herself to make reforms than to hinder them; many dissensions and many losses would thus be spared her. The degeneration was a scandal which could no longer be cloaked: that the Church accepted it only showed how far it had strayed from Christianity.

But beneath the surface, recognised only by a few members of the Church, there was an issue that could not be decided so easily and which today even is not finally decided. Should the Church be preserved through tradition and obedience or should she, and Christianity in general, be endangered for the sake of freedom? Freedom alone seems reconcilable with Christianity; the decision for Christ is only valuable when it is the personal decision of each individual. Yet the call to obedience is seductive and has been effective through the centuries, for is mankind really capable of living up to freedom or must it not degenerate? Is the Church not wise, nay in duty bound, to relieve the faithful of this decision in order to lead them more safely to salvation? The Church only apparently entered into argument with Hus and almost always for ignoble ends. Yet today we must hesitate simply to condemn her out of hand, for behind her unworthy excuses we feel this greater problem which might have been sufficient to justify her.

The great achievement of Hus, however, was that his life, which towered far above the church dispute, answered this ageless question. His example showed that for Christians it must be freedom, without regard to the dangers that may arise from it. In this sense Hus's useless appeal to Christ, which his age with a certain amount of right scorned and rejected, was not in vain. It gave him the strength to endure to the end the hard path of mankind awakening to the call of the future. And that gives him, who is much more important than all his own teaching, his greatness.

But for this very reason the appeal to Christ could not save him. It strengthened his inner calm and made it possible for him to face exile but in exile he was to find no rest. He must tread his path to the end.

Hus's decision to leave Prague began gradually to affect his cause favourably.

The Church seemed to be triumphing when he fled. Many people attended the energetic sermons of Palec and Stanislav. The Prior of Dola published an " Antihussus " in which he called Wyclif the Arius of his age, Hus his son and the Bethlehem Chapel the Satanic school of the Wyclifites, a dangerous ambush, a den that infected the whole of Prague. This extreme severity seemed to have good results. In his first letters Hus conjured the people of Prague to remain true to the word of God and shun the example of Palec and Stanislav: there were obviously many backsliders and Hus feared an increase in the number. He never tired of describing the simple life of the Saviour, the persecutions, the humiliations and the shame that He and His disciples had borne. He hoped thus to prevent the people of Prague from being blinded by the success of power and the outward abasement of the Wyclifites. The Saviour Himself had been condemned to the basest punishment as a heretic and criminal: what was the ban on Hus in comparison? Untiringly he called upon them to protect the beloved Bethlehem Chapel, for there was the constant danger that it might be destroyed.

At the beginning of 1413 Hus's letters seemed much more assured and calm. Anxious conjurations had given way to gratitude for the self-sacrificing loyalty of his congregation, joy at the success of the Masters in asserting themselves, emotion over the longing of the people of Prague to see him again and their sorrow at his lot. " Beloved," he wrote to them, " I most urgently beg you not to give way to fear, because I am not with you. I rejoice that you continually hear the word of God and that the merciful Redeemer has vouchsafed you many steadfast leaders towards the truth."

The blindness of the Church contributed much to this change. Even in Prague they still did not grasp what the issue was and again staged a drama that simply played into the hands of their enemies.

Archbishop Albik was not equal to the demands made on him by high office in those troublous times. He would gladly have retired but did not want to lose his income. With all publicity a plain business deal was therefore made. Albik received the sonorous but empty title of Bishop of New Cæsarea and at the same time the very concrete income of a Provost of Vysehrad : the former Provost became Bishop of Olomouc, and the Bishop of this city, Conrad of Vechta, became Archbishop of Prague, the two latter, who took over much more highly paid offices, having also to pay a suitable amount of " release money." And the Pope who condemned Hus so severely approved and consented to this bartering. What better proof was needed that the most degraded simony was rife in the Church ? Hus seized this opportunity for a treatise against simony : he could seldom have found it easier to prove his point, the more so as Conrad was one of the most notorious pluralists of the time. When he became Bishop of Olomouc he was already Provost of Melnik, Under-Chamberlain and Master of the Mint. He lived in Prague and farmed his bishopric : the Church had to coerce him into giving up at least the rich provostship, which he regarded only as a source of income and not as an office.

Nevertheless this exchange of offices ultimately worked out in Hus's favour, simony though it was. Conrad, the " limping German," came from Westphalia and therefore to a greater extent than Albik and Zbynek stood above party and consequently inclined to the Hussites, a further proof that national questions were not the issue. He skilfully and energetically pursued the policy of the king, aimed ultimately at protecting Hus. He, too, urged Hus to leave Prague and assisted him substantially in many ways.

The king's efforts to promote an understanding did not flag. It is significant that the obvious way of restoring the longed-for quiet was not considered : there was never any idea of carrying out the Pope's orders. Efforts were directed only towards rendering the orders harmless by a partial compliance. A matter of equal concern for the king was the reputation of Bohemia, which lay as near his heart as his longing for peace and quiet. Bohemia was decried and condemned as a seat of heresy throughout Europe. This disgrace, intolerable in the Middle Ages, had to cease : otherwise a crusade might be proclaimed against Bohemia. But this end too had to be achieved without the sacrifice of Hus or one of his followers. This proves how great was the influence of Hus in spite of all setbacks.

It was not political considerations alone that counted : it was not the power of Hus and the number of his followers that decided the king and his advisers. The teachings of Hus had already become a part of the flesh and blood of the nation. Without realising it and without confessing it, the king and his advisers were fundamentally Hussites. The justice of Hus's reproaches to the Church was all too obvious : the figure of Hus stood out all too greatly and nobly beside his pygmy opponents who, even at their most malicious, could never question his personal integrity. His immaculate, simple and Christ-like life was as patent as the moral weakness of most of his antagonists. For all these reasons Hus's exile proved fruitful. He could safely entrust his cause to the people of Prague. After their first hesitation the majority stood again with him. His very absence gave a new weight to his letters, counsels and admonitions.

It was no easy task for the king to resume his forlorn attempts at arbitration. In December 1412, under his presidency, however, the highest provincial court met in Prague. The king put to it the question of " how peace and the good name of Bohemia could best be restored." In despair a new synod was summoned and met on February 6, 1412. However, the irreconcilable differences between the two parties only became more apparent through this and it dispersed with nothing achieved. A court of arbitration was then set up and both parties bound over in advance to accept its decision under pain of exile. Surprisingly enough it really made some headway.

The president of the court asked each party, " Will you submit yourself to the decision of the Holy Roman Church ? " Palec answered, " Yes, in so far as by the Roman Church is understood the Church of which the Pope is the head and the College of Cardinals the body." John of Jesenice answered, " We wish to obey the orders and decisions of the holy mother, the Roman and universal Church, in all matters in which a devout and faithful Christian is bound to obey." At this the president announced, " The Doctors and Masters are therein agreed that they will submit themselves to the orders and decisions of the holy universal Church in all, as faithful and devout Christians should submit themselves." And on this peaceful basis he wanted to begin work.

This scholastically subtle formula, which must apparently be acceptible to every Christian, plainly inclined to the Hussite point of view. It is therefore not surprising that the Doctors protested against it. Stanislav excitedly exclaimed that the corollary " as faithful and devout Christians should submit themselves " certainly sounded very fine but contained poison. The Doctors demanded the explicit recognition of John XXIII. The age, however, was so accustomed to such subtle compromises and the appeal to John XXIII, who was still only one of three

Popes, seemed so unessential that suddenly the Doctors appeared as the real stumbling-block in the way of peace. They thereby defeated the court's undeclared intention of maintaining an appearance of loyalty to the Church without yielding in fact. The lightly roused wrath of the King suddenly descended upon them. " To chastise their open and criminal malice " he banned Palec, Stanislav, Peter of Znojmo and John Eliae from the kingdom. With one stroke the Church party was thus deprived of its leaders. The ban was actually enforced. Only Palec turned up in Rome some time later. The other leaders dropped out of the struggle for good and seem to have died in exile soon after. Soon afterwards the Church party suffered a second equally heavy blow. Wenceslas changed the proportion of representation on the Old Town Council which had hitherto been a Church stronghold. He decreed that in future nine Germans and nine Czechs should hold office.

Even this surprise change brought no final settlement. Prague was in a state of constant turmoil. Whenever Hus returned to Prague the interdict came into force again and threatened to destroy all his previous successes. Soon after they had taken up office, two of the new Czech town councillors were executed for reasons not known. Palec proved more dangerous in Rome than he had been in Prague. Together with Michael de Causis he sought revenge for the disgrace he had suffered and fought more ruthlessly against Hus, his former friend, than any of his non-Bohemian enemies. Hus did not find in his king the protector he needed for the work of reform to proceed vigorously. The king dared not openly confess himself a follower of Hus and took pains not to clarify his attitude. Everything was in a dangerous and irritating state of flux that must in the long run prove intolerable.

That there were no public outbursts of passion to decide matters for good or ill was mainly due to the fact that Jerome had had to leave Prague about the same time as Hus. Jerome had probably attempted to end the eternal vacillation and hesitation : most sources ascribe to his influence the more energetic steps of the king, such as the changes in the Old Town Council, even though he was certainly not in Prague at this time. Perhaps it was his realisation that he could not permanently overcome the vacillation of the king that once more brought to a head his old restlessness. He set out on another of his long journeys.

On this journey he attempted to carry out that grandiloquent scheme which, had it succeeded, would have changed the direction of development in Europe. He attempted to bring about a

Czech–Eastern–Slav rapprochement and to find an ally against the Pope in the Orthodox Church. He went first to Poland, whose king was well disposed towards him. Hus had kept him informed of events in Prague. Among the Poles there were many adherents of the Hussite party who would later take up the cudgels for him in Constance. But in Poland too the Catholic Church was overwhelmingly strong. Jerome, whose reputation as a heretic had preceeded him, had soon to flee. A meeting with him made a deep impression on the Bishop of Cracow. He reported to King Wenceslas that the people could not grasp "the dogmas of such a great philosopher" and thereby involuntarily admitted the greatness of the man he was fighting.

Jerome continued his journey to Lithuania and Russia. The charge in Constance reported, "In Russia there has been from earliest times a populous city called Vitebsk. The inhabitants of this city are mainly Russians, schismatics, belonging to the Greek sect, which deviates in many ways from Christian belief and persists in false doctrine. In the year of our Lord 1413 in the month of April there came to this city Prince Witold, the brother of the King of Poland, with a large host and a train of followers, among whom there was also Jerome of Prague. The clergy and the devout Christians of this city went out to meet the aforesaid prince in a procession with banners and relics. The aforesaid Russians too, the schismatics, also came forth from the city with their false relics after their accursed custom in their accursed procession, and greeted the prince on his entry. Then the aforesaid Jerome contemptuously left the procession of the monks, friars and catholics and joined the procession of the Russians, schismatics and unbelievers. And in the presence of from four to five thousand people of both sexes, he knelt down and began to bow himself before the false relics and pictures, publicly and openly making common cause with the sect of the unbelieving schismatics and Russians and turning aside from the confession of the true Christians. This same Jerome made every effort, as far as he could, to turn the aforesaid prince with all his Christian following from the Christian faith and to move them to enter the sect of the Russians and unbelievers. With an impure mouth he confirmed his false teaching and to the disgrace of the Christian faith he stated with certainty that he believed that the aforesaid schismatics were good Christians and he persisted in this error and praised the Russians and their wrong belief."

It is not clear to what extent these negotiations prospered and what reception the proposals of Jerome received, for his efforts were brought to a sudden end by a shattering event. It is also uncertain whether these negotiations received support in Prague. Hus was certainly still mindful of his friend : for he wrote in his defence one of the most passionate of his letters. This letter betrayed that these plans of Jerome, of which so few traces have remained, must have been well known at that time and that a further mission to the Southern Slavs was intended. Master Sybart of the University of Vienna warned the Bishop of Zagreb against the heretic Jerome. Therefore Hus wrote to him, "He who brings his neighbour into ill repute with heavy-weighing lies does not deserve a greeting. See here, you professor, you, not of holy theology but of the notion of injustice, why do you assert that Jerome is a disseminator of heresy and by no means the least, when you know nothing of his faith, and why do you so boastfully add the lie that he went to the King of Poland and his brother in order to plot an upheaval ? Have you then such a knowledge of the human heart that even at such a distance you can read a man's thoughts ? Do you confess the laws of Christ when you thus speak ill of your neighbour ? This honourable Master was not enough for your sharp teeth : the Bohemians too, were not enough : you had even in your devilish craziness to impute heresy to the Kingdom of the Slavs. On the Day of Judgment you will have to give an account of every word before the most severe Judge. In name you may be a professor of theology but in reality you are a professor of confusion who throws men into uncertainty, who lyingly tosses the disgrace of heresy upon your brother. You are certainly badly instructed in the theology of love. May God give you the spirit of truth."

Jerome's effort remained unsuccessful and must inevitably have remained so : the times were far from ripe for such deep political changes. Jerome's ideas were far ahead of the times. They were taken up later by the Hussites but only hesitatingly and when it was already too late. This vast and attractive political plan only showed afresh how right was the road taken by Hus : first the inward road had to be trodden to the end before its lessons could be put into effect in the external world. Spiritual gains could not be lost like external things attempted prematurely, even though they might be mysteriously transmuted in the course of time. The road of Jerome needs must soon join the road of Hus.

When he decided to go into exile Hus turned his steps towards his native Southern Bohemia which he had left more than twenty years earlier. He found asylum with one of his nobly-born adherents in the stronghold Kozi Hradek. And here this exile, forced upon him by his enemies to bring about his downfall and accepted only fearfully and hesitatingly, turned out to be a decisive factor in his own development and that of his cause. For here he completed work that he had begun in Prague, including the translation of the Bible, and in addition wrote such an abundance of new works as seems almost impossible in so short a time. Exile lasted less than two years and was repeatedly interrupted by visits to Prague. His experiences and teachings, his intentions and thoughts had in the last years been crystallising within him and his exile thus represented only a saving opportunity of at last saying all that he had to say. Apart from innumerable short tracts, answers to the voluminous writings of his enemies, expositions of the faith, some text books and many letters, he also wrote his major work, a collection of his Czech sermons and homilies, and the Latin work " De Ecclesia " in which he expounded all he had to say about the Church.

In these works Hus's intellectual achievement found its final expression. He still preached and taught whenever occasion offered. " Pray for me," he wrote to the people of Prague, " that God may bless me in the preaching of His word, as I preach it now wherever I may and as need arises, in the towns and villages, in castles, in the open fields or in the woods. I would use every opportunity that the Word of God may not lie buried within me." Through these sermons his feelings too were strengthened and deepened. The decision which he had made in obedience to his feelings was proving right and his whole personality was approaching its maturity.

The falling-off among people, even though not so widespread as had at first appeared, had changed Hus. In utter self-oblivion he was now simply an instrument for preaching the word of God. The confusion in Prague sank more and more into the background of his mind, no longer rending him, amid the quiet of the lovely south Bohemian landscape. The attachment of the simple peasants and the local townspeople brought him ever deeper happiness. He preached where he could, from carts, by the hedgerows, at the annual fairs, at weddings and christenings and funerals, and ever more people streamed to him, coming long distances to hear him. They came afoot, on horseback, in carts, only to drink in more of his words and not to miss one of the precious sermons. He relived his experience with the Bethlehem Chapel but purified, deepened and clarified. For now no office bound him, no goal beckoned him on, no ambition spurred him : no duties demanded fulfilment, no rank lay ahead, no earthly greatness lured him. He lived the life of his Lord. He moved about the countryside, simple and poor, a man among men : he had come from Bethlehem to Galilee. More strictly than ever he strove to live up to the standards he set himself. " He who serves the altar should live from the altar like the apostles, having food and clothing and being satisfied with that. He must indeed live, but not be haughty of spirit, not enrich himself, and not win earthly goods by his priesthood." He went about the countryside scattering the precious seed of the word of God. The whole countryside came under the spell of his mild and gracious personality. The seed he set was to grow well and yield a splendid harvest. Soon after his death his most pious disciples were to build here the city of Tabor for the defence of the undefiled word of God, for the defence of his doctrine and memory.

In this serene atmosphere his readiness to die was transformed to ripeness for death. " I assure you," he wrote to his friends, " that it is not persecution but my own sins and the perversity of Christian peoples that sadden me. What suffering can it cause me when the riches of this world, which are but chaff, are taken from me ? What can the loss of the favour of the world matter, when it so lightly leads one astray from the path of Christ ? What matters the disgrace which, humbly borne, so purifies and enlightens the children of God that they shine like the sun in the kingdom of their Father ? What would it matter to me, finally, if my life were taken which is but death and by whose loss we first may find true life ? Men blinded by pride, ambition and greed do not understand that. Neither do they who, fearing where no fear is, have turned from truth to where patience, charity and the other virtues waste away, and who are wondrously confused within, because the recognition of the truth presses upon them, but also the fear that they must lose their names and sacrifice their miserable bodies to death. But I will willingly offer this body, trusting in the Lord Jesus who may give me the grace thereunto, because I do not long to live in this evil world unless by God's will I may lead myself and others to penitence. Know that I shall not flee when I must expose this wretched body to the danger of death, for I know that in God's word we lack nothing and the truth of the gospels will always continue to be spread."

But how was he to recognise the hour of his death, how was he to know when to give up his body without uselessly squandering this unique and precious life ? This life, too, had been lent him by God that he might piously make use of it. Again and again this question snatched him from his peace of mind, forced upon him by his longing for martyrdom. The consciousness that he must preach the word of God held him back from an over-hasty answer. But Jesus Christ finally went from the countryside to

Jerusalem, Jesus, too, did not always go about in Galilee : when His hour came He finished His preaching of the Word of God and strengthened His teaching by His sacrifice. Exile was a profound and happy experience for Hus, but he could not bear it perpetually. His disciples were ready to end what he had begun. But the situation in Prague betrayed clearly enough that a last deed, a last act of suffering, was necessary to secure the final efficacy of his teaching and to break the fetters that still hampered the word of God. Such fetters were the fears of his followers for his life. When must he make the purposeful sacrifice that would free them from his care ?

On June 21, 1413 Hus was once more in Prague. He brought with him a gift for his congregation. He stuck up on the walls of the Bethlehem Chapel the treatise " On the six errors," in which he tersely and clearly summarised the reproaches he made against the Church. The six errors of the Church were : that the priest in the Mass created the body of Christ : that the Virgin Mary, the Pope and all the saints were to be believed in, when only God was to be believed in : that priests could at their pleasure remit sins and absolve from punishment and guilt : that members of the Church must give unconditional obedience to all orders of their ecclesiastical overlords without consideration as to whether these were in accordance with the commands of God : that any excommunication, just or unjust, injures the person against whom it is proclaimed : and finally simony, with which most of the clergy were tainted. This short and simple exposition showed how inwardly clear Hus was : his work was completed and he was ready. To strengthen this preparedness and to test once more how his cause stood in Prague, he stated at the conclusion of this tract that he had publicly been in Prague without the interdict being enforced.

Many things had indeed changed in Prague in the meantime. Following the example of Hus, many of the Masters now made preaching their main activity. They now called themselves the " evangelical priesthood " in contrast to that of the Church which they called " Mahommedistic " because, like this false prophet, it courted worldly might. The appointment of Hussite preachers in the Church was enforced more and more. The people broke the recognised custom of confessing only in the Church to which they belonged and went to the Hussite priests. A Hussite frequently was called to preach in a strange church. The priests who respected the interdict were driven out and their places taken by Hussites ; and even if the Archbishop refused to confirm such a change he could not prevent it. But all this did not suffice to bring about a real transformation. When Hus mentioned the lapse of the interdict, it was once more re-imposed in full force and it was still strong enough to force Hus to leave Prague. Bethlehem Chapel waxed but the University, which Hus cherished equally, declined : in the year 1413 no Bachelors' examination took place there and in the following year there was for the first time no Quodlibet. Every success of the Hussites only increased the tormenting disquiet in Prague.

To this must be added that the catholic world, which was a self-contained and homogeneous world, was increasingly meddling in the Prague turmoil. " For the whole world resounded with the cry : Bohemians are the sons of heretical degradation," as Ludolf of Sagan, a German from the Empire, put it. The Paris University denounced twenty articles from Hus's " De Ecclesia." Its Chancellor Gerson was a protagonist of reform, but he wanted to see it only within the church and he saw that Hus was bursting these limits. He therefore keenly opposed him although for more honest reasons than the simonists. He repeatedly urged the Archbishop and Prague University to take measures against Hus : " For many years now a most harmful tare of various errors has been spreading in shocking quantities in the Prague diocese, errors that have their ill-famed origin in the books of John Wyclif and which are being defended there with the most provocative insolence." He demanded the destruction of the Wyclifites " with fire and sword." His insistence was supported by many Church and lay dignitaries. The respected Cardinal Simon of Rheims complained, " That old enemy in the kingdom has gained such power " : the Pope tried to force the king to redress things : the Germans, including Master Sybart of Vienna, pressed Sigismund, the heir to Bohemia, and all the German universities lent the necessary emphasis to this protest. What did it help that when a new war of the Poles against the Order of Teutonic Knights broke out the Bohemians supported the Poles again and thus won many friends to the cause of Hus ; the east was still far too weak and undeveloped to be in a position to exploit the situation to its own advantage and help the Bohemians. The king and the Archbishop tried to help : the Archbishop promised that the errors of " that most harmful arch-heretic John Wyclif " should be eradicated in order to appease the world : in reality however both king and Archbishop were completely helpless in the face of Prague and the world. A storm which would destroy the Bohemian kingdom began to gather over Prague.

On June 26, 1414 Hus was forced to leave Kozi Hradek because his benefactor died and his heir was not so much attached to Hus. He found a new haven in Krakovec Castle which was nearer Prague. This change increased not merely the physical proximity of Hus to Prague. Once again he began to preach. As he travelled through the land spreading the word of God people again thronged to hear him and would not depart from him. And yet something had changed. The repetition of this activity did not have the same redeeming power for Hus. The seed was sown and the sower must turn to other tasks. Was he not responsible for the happenings in Prague, for all the misery and dangers which threatened to destroy the kingdom? It could not go on like this for ever. The last decisive act for the Faith was becoming more urgently necessary. Again and again he asked himself, torn with inward perplexity, when his hour would finally come. But what could he do? To submit to death at the stake appeared in the last resort impossible of execution: for as before, the road to Rome seemed to him senseless and wicked. Should he then submit to the Antichrist? That could not, must not be the meaning of his life. But just as he began to despair Rome was preparing for him the solution to his torments.

If you looked at Rome and Prague at that time, the contrast was sad and moving. In Prague, there was a host of upright, self-sacrificing and God-fearing men, ready to offer up all for the word of God. Their only guilt was that they would not submit to a Church whose degeneration they recognised. Yet persecuted by all catholic powers for the sake of their pure faith, their survival seemed impossible. In Rome, however, which should be the safeguard of this faith, there was a diabolical degeneracy which made a mockery of Christianity, a church rule which demonstrated the justice of all the charges brought by the Hussites. And this Rome was still wooed by all the catholic powers and held in its hands the destiny of the Hussites. It was only thanks to the greatness of Hus that this unequal struggle was raised from a desperate forlorn battle to the pure heights of a vast spiritual struggle.

The treacherous peace between John XXIII and Ladislas of Naples did not last long. In May 1413 Ladislas abrogated all his treaties and invaded the Church state. John fled, wandering long in Italy. None of the cities would tolerate the presence of this most hated of all Popes. Florence at last unwillingly admitted him to make an end to the scandal. The Neapolitan troops met no resistance in Rome. The town and the churches were pillaged and horses stabled in St. Peter's. Once again a king rode into a cathedral. When Ladislas solemnly entered

Rome on March 14, 1414 he rode into the most sacred Church in all Christendom, the Lateran Church, and scornfully seated on horseback had the heads of the Apostles shown him. This ride, unlike that of Wenceslas in Prague, was senseless : it was only a sign of arrogance and autocracy. The truly shocking thing about the war, however, was that it was certainly John himself who had inspired this new breach of treaty. He wanted to save himself from the council that seemed imminent. For John, rightly as it turned out, feared this council more than any enemy and any crime. Like Gregory he would deliver up Rome to keep it at bay.

John's peace with Ladislas had for the first time made the healing of the schism seem near. From that time Gregory XII had resided impotently in Rimini, and Benedict XIII equally impotently in a Spanish castle : both indeed were out of harm's way, but they had practically no influence left. The whole world was clamouring again for the summoning of the council to heal, finally and for ever, the schism which had already lasted far too long. Nothing had indeed been left for John to do but to summon a council to Rome for 1412. But as his authority was already weak few took part in this council and so he succeeded in diverting its attention from the schism. The one achievement of the council was to wage war on the books of Wyclif, which were publicly burnt in Rome on February 10, 1413, in front of St. Peter's. This council did, however, extort from John a promise to summon a new council in the same year and this one would prove more dangerous since Sigismund was also insisting on it. The plot of John and Ladislas relieved John from the necessity of keeping his promise.

John had, however, not reckoned with the complete treachery of Ladislas who carried on a real war endangering John himself, instead of only a sham war.

This made his plan fail. Ladislas drove John into the arms of Sigismund whom he had wanted to avoid. There was nothing for it but to do as Sigismund wanted. In despair he tried to prevail upon Sigismund to choose at least an Italian town as the venue of the council, but Sigismund had by then gained such a preponderance that he would not consider it. He insisted on a German town which would protect the council against Italian scheming. Moreover, Ladislas died soon after : when he was launching his campaign against Bologna the pretty daughter of an apothecary in Perugia poisoned him. John lost his welcome enemy and was finally committed to the council. He still tried, however, to postpone the council on the plea that now, after the death of Ladislas, he had first to reconquer Rome, but his own cardinals forced him to attend the council. All his subterfuges were in vain.

The announcement was made by King Sigismund on October 30, 1413, and by Pope John XXIII on December 10 of the same year, that a general Council of Christendom would take place in the free Imperial city of Constance on November 1 of the next year. To his horror John saw that the Council, to which Germany lent the authority of the Empire and France the light of science, would become one of those great councils general determining the order of the Church for long to come. That was exactly what John wanted to avoid. Sigismund knew that his regal power depended on the success of this Council: after a long interval the King of the German Empire was again a protector of Christendom: he could lend his kingdom fresh power and authority if he stood the test of his office. That is why he strove to make the Council as comprehensive as possible: in spite of John's protests invitations were sent to the other two Popes, Gregory and Benedict; the King of France was invited and the King of Aragon, the last follower of Benedict. It was really to be a council of the whole Catholic world. At the same time, Sigismund wanted to free himself and that catholic world from another great anxiety: he invited Hus, too, to appear before the Council of Constance.

At Christmas of the year 1413, King Sigismund and Pope John met at Cremona to discuss the preparations for the Council and to wrest from one another as many concessions as possible. Gabrino Fondulo, the tyrant of Cremona, led the two rulers to a tower to show them the city. There he was seized by the satanic thought, as he himself later proudly confessed, of pushing the two highest princes of Christendom from the tower. It appears that only an accident prevented the carrying-out of this sudden inspiration which would have prevented the Council from meeting and would have had immeasurable consequences for the whole world. The Renaissance was here announcing itself and opening up new depths of the human soul. Soon its rule would begin. Before that, however, the Council provided a fearful and yet magnificent closing chapter to the Middle Ages by its invitation to Hus.

This invitation was for Hus the longed-for sign of salvation. Sigismund promised him protection and safe conduct, but Hus had no illusions about these promises. Indeed, one of the royal envoys even warned him, "Know for certain, Master, that you will be condemned." His friendly nobles who knew the character of Sigismund implored him, "Beware of his safe conduct. He will deliver you into the hands of your enemies." But why should death frighten him? Here at last was the opportunity of putting an end to this unbearable waiting and uncertainty. And what an opportunity it was, too. Sigismund promised him that he would be given a free hearing. Hus could stand up before all Christendom to proclaim his teachings and prove his innocence. And Constance was not Rome: there not only his enemies were assembled, but representatives of the whole Church and of the universities, and perhaps he would succeed in convincing them: perhaps he would succeed in winning the battle for pure Christianity and save the Church of Christ. Dare he shirk this task? Even if he failed, he had at any rate fulfilled his duty to the last and in full measure: he could then face death calmly. For such a death, suffered before the world for the sake of Christ, was no longer meaningless. At last his hour had come.

And Hus did not hesitate for a moment to accept the invitation to Constance. He did not fear for his life. He only prayed fervently that Christ would give him the strength not to depart from the truth, not even a hair's breadth, up to the last moment. Would Hus's prayer be heard? His road to Golgatha had begun.

BOOK THREE

THE TEST

CHRISTENDOM IN SESSION

The Council of Constance, which opened on November 5, 1414, and was dissolved on April 22, 1418, thus lasting three years, five months and eighteen days, was one of the most dazzling assemblies in all history. Not only were the highest dignitaries of the Church assembled with hardly an exception : not only was it a congress of the theological faculties of practically all the universities, with hardly a great academic authority missing : it was also a German parliament such as had not met for many years, and a pan-European conference having repercussions in Spain and England, in Scandinavia, Greece and Russia.

At this Council three Popes were deposed, a fourth nominated, and important Church offices distributed. The Pope ratified Sigismund's position of Roman King and Sigismund himself reaffirmed the tenures of the German and Hungarian fiefs or withdrew them and bestowed them afresh. Brandenburg was finally given to the Hohenzollerns. A delegation from the Greek king and the Archbishop of Kiev, with eighteen Greek-Catholic bishops from White Russia, Lithuania, Tartary and Turkey, made still another attempt to reunite the two Christian churches by healing the Greek schism too. The Queen of Bosnia appealed for help against the Turks. The pagan Samogitens, whose home was south of Courland, begged that priests and scholars might be sent to instruct them in the Christian faith and to protect them from conversion at the point of the sword by the Teutonic Knights. The Knights themselves begged help against Poland. Once again the unique position of the Church in the organisation of the mediæval world was strikingly expressed. Major and minor military campaigns to ensure the carrying-out of the Council's commands and to keep order in the vicinity of Constance interrupted proceedings from time to time. Throughout these years the king was either in Constance or travelling on business connected with the Council : one of his journeys was devoted to bringing to an end the interminable Anglo-French war. This Council was not concerned, like so many previous ones, with individual thorny points of the faith, but with all the vital questions of Christendom as a world-order.

The simple and apparently reliable list of persons attending the Council, drawn up soon afterwards by the Constance citizen

Ulrich of Richental, clearly shows the importance of this assembly. He notes the people either permanently present at the Council or attending it for a period. Richental reports, "Pope John XXIII came with six hundred persons. Pope Martin who was elected in Constance came with thirty persons. Five patriarchs with one hundred and eighteen persons. Thirty-three cardinals with three thousand and fifty-six persons. Forty-seven archbishops with four thousand seven hundred persons. One hundred and forty-five bishops with six thousand persons. Ninety-three suffragan bishops with three hundred and sixty persons. More than five hundred Church princes with four thousand persons. One hundred and thirty-two abbots with two thousand persons. One hundred and fifty-five provosts with one thousand six hundred persons. Our Lord the King, two queens and five princesses. Thirty-nine dukes, thirty-two princes and royal counts. One hundred and forty-one counts. Seventy-one barons. More than one thousand five hundred knights. Twenty-four auditors and secretaries with three hundred persons. Thirty-seven from the High Schools with two thousand persons. Two hundred and seventeen doctors of theology with two thousand six hundred persons. Three hundred and sixty-one doctors of both laws with one thousand two hundred and sixty persons. One hundred and seventy-one physicians with one thousand six hundred persons. One thousand four hundred Masters of Arts with three thousand persons. Five thousand three hundred simple priests and scholars. The apothecaries came with three hundred persons, including sixteen masters. Seventy-two goldsmiths and more than fourteen hundred merchants, retailers, furriers, smiths, shoemakers, tavern keepers, and other craftsmen. Twenty-four royal heralds with their attendants. Seventeen hundred trumpeters, pipers, fiddlers, and other musicians. More than seven hundred public courtesans in the brothels, and others who had rented their own houses and, in addition, many private ones whose number cannot be reckoned. To the Pope were attached twenty-four secretaries with two hundred persons, sixteen porters, twelve court officers with silver wands, and moreover, sixty servants of the cardinals and auditors and many old women who washed and mended the clothes of the Roman gentlemen. More than twenty thousand squires. More than eighty-three kings from Asia, Africa and Europe sent their envoys plenipotentiary. Those of the other gentlemen were innumerable because they were daily coming and going, but there may well have been five thousand. Four hundred and seventy-two legations of the towns of the Empire,

B. Picart In. 1723. FRIDERIC ELECTEUR DE BRANDEBOURG.

Three hundred and fifty-two legations of the provincial towns. Altogether, seventy-two thousand four hundred and sixty persons."

For several years Constance was the capital of the world. Its citizens lived in an abundance and variety rarely enjoyed in the Middle Ages. Magnificent processions were constantly going through its streets, the Pope could be seen riding on his gold-decked white horse with the king himself and a prince holding the bridle. The cardinals follow in their red hats. The Corpus Christi procession included " nineteen cardinals, two patriarchs, twenty-six archbishops, seventy-seven bishops, twenty abbots, all with mitres, and four more bishops without mitres." Richental added admiringly, " Each carried in his hand a burning candle ; there were more than two hundred and seventy candles. So many I counted myself, and each weighed half a pound." The Pope read Mass. At Candlemas the Pope consecrated the candles and from his balcony threw them among the people. Then there was a splendid tournament in which the king himself fought. The Cathedral, where the spiritual court met, was gorgeously decorated. Heretics could be seen burning at the stake. Then the most famous lords of the German Empire rode forth to war against Frederick of Habsburg. The envoys of foreign kings came and went, vying with each other in pomp and extravagance. The King of Poland sent a salted bison which was publicly displayed that all might admire this rare animal. The guard bringing it related that transport alone had cost more than four hundred Hungarian guldens. Then pagans appeared wearing strange garments such as none had seen before. King Sigismund rode through the streets with the Order of the Golden Rose which the Pope had conferred upon him. The large store-house of the town was rebuilt, its windows sealed up and the whole square in which it stood cordoned off by soldiers from the lake and land so that Conclave electing the new Pope might observe all the due regulations. Eighty thousand curious people watched the special examination of the food that was taken to the walled-in Conclave to make sure that it contained neither messages nor poison. For the only time the cry resounded in Constance, " We have a Pope ! " A miracle happened. Crows and daws habitually sat on the roof of the store-house. While Conclave sat not a bird was to be seen. When the Pope had been elected there came " very many small birds, such as titmice, siskins, chaffinches, goldfinches, redstarts and others. One flight came after another, there must have been two thousand that perched on the roof of the store-house so that everyone saw them and wondered." Once again the Cathedral was decorated, even more gorgeously than before. A new Pope was to be crowned. Another miracle happened. Provost Henry of Lucerne was murdered. When the murderer was sentenced, the corpse began to bleed and "became fine and red, as no one had previously seen him." At the desire of Sweden the blessed Bridget was canonised with all due pomp. Again the people crowded to the Cathedral : Sigismund was crowned Roman King by the Pope. In the market-place Burgrave Frederick of Nuremberg received the fief of Brandenburg. In the presence of the Pope, King Sigismund knighted the Mayor. Masses were celebrated with strange Greek rites. Foreign vendors offered goods and foods such as the people of Constance had never seen or bought before. The trumpeters, pipers and fiddlers played for splendid balls. And as always in the Middle Ages the solemn went hand in hand with the obscene. The pious citizens sighed that a hundred years would not suffice to cleanse Constance of all the sins committed while the Council sat there.

Constance offered a cross-section of time as well as of the world. The pagans represented the age before Christ. Early Christianity was typified in the Greek Catholic envoys. There was still, though for not much longer, a Patriarch of Byzantium, and he, too, took part in the Council. Hus and his followers represented realism, that is, early scholasticism, and at the same time foreshadowed future developments. The Parisians, with Gerson and Peter d'Ailly at their head, with the fame of whose scholarship the world was ringing, represented "modern thought" of their period. Among the papal secretaries was the Florentine Poggio, one of the first of the famous humanists : he was the sign of the Renaissance that was at hand. King Sigismund and his lieges embodied the splendour of the mediæval crown of the Holy Roman Empire of the German Nation.

But the proximity of the new age was revealed in the townsmen. The town councillors and the shopkeepers managed without a hitch the vast influx of people into the little town of Constance, Food, fodder for the innumerable horses, wood, hay and straw. and all the other goods needed, were supplied so smoothly that even the initial high prices sank again to normal. There was hardly a complaint about the quarters provided for the numberless visitors, and, a rare thing in the Middle Ages, there was not one fire. The level of general safety was exceptionally high. A single robber knight interfered with transport : he was captured and his castle razed to the ground. Only twenty-two men were executed for public crime. Richental mentions this several times as a matter for special congratulation, and it must have been an infinitesimally small number for the times. The king and the princes certainly handed over many more people to the municipal court, but this was a humane body and if the people charged had not done anything too serious they could discreetly vanish over the Alps. Public order was so well maintained that even debtors did not succeed in escaping ; only King Sigismund managed to cheat the town of the debts he and his followers had contracted by giving unmarketable pledges. His, too, were the Hungarian troops which were not amenable to discipline and were therefore quartered well out of the town. The town on the whole proved almost as capable of managing this vast influx as any modern capital.

That was the lively background for the forty-five main sessions of the Council and the innumerable smaller meetings and talks. The three main tasks for them were to substitute one Pope for three and thus heal the schism, to reform the Church root and branch, and to extirpate heresy in Bohemia. The removal of the Greek schism, which might have been the greatest task of all, took only an obscure place on the agenda, its vast importance apparently being grasped by nobody. The immediate but smaller problems were so urgent that main tasks were often crowded out by them. The problem of reunion with the Greek Church, too, could only be solved if serious reform were undertaken : Rome in its degeneracy had no attraction for the Greeks. And in spite of all appearances this Council, too, failed as did the Council of Pisa in this most critical task. The Council's achievement was only great in the negative : in its positive work it contented itself with half solutions which could not change the shape of things to come for Catholicism.

The strength and weakness of the Council was apparent in the two figures which dominated it. The first of them was King Sigismund. The Council was undoubtedly his personal triumph, and an outstanding one. No one would dare henceforth to dispute the German kingdom with him. King Wenceslas declined finally into the ruler of the little kingdom of Bohemia. It was Sigismund who had brought the Council about in the teeth of years of desperate resistance by John XXIII. He it was, therefore, who saw to it that a vast attendance at the Council guaranteed its importance. He spared no pains to bring all three Popes and the most important kings to Constance. When all his invitations were not accepted, he personally went to France, England and Spain to ensure the recognition of the decisions of the Council by the entire Catholic world : he thought thus to arrest its decay. When John XXIII fled from Constance, and the whole Council hung in the balance, it was Sigismund's rapid decision and energy that saved the situation. This all proved that he had emerged from his doubtful and contradictory youth to be a king who had deservedly won back the imperial throne : he was one of the most impressive and important of the German emperors. He still lacked character, however, and that is why his deeds and crimes had no clear direction or permanent meaning.

How little he had changed fundamentally was clearly seen in his behaviour to Hus. He offered him protection in Constance and wrote him a letter of safe conduct to give weight to this promise. This much-contested letter ran : " We Sigismund, by the grace of God Roman King, greet and wish all prosperity to all princes, counts, barons, nobles, gentlemen, knights, captains, governors and officials, overseers, customs officers of the common-weal and mayors of the towns and districts and all other subjects of us and of the Holy Roman Empire. Reverend, wellborn, noble, beloved and true ! We commend to you the honourable Master John Hus, Bachelor of Theology and Master of Arts of the Kingdom of Bohemia, who is on his way to the Council of Constance about to be held ; him we have taken under the protection and shelter of the Holy Roman Empire, desiring you individually and collectively that when he comes to you you receive him with attachment and honestly entertain him. And in all that serves the security and furtherance of his journey, by land or by water, be helpful and prove your friendly will ; and with all his servants and horses and all that he has with him, without hindrance, by all roads, harbours, bridges, lands, counties, districts, courts, towns, markets, hamlets, villages and all places, without any sort of toll, tax or charge, let him freely pass and receive accommodation for the night, and allow him to return, when need demands providing him and his with a secure escort, all out of due reverence of Our Majesty. Given at Speier this 18 October, 1414."

There are various interpretations of this safe conduct. Sigismund's defenders regard it simply as a document commonly granted to travellers at the time, wishing thus to invalidate the words " and allow him to return," which seemed to guarantee an unmolested return to Bohemia. Others regard it as being valueless from the outset since Hus was summoned to an ecclesiastical court over which Sigismund had no jurisdiction. Hus did not await the arrival of the king's letter, but left without it, which would seem to question its efficacy : but he travelled with the king's messenger, a " living safe-conduct," which signified the same as the letter, and the letter arrived in Constance one day after him. Hus's contemporaries obviously believed that the letter was a sacred promise that Hus would return safely to Bohemia: for the Council first sought to forge the date of the letter so that it looked as though it had been drawn up after Hus had already been taken prisoner: and then the Council several times assured Sigismund that he need not keep a promise to a heretic. Finally, all letters of safe conduct granted for the Council were subsequently declared invalid.

However that may be, Sigismund himself undoubtedly recognised the face-value of his solemn word: when he learnt that Hus had been thrown into prison he felt this to be a violation of his safe conduct and wanted to free Hus. He even left Constance when he failed and only when he saw that the whole Council might thereby be jeopardised did he unwillingly yield. Then his lack of character became apparent: having once yielded he washed his hands of his promise and gave Hus not a further shred of protection although he might still have considerably improved the situation or even saved it. It must certainly be admitted that Sigismund was in a dilemma. Even had he been of good-will he could scarcely have found a way out, for he who protected heretics himself became a heretic; he betrayed all too clearly, however, that his promise in no way influenced his conduct. He finally went so far as to urge the fathers to burn Hus, falling without inhibition from one extreme to another. This cheated him of real success.

Sigismund had imagined that things would take a different course. He was surrounded by Hussites who believed that their Master would easily clear himself of the unjust charges. Pope John had given him far-reaching assurances of a favourable outcome to the affair—for John was anxious to get into Sigismund's favour and the absolution of Hus would not be too high a price to pay for it. But the charge against Hus proved to be serious. Moreover, from the beginning the Council took the affair completely out of the hands of the weak Pope. John found he had to fight for his own life: how could he be bothered with Hus. The promise that Sigismund had given in anticipation of an unimportant affair would be put to the test under far more complicated circumstances. It became apparent too that Hus was of an unyielding character and would accept no compromise that would let him down lightly. Sigismund, for whom life was one compromise after another, could forgive him this least of all. How easily the whole affair could have been smoothed over by an apparently honourable recantation, a few words that to Sigismund meant nothing more than empty phrases. But no : Hus would not pronounce those few words that would relieve the king of his inconvenient promise. Well, let Hus pay for it.

Sigismund's anger, as ready as his promises, drowned any second thoughts ; loyalty and good faith meant nothing to him. He himself now urged the cardinals to burn the obstinate man. Hus and all things were for Sigismund simply bargaining counters to be valued according to the purpose they served ; moral integrity was an empty phrase. With Sigismund as with the whole Council, there was no real passion for a Christian solution of the issues. They were seeking a momentary advantage which would preserve an outward appearance of progress in the business of the Council. That, however, was not enough for the task of reform. Faithlessness was not only wicked but also a bad political weapon. It delivered Sigismund completely into the hands of the cardinals and he was unable to force them to make reforms afterwards. The whole Council became the stage for Hus's greatness and for many decades Bohemia was lost to Catholicism and Sigismund.

The second great figure of the Council was Gerson, the Chancellor of the University of Paris, who, together with his teacher Peter d'Ailly, championed reform. He was one of the few not tainted with the general character of the Council : he was deeply concerned with the cause for which he passionately fought, he vouched for his deeds with his conscience, he was perhaps the only one who for purity and firmness of character was Hus's equal. But his fate was a further proof of the extent to which the Council as a whole resembled Sigismund.

Gerson fought the vices of the Church no less than did Hus. " How dare the Pope," he wrote, " issue decrees only to obtain money, as also to apportion bishoprics and abbacies which are nothing to do with him, how dare he indulge in this accursed and predatory sale of benefices, of which one heard nothing in the early Church when the Popes were holy." When a Pope said that he had the power to bind or loosen in heaven or on earth, he was for Gerson " a son of perdition, a simonist, a miser, liar, whoremonger, extortionist, and arrogant, worse than the devil." The Roman Curia seemed to him a large market, where " the more you brought with you, the more you could get," and where Christ was not merely sold once, as he was by Judas, but a hundred times a day, and not for thirty but for hundreds and thousands of pieces of silver. He, too, limited obedience to what was good and what was allowed : nay, more, he even justified the intervention of the secular power in the realm of a rotten church : but at this point his way deviated from that of Hus.

For Gerson secular intervention was a remedy that was in itself wicked and was only permissible in the most drastic emergencies : he was in favour of an autocratic church to which the secular power had unconditionally to be subordinated. When he fought the Pope he championed the more energetically the power of the Council, at whose behest alone the secular power should intervene. The unity of the Church must not be encroached upon, its regeneration must not come from outside. The secular power was to blame that the contemporary age in which the Church failed was a period of hopeless chaos. For where could a man wanting order look for support : to England and France, rending each other, or to that ramshackle monstrosity, wasted by eternal civil war, the still Holy Roman Empire of the German Nation, or to Italy, disintegrating into ever more city states inhumanly fighting each other ? A pure regenerated Church seemed to Gerson the only worthy government for this world. But he knew that such a Church could only be built up on a foundation of what existed, for however rotten it might be it was the only basis for restoration. Nominalism had led all too plainly to the limits of thought beyond which a Church could not be built ; and if this limit were passed, the Catholic world would disintegrate into a hopeless multiplicity of impotent states.

Gerson had a fanatical hatred of the rule of feeling and scorned mere credulity. The new Church, it seemed to him, could only be realised by means of superior reason which would at once preserve and renew what already existed. What would it help if moral indignation, however justified, in sweeping away the immoral priests at the same time destroyed the foundations on which the new structure could be raised ? At last came the great Council for which Gerson had been working for years. This could realise his demands. He succeeded in overthrowing the incapable Pope and establishing the power of the Council : and then came along those two fools Hus and Jerome and with their tempestuous demands threatened to reduce all to nothing. For him, the most modern of the thinkers of his age, realism, which could be justified by feeling alone, was contemptible. Hus and his followers preached sheer reaction which could never build up the Church. As he worked to a rational plan and not from moral feeling, their teaching appeared to him chaotic and unwise. But above all it undermined the foundations of the Roman Church on which alone it was possible to build.

B. Picart delin. 1712. L. Surugue Sculps.

And thus he demanded against them, with whom it hardly seemed worth his while to enter into discussion, the secular sword: the court for heretics was welcome to him if it re-established the power and mastery of the Church. Now the two extremes working against the Church were removed: the worldliness of the Pope whose one thought was his own well-being, and the superabundance of feeling that forgot the earth in thoughts of Heaven. Nothing could now stand in the way of successful reform. The framework of the Church saved, new contents could now be created for it.

Gerson, the man defeated by the Council, was a truly tragic figure. He was so fanatically rooted in his own ideas that he forgot the fate his demands had already suffered at the Council of Pisa. The Cardinals, eager for reform, could not prevent the election of a new Pope before reform started, and the new Pope, no better than the old, had prevented reform. Gerson suffered exactly the same fate in Constance. The Council gladly followed him as long as his attacks were directed against a Pope who could not be kept in office, against schism, which even the blindest could now see was intolerable, and against Hus and Jerome who were less the opponents of Gerson than of the degenerate Church. Hardly had these enemies been destroyed before Gerson himself was defeated, too. For the next step would have to be an assault on simony and all the customs that safeguarded the incomes and prosperity of the clergy; Christianity would have to be taken seriously and an attack launched on greed and lust and worldly power, on riches, pomp and circumstance, and the exploitation of the laxly ruled flock. Could the high Church dignitaries from being the equals of the highest worldly rulers suddenly become the least of their servants, transforming themselves into poor ministers of Christ?

Gerson found against him a united front of all the clergy. He did not indeed even demand evangelical poverty but only purity of morals: but the best intentioned of those on the other side wanted to remove abuses only in so far as they were dangerous to the authority of the Church. Gerson had deprived himself of the support that could have compelled reform, for the Church he wanted could only be brought about by the force of feeling in revolt. The degenerate Church would only yield if confronted with an opponent determined if necessary to go on over its dead body. Once again, against Gerson's wishes, the new Pope was elected before reform was tackled: and once again the new Pope, although he might be better than the wretched John, was against any fundamental reform. All remained so very much the same that a hundred years later Luther could make the same reproaches against the Church that Hus and Gerson did.

The Church lost the last opportunity of restoring the unity not only of the catholic but of the whole Christian world. Hus was a pacific antagonist who valued the impressive Church organisation: he did not wish to destroy the Church but for its own good lead it back to pure Christian doctrine. He was not aware of the scope of his own demands, not aware that he was demanding freedom of conscience and personal responsibility: he believed that his teaching was possible within the framework of the existing Church. Ethical force, his strong moral feeling and his love of Christ shaped his actions. He thus did not yield in blind obedience which he considered immoral as soon as faith was lacking, but demanded that he should be taught and convinced. He wanted first and foremost a thorough moral reform of the Church, and had the Church carried out such a moral reform he would have accepted its dogma: for it was the degeneration of the Church that first shook his belief in it and led him to Wyclif and the Holy Scriptures. Instead the Church did everything to force the new and still unconscious moral demands to a decisive breach. It refused all teaching and all discussion and questionings, demanding unconditional submission although it continued in all its degeneracy. Because it acted irresponsibly it compelled Hus to declare plainly that even the most important Council could not relieve him of his personal responsibility. The Church itself helped on the expression of the demand for freedom of thought and conscience and it was the Council itself that turned Hus from a fighter for the internal reform of the Church to a martyr of the reformation. The Church was certainly right from its own point of view when it demanded unconditional obedience, but then it had also to be equal to unconditional demands. At a time when the Pope himself, the Vicar of God on earth, had to be deposed for the basest crimes, that commonsense to which Gerson appealed would demand that a high moral force such as Hus should be used and not destroyed. Hus's unawareness of the revolutionary character of his demands created an opportunity bordering almost on the miraculous. Through Hus the Church might have succeeded in cleansing itself, even in the eyes of the most pious, of all reproaches made against it. What a triumph for Catholicism if not only Hus but also the Greek Church, demanding the same reforms as Hus, had been led back into the bosom of the Catholic Church. But Gerson was too fanatical and the Church too small to use this last chance, and when Gerson himself was defeated there was nothing left for the truly faithful but to oppose the Church. Instead of bringing peace the Church thus unleashed that war for Hus which led to the greater wars which afterwards rent Christendom and finally undermined it.

The Council did not succeed in suppressing the more flagrant immoralities and abuses among the clergy even for the duration of its sessions. Externally magnificent, it was inwardly stained with simony and excess, corruption and pettiness : in spite of the goodwill of several cardinals it was all too deficient in virtuous personalities and yielded Hus ever fresh proofs of the justice of his charges.

John XXIII went to Constance in October 1414, to open the Council which he had been forced to call. He had decided upon the journey only when there was no longer any way out. He would gladly have sacrificed the whole Church for his personal well-being. In Meran he took Duke Frederick of Habsburg into his services for six thousand gulden annually. He sought every worldly means of shielding himself from the looming dangers. He had no thought of surrender but only of selling office and life as dearly as possible. When his carriage overturned on the Arlberg those rushing to his assistance heard him cursing, " Here I lie, in the devil's name ! " And when he first caught sight of Lake Constance and the city beside it he cried out, " That's the way to catch foxes." He knew what lay ahead of him and he did not find it worth while even to put up a pretence of papal dignity.

Yet this Pope, whose shameful deeds were known to every cardinal, was received in Constance with all ceremony when he entered the town on October 28. Richental gives an enraptured description of the splendid procession. " Our Holy Father Pope John XXIII," he wrote, " mounted a white horse before the Kreuzling Gate and was robed in vestments like a priest at the altar for the Mass. He was all in white with a simple white bishop's mitre on his head. Over his head was held a golden canopy, a gift from the people of Constance. Four citizens, Heinrich Schiltern, Heinrich Ehinger Hans Hagen the judge, and Heinrich of Ulm, the mayor, carried it above him on four rods. On foot beside him were Count Berthold of Orsini, a Roman who had come with him, and Count Rudolf of Montfort, who held the bridle. Before him were nine white horses with red saddlecloths. Eight of them were laden with sacks of clothing, and on the ninth there was a silver gilt chest containing the Holy Sacrament. This horse, too, had a red saddlecloth on which stood two lighted candles and a bell at its neck, and a man on horseback following it carried in his hand a long wand which was set up on the saddle On this wand was a covering of cloth, made of red and golden pieces, which was so broad that it might well have covered three horses. On top of it there was a golden pommel on which stood a golden angel holding a cross. Behind it there rode nine cardinals on horseback with long red robes and red cloaks, and each had a broad red hat on his head. All the bells were rung."

Did not this sound like a confirmation of what Hus had said : " Christ the Lord rode upon an ass and he, the Pope, on a magnificent steed or a stallion, his bridle decked with gold and set with costly stones, as were the chest straps and other harness, while purple tassels and the saddlecloth on which he sat hung to the ground." Was not Hus right when he exclaimed, " O, how vastly are they deceived who approve all this in the Pope as the cardinals do who also ride with him with the same pomp except that no canopy is held over them and they have not shoes of gold." In view of this Pope there can be no doubt that truth was on the side of Hus when he said, " Those, too, deceive themselves who kneel before the Pope and approve all as I, too, approved it when I knew not the Scriptures and the life of my true Saviour. Now I know it and hold all this for blasphemy and true Antichristianity which brushes aside the holy Scriptures with such antics and Christ is despised."

To such a man, earnestly striving to live in accordance with the life of Christ, the Church would give no hearing. Hus, too, was nearing Constance at this time ; but his way was infinitely more like Christ's to Jerusalem than was that of the Pope who should have been Christ's vicar on earth. But Hus, the believing and immaculate Christian, was not solemnly welcomed by the Council : there were no such honours for him as were squandered on the despicable Pope. Soon the Council would treat Hus as a criminal and have only hatred and scorn for the greatest among them.

"WITHOUT the letter of safe conduct I am now beginning my journey to my very great and very numerous enemies, among whom the worst are of my native land, as you will recognise from their testimonies against me and the proceedings of the Council. Many more enemies will rise up against me than once against our merciful Saviour : Bishops and Masters and temporal rulers and books of the law. But I trust in my loving, wise and mighty Redeemer, that He, thanks to His promise and to your true prayers, will grant me the wisdom and steadfastness of the Holy Spirit, that I may endure to the end and not be lured to the wrong side, even though He let me suffer temptation, scorn, prison and death as He Himself had to endure them and as He lets His dearest servants endure them. For He has given us an example that we for our own salvation and for Him take upon ourselves suffering. He is God and we are His creatures, He the Master and we His servants, He is the King of all the world and and we cowardly little creatures, He the sinless and we the sinful, He the needless and we the needy. He suffered : why should we then not suffer? Therefore, beloved brothers and sisters, pray fervently that He may give me steadfastness and cleanse me from every stain. And if my death may serve His glory and your well-being, may He help me that fearlessly before all I may take evil upon me."

Hus looked thoughtfully at the letter which he was writing to his beloved people of Prague. A few weeks previously he had returned from Prague to the castle of Krakovec in order to steel himself in quiet retirement for the hard road to Constance. He had always thought that he might be able to take leave of his congregation in a sermon : but the time had slipped past and he had to do it by letter. He was to leave the following day, October 11, 1414, without visiting Prague. Was he ever to see it again? He was in a mood to take death as a grace vouchsafed to him, the longed-for martyrdom was in his thoughts. Perhaps, however, God in His grace had decided otherwise : perhaps His grace was so great that he would return as victor. "If my death serves His glory and your well-being," he had just written. Could his life perhaps not prove of still greater service to

Christendom and to Christ? He had meant to conclude the letter, but then he continued writing:

"If, however, it is for the best that by His grace I return to you, then may He let me both there and here endure all without a stain, that we may continue mutually in His laws, tearing the snares of the Antichrist and leaving behind a good example for the coming brethren. Perhaps you will not see me in Prague again before my death: but if Almighty God in His grace allows me to return to you, we shall with the more joy see each other."

Hus hesitated to end his letter. In his ears still rang the words that his true follower, the Polish shoemaker Andrew, had called to him as he left Prague, "God be with you. I do not think you will come here again." The words had touched him, but he had not immediately grasped their entire meaning. Recently too he had written to King Sigismund to say that he was concerned only with a free and public hearing: the safe conduct should serve only to give him a chance to proclaim and defend his teaching before the whole Council and the whole of Christendom. Perhaps this had been unwise of him, but dissimulation was foreign to him and he had fearlessly written the words, "I beg the favour that I may come in peace and publicly confess my faith before the general assembly. For I hope that I shall not be afraid to confess Christ and His laws and if it be necessary to suffer death." But the more he pondered the more apparent it became that his task might not yet be fulfilled. He must in any case fight, fight to the last breath, using all possible means, even the safe conduct: only then could he be certain that he had not wantonly thrown away his life. For the victory of his teaching, the restoration of a pure Christian Church, the victory of the Scriptures, would be finer than death and of more service to man and to Catholicism. He must shake off the weariness that he now felt. With all these clergy to be confronted he must not allow himself any weakness whether in the face of death or of life.

The letter still lay unfinished before him. Was this really the hour for death? Full of care he thought of his circle of followers: who would lead them when he was no longer there? They were devout, firm in the faith and of good will, but each insisted too much on what he thought was his right. They obeyed his words, thanks to the grace of God, but would not quarrelling break out once he was no more there? Full of love he thought of Jerome the turbulent: who would bridle him? Little Jacobellus was already impatient of this force and vitality. Would he not openly fight against him? Certainly Jacobellus best knew the Scriptures, but he was too rigid and narrow and would not make a concession even if all were at stake. There was John of Jesenice, his true and courageous advocate, who had learnt much in Rome. He was leading the congregation ever better, but he still lacked the authority needed to make his word prevail. And his good "cardinal" John of Reinstein, so like John of Jesenice, so capable and brave: this staunch follower was accompanying him to Constance and how would it fare with him there? Or Christian of Prachatice, his old teacher: he could not think of him without emotion. No ban had ever been read against him in his church. But Christian was old and tired: he understood Hus, but would he understand Jacobellus? Was not much work still needed to secure his teachings even in the very circle of his followers?

However that might be, he agreed to the great step, fixing his departure for the following day and nothing now depended on him. All was in the hands of God. There was no need for him to torment himself: he could wait for God's decision. And thus he finished his letter. "Jesus Christ be praised for He is eternal with all the elect. Those who endure in His truth will know heavenly joy with Him." Beneath he wrote a bold "Amen."

No other decision was possible. He had to go to Constance if he did not want to aggravate the intolerable situation in Bohemia. Any other decision would have compelled him to hide his face in shame. Now, however, he was glad that the touching care of his friends had compelled him to do everything in Prague that could help him in Constance. On the occasion of a synod he had nailed up notices all over Prague that he was ready to face his accusers but the synod had not accepted his challenge and none had put in an appearance against him. He took with him a notary's certificate to this effect: would it not weaken the charges of his opponents that they had refused to face him, and instead had secretly collected statements against him to use in Constance. His friends had procured him copies and he was able to prepare his reply, which appeared to him convincing. The Inquisitor himself had explicitly declared that he could find no heresy or false doctrine in him and in frequent talks and upon examining his sermons had found him to be an orthodox catholic. The Archbishop at first avoided his friends, but finally he, too, told them publicly that he was not charging Hus with false doctrine or heresy: his fault was simply his failure to obey the papal summons to Rome. This disobedience was now effaced by his going of his own accord to Constance. Truly he had done all he might to assist his victory at Constance.

His good friends did not overlook his creature comforts, making a collection on his behalf. King Wenceslas and the Queen were among the donors. To him, so modest in his demands, the sum appeared large. In Constance it would prove all too little in spite of his simple habits. The nobles provided a carriage and horses, and Pflug of Rabstein gave him a magnificent stallion on which he could worthily appear in the king's retinue. He smiled, for he did not care for such outward shows. Yet they were important : they demonstrated to the world that this journey was voluntary and independent. No command and no foreign favour but the love of his own people paved his long way.

Hus decided not to wait for the safe conduct for only by setting off now could he be in Constance in time. Originally he had not sensed any danger in this, but now, thinking not only of death but also of life, he had misgivings. He had been warned not to trust Sigismund many a time and his journey took him through the land of the Germans whom he believed to be his worst enemies. But these misgivings, later to play such an important part in the dispute over the safe conduct, now appeared to him undue. Was not the "living safe conduct" with him, consisting of John of Chlum, a faithful follower, and Wenceslas of Duba, who was well disposed to him ? He was to be joined during the journey by Henry of Chlum, too. These chivalrous Bohemian barons would be able to protect him. Moreover, he was to meet Sigismund in Germany. Impossible to delay the journey on account of a few childish fears.

And so on the morning of October 11 a very modest convoy of several carriages and about thirty riders left the castle of Krakovec. The barons had provided a number of soldiers, and John of Chlum had with him in addition a pupil of Hus's, Peter Mladenovic, as secretary. He was to record the events in Constance in a simple chronicle. Hus was accompanied by his " cardinal " and a few of his followers who, thinking that they might help their beloved master, would not be dissuaded from going too. Hus was to have drawn his hood over his head to remain unrecognised but he declined, declaring that he would travel openly as he had nothing to conceal. Would the merchants who overtook them spread the news that he was coming ? He carried a large number of placards, to be put up in the German towns, announcing that he was going to Constance " to attest to his faith, the faith which he had hitherto confessed, was now confessing and, God willing, would confess to his death."

He begged the Germans as he had done the Bohemians that " if there were anyone who wished to charge him with heresy or false doctrine would he proceed to the Council. For Master John Hus was ready there to give account of his faith to any opponent." For that was the meaning of his journey: he would give account to all his enemies, and proclaim his teachings to all Christendom. With one stroke his opponents would be silenced.

He crossed the frontiers to the Palatinate with fear, thinking he was entering the country of a bitter enemy. But at Pernau, the first place on German soil that he passed a night at, he was pleasantly disappointed. The parish priest himself came to meet him and presented him with a large can of wine as a sign of welcome. The priest had called together all his colleagues and in love and friendship they listened to an exposition of his teaching, assuring him that they had always been his friends. This continued. Everywhere, at Neustadt as in Weyda, Hus received a friendly greeting from the people. In Sulzbach a provincial court was sitting under the count, and Hus entered the court-room and cried out, "Lo, I am Master Hus, of whom, I believe, you have already heard much evil. Now examine me!" A great discussion developed, but it took a very favourable course, Hus reported. The same thing was repeated in Lauff. "Here the priest came, a great lawyer with his curates, and I discussed everything with him and he accepted all with favour." Hus could hardly believe it. His reputation had reached beyond the frontier and the seed of his word had fallen on fruitful soil. Even the Germans paid attention to his teaching and ignored the long-finished national dispute.

On October 19 Hus entered the free imperial city of Nuremberg, of great importance in those days. Some merchants had announced his approach and a crowd gathered to greet him. The next morning John Helwel, the priest of St. Laurence's, came to dispute with him. In the meantime the citizens and Masters gathered to listen. They wanted to speak to him privately, but he said, "I preach publicly and desire that all who wish may hear me." This great debate lasted from morning until far into the night. Hus noticed that Master Albert, the priest of St. Sebald's, was displeased that the citizens agreed with him but finally he succeeded in convincing the Master, too. The whole gathering supported him, saying, "Certainly, Master, what we have heard is Catholicism. We have been teaching it for many years, we stand by it and believe it: if there is nothing more against you than this you will certainly leave the Council with honour and return home." Hus was deeply moved by his reception. God visibly had him in His hand. He reported to the people of Prague, " Know that up till now I have met no enemy. And thus I recognise that there is no greater enmity against me than from the side of some people of Bohemia."

Fateful consequences followed, however. Hus heard that Pope John was already approaching Constance while King Sigismund was still at the Rhine, which meant for Hus a detour of sixty miles. In view of his good reception in Germany this appeared unnecessary and he decided that it would be better to go directly to Constance to arrive soon after the Pope. He was not travelling, as he had expected, through an enemy country and so he could equally well await the arrival of the king in Constance. He merely sent Wenceslas of Duba to Sigismund to tell him of the change of plan and to fetch the letter of safe conduct. King Sigismund was greatly pleased by the news : Hus's zeal seemed to promise that his position would not be too difficult when he faced the Council. Later, however, Sigismund would use this change of plan against Hus in order to wash his hands of responsibility for his death. Truly Hus would have been differently treated by the Council if he had come in the king's retinue, and Sigismund, too, would not have abandoned him so lightly. But to Hus this journey appeared a splendid continuation of his journey through Bohemia, again he thought of himself as being in Galilee. How could thoughts of his own safety intrude ? He hastened to Constance for the final fight for his faith : perhaps he would succeed in convincing the Council as he had done all whom he had encountered on the way.

From Nuremberg onwards, Hus reported, he was preceded by a Bishop of Lebus, " who rode a day's journey ahead and spread rumours that I was being brought in chains in a cart and that people should beware of me because I read their thoughts." But this warning of the zealous Catholic, who noticed with horror the growing effect of Hus's journey, did not help. The only consequence was that " crowds gathered as at a theatre " and were convinced by Hus. " The enemy's lie became patent and the people inclined to me as soon as they heard the truth." Hus was in Galilee and his path was the path of the Lord who converted the people to Him.

Throughout the journey he read Mass for those with him, and the interdict that should have followed Hus's presence was never proclaimed. In all the towns of the Empire, including Ulm, he had discussions with the Masters, and nowhere did he find enmity. The blessings of all accompanied him to the Council and the hearts of the simple people went out to him. To each of his nightly hosts he gave a copy of his explanation of the ten commandments : everywhere it was accepted with thanks and emotion and people came from far around to read it and believe. His " living safe conduct " surrounded him with loving care. " Wenceslas of Duba and John of Chlum are kind and good to me and are at the same time the proclaimers, or better, the protectors of the truth. With them, with the help of God, all can only go well." In Biberach in a discussion John of Chlum defended the teaching of Hus so enthusiastically and learnedly that all took him for a Doctor of Theology. Hus jokingly called him " the Doctor of Biberach " after that. Hus could take his first glance at Constance across the lake from Buchhorn with a stout heart.

The journey had forced into the background his premonitions of death and increased his determination to stake all on a victory of the truth. It seemed a good omen to him that Constance meant " steadfastness " as well as " constancy " in Latin : God who had led him so far would give him both qualities ! " Beloved," he wrote to the people of Prague, " know that all is well with me. I dread nothing since I hope that after such a great fight the victory is the greater, and after the victory the reward ; and the greater is also the confusion of the persecutors. Jesus Christ is certainly with me, the most courageous of all warriors, and therefore I fear nothing that the enemy may do unto me."

This hope of victory, which contrasted strangely with his unweakened longing for martyrdom, did not leave him until the terrible end. This hope gave rise to his last hesitation and wavering, never expressed in his deeds which only grew more decisive, but in his utterances and letters. He accepted prematurely as signs of God things meant only as final consolation. But is not that understandable ? He expected to reach Golgatha along the way of shame and mockery, scourging and the crown of thorns ; instead his way was the mild road of the sower of Galilee. Hus forgot that he had met only the people and the simple priests whose hearts still remained open to pure Christianity : he had not yet met those in high places who would lose everything if he won.

This hope, too, was used against Hus by his later opponents. If he was ready to die, if he wanted to be a martyr, why did he cling to the safe conduct, why did he reproach Sigismund ? But the late opponents of Hus should, of all people, understand Hus's anxieties. Perhaps he really died too early, perhaps if he had lived longer the Hussite movement might have developed more fruitfully. He alone could have prevented the split among his followers. In fact this delusive hope lent a last lustre to Hus's road. He remained cheerfully ready for martyrdom but he did not resign himself fatalistically to it. What he had dimly realised in the last few days in the Krakovec castle had now become certainty. All weariness disappeared. Unbroken by the tortures of his prisons he fought bravely to the last moment of a life devoted to the service of truth : but his longing for martyrdom, however, finally transfigured his death.

On November 3, 1414, Hus embarked on the ship that took him across the lake to Constance. Simply and almost unobserved but of good courage he entered the town which he would never leave again. He was directed to lodgings at the house of Fida, a baker's widow living in Paul Street. She received him in a kind and friendly fashion. "A second widow of Sarepta," he described her in his letters, "who has given lodging to us all." "She served him with all her heart," wrote Richental. Hus was ready and equipped for the fight. On the first day John and Henry of Chlum had to report his arrival to the Pope, and Henry had to ride on to give the same news to Sigismund. A day later Wenceslas of Duba arrived with the letter of safe conduct and reported that Sigismund was well satisfied that Hus had gone directly to Constance. A good sign. Hus began to believe that his struggle might be successful. He settled down in his new house, again read Mass daily and continued his work at the evidence and the great sermons which were to decide his fate.

Hus's Bohemian opponents were making equally good use of the time. While Hus was openly working at his vindication they were secretly collecting any evidence that could be used against him, however old it might be, however unconvincing it might sound.

Many of the statements deposed went back as far as 1399. The priest Protiva swore to utterances about John of Nepomuk and the Church made twelve years previously. Hus could not think without bitterness of how long his words had been secretly cherished by certain of his enemies. If they had really thought them dangerous to Christianity, they should immediately have leapt to its defence. Instead, cowardly and crafty, they stowed away his words until it seemed safe to attack. The false charges that Hus interpreted holy communion in the Wyclifian way and that he taught that a priest in mortal sin could not pronounce absolution were made again. Andrew of Brod accused him of expelling the Germans although he himself had played a part in changing the voting system at the University. Hus was accused of defending the forty-five articles of Wyclif and of attacking the Pope : nothing was lacking to complete the picture of a hardened heretic. In his answers Hus angrily rejected the straightforward lies : other evidence he attempted to trace back to his original words, which had been distorted either maliciously or unintentionally.

In answering these statements and the first charges of Michael de Causis and Palec, the desperate fight of Hus for the true meaning of his words began. His enemies reproached him with having asserted that no one can be excommunicated except by God. Hus answered, "Yes, in a just way." His adversaries said that he had described all the commandments of God as corn and all the statutes of men as chaff. Hus agreed, but added that he had called "chaff" only laws not based on God's laws and contradicting them. It was asserted that he had denounced the Roman Church. Hus returned, "I have never denounced the Roman Church : but by the Roman Church I understand all Christians who hold fast to their faith in Christ. And it is clear that the Antichrist has begun his reign in order to destroy the Christian faith, and first and foremost in the Roman Curia." Michael de

Causis then accused him of plainly declaring the Pope to be Antichrist. Hus defended himself, " The Pope is Antichrist only when he sells offices, is proud and grasping and lives in disharmony with the way of Christ. It does not follow that every Pope is Antichrist. A good Pope like Saint Gregory never was or is." Thus it continued endlessly. The accusers always took the utterances of Hus as absolute and applied them to the Church and all its institutions whereas Hus meant them relatively and only in application to the degenerate Church and its unworthy ministers. Were the clergy true Christians he would have had nothing against the Pope or his laws or any of the offices of the Church. Surely the Council, whose aim it was to reform the Church root and branch, must have approved. For this very reason the accusations against Hus were given a heretical twist : and the Council gladly acquiesced in this as it would otherwise feel a breeze itself. Moreover, it feared reform and public castigation of abuses more than the abuses themselves.

True, in some cases Hus was himself to blame that his words were so capable of misinterpretation. In his attacks he did not always distinguish sharply between the office and those holding it. He made every effort to clarify any such obscurities at the Council, but what could that avail him. Not even proven lies were dropped from the charge, which at times rose to such heights of absurdity that it is hard to understand how even his most malicious enemies could take it seriously. It was asserted, for example, that Hus had designated himself the fourth person of the Godhead, adding himself to the Holy Trinity. It is not strange that Hus's defence was at times irascible : it is rather strange that this irascibility is held against him even in modern times.

The cleavage between Hus and the Council was more obvious over questions of the doctrines of Wyclif. Hus's debt to Wyclif was stressed because this would bolster up the false charges about holy communion and priests in mortal sin : if Hus were proved a follower of Wyclif it could be assumed that he had adopted these unquestionably heretical beliefs. This would be of great importance in securing his condemnation. But quite apart from this there remained real differences between Hus and the Church, even a serious and conscientious Church. Hus indeed defended himself, " What Wyclif taught of truth, that I accept, not because it is the truth of Wyclif but the truth of Christ." The doctrine of predestination had, however, been rejected by the Church. Centuries of conflict have shown that the Scriptures yield abundant arguments for and against this doctrine. It was one of the crucial problems of scholasticism and it is still a problem which simply admits of no straightforward solution. The Church was therefore right when it decided in favour of one solution and rejected another, for such important issues cannot be left in the balance.

Nevertheless the proceedings of the Council in this respect seem hard to justify. Wyclif had been forced back on this doctrine because he could not but doubt the existing Church. The visible Church had degenerated to such an extent that nothing remained but to oppose it with the invisible Church if faith were to survive. A church willing to reform itself need not have feared this doctrine. It appeared so dangerous since it clearly made the greatest demands on the clergy, denied the power of degraded and wicked priests over holy and elect laymen, and also conceded to the secular power authority over a degenerate priesthood.

But even apart from the practical consequences which gave the dispute double bitterness, and with only a theoretical unity such as any church must demand kept in mind, the proceedings of the Council were not justified. Hus cried again and again, with an unwearying and almost monotonous persistence, "Teach me!" He asked, begged, beseeched, that he might be shown passages in the Scriptures that were apter, more evident, more convincing than those he produced, and this might indeed have been possible, for there is good reason why the dispute on predestination has been drawn out inconclusively through the centuries with those on each side basing their arguments on the Scriptures, and there is no evidence that Hus might not have been convinced. But the Council would give no instruction, admit of no discussion; the only argument regarded by them as pertinent was, "We have rejected the teaching of Wyclif as heretical and you must therefore unconditionally abjure it since otherwise you are a heretic." But how could Hus comply when he knew that the Council had not the moral right to reject any teaching as heretical and when he could not but believe that Wyclif's teaching was far nearer to the true Church than was the Council?

That was the crux of the whole case. Only dogmatic questions were discussed since the Council must avoid moral questions and Hus was always concerned with the moral aspect of questions. That gave the case an apparent confusion that seemed to tell against Hus. He cried unwearyingly, "Teach me!": he could not understand the refusal since these questions seemed to admit of discussion: he felt he was beating against invisible walls. He demanded instruction so often that it seemed incomprehensible why he did not simply comply: and then again he became involved in apparent contradictions, as when he declared he was no heretic and yet held firmly to the teaching of Wyclif which had been rejected as heretical. Beneath it all, however, his feelings led him aright. He could not and must not submit because it would be immoral to yield to an authority which he could not recognise as Christian and which used no Christian means to prove itself. The Council in its turn had to erect this invisible wall in self-protection. It could easily maintain an appearance of right in the eyes of the majority on questions of dogma, but on moral questions it would be lost. And as Hus thought that these dogmatic questions really conditioned reform while his moral resistance and his rejection of authority still remained on the unconscious level he could not explain this opposition between thought and feeling, between the spoken and the unspoken, and he could never bring the discussion to the moral, the feeling, level. The Council therefore succeeded in maintaining this saving confusion throughout the whole trial. Only the death of Hus broke through the invisible walls, tore all protective veils, and shifted the emphasis from dogma to moral conduct. Only then did Hus's ethical conduct in the face of an immoral Council become apparent.

Through this planned confusion Hus was lost from the beginning. These dogmatic questions, surely capable of solution, seemed to confront him with the alternatives of recantation or death. He was lost in any case since he was incapable of implicit obedience, but the course of the proceedings might have been clearer and less frustrating. Their outcome, however, could not have been changed by any defence of Hus.

In its desire to avoid reform the Council was mainly thrown back on political intrigue. Hus could have been saved had any statesman ruthlessly and immorally exploited the degeneration of the Church for his own ends. That was the point of the agreement between Sigismund and John XXIII : the fall of John opened the way to the death of Hus. It was ironical that Sigismund and Gerson handed over Hus in an attempt to save the Council and with it the cause of reform, and thus the only true reformer was overthrown in the name of reform. For like John the Council had in the meantime realised how well this case might further their own ends : without any great sacrifice they could magnificently champion the cause of the Church. The Council's glory could only be enhanced either by the recantation of Hus, welcome as a sop to Sigismund, or by his death. What a way of diverting attention from reform !

It was mainly thanks to the Bohemian adversaries of Hus that the Council was urged along this way. It was they who first pointed out to the cardinals how well the Hus case could be used for the secret ends of the Council. Hus rightly complained about them, for while the Pope still tried to gloss the matter over, they used every means to give it publicity. They laid charge after charge before the Council, and ran from one cardinal to another painting in the gloomiest colours the danger represented by heresy in Bohemia. Almost every deterioration in the position of Hus can be traced back to them.

The day after Hus's arrival Michael de Causis made an attack on the " excommunicated, stubborn John Hus who was under suspicion of heresy " and tried to incite the people against him. When his arrival had been reported the Pope had still reassured him, " As far as it lies with me I will in no wise allow that an injustice be done him as long as he remains in Constance —even though he had killed my own brother." But now when John of Chlum complained he simply shrugged his shoulders, saying, " What can I do? This is the doing of your own countrymen ! "

This first plot did not seem particularly dangerous. The Pope tried to help Hus, first seeking the easiest solution. He sent two bishops and a lawyer to Hus to ask him to submit silently. Hus refused. The demand only strengthened him in his resistance, in view of the obvious deduction that they were afraid of his preaching. " We have had it reliably brought to our experience," wrote John of Reinstein, " that all are afraid of the imminent sermon before the clergy that Master Hus intends to preach." Nevertheless, the Pope, in spite of the resistance of the cardinals, raised the ban and the interdict against Hus and allowed him to go out and to attend church : he was only not allowed to attend the solemn Masses of the Council. Hus accepted this limitation. He even did not leave his house or preach, on the advice of Sigismund who had sent him a message to the effect that until he arrived in Constance he should refrain from any steps. But material enough for a quarrel was already at hand and the Czech opponents of Hus knew how to make the most of it. Hus read Mass every day in his own house and many attended it. Why did the simple people go so eagerly? What did Hus say to them after Mass? The Bishop of Constance requested him to stop celebrating Mass. But Hus would not agree to give up his services. Thereupon people were forbidden to attend his Masses and Hus was kept under suspicious observation.

In the meantime the Council was not yet under way. The

most important members had still not arrived. Sigismund was to be crowned king in Aix-la-Chapelle on November 8 and so he and most of the German rulers could not reach Constance before Christmas. Gerson, too, was not there, nor were the delegations of the other two Popes. The opening of the Council was therefore postponed until November 5 and the first solemn session was to be on November 16.

The solemnity of the Council was magnificently expressed in this session. The Pope, whose self-confidence had been shaken, could once again feel himself head of the Church, as he had just received the news that Naples had been conquered and Rome regained. The cardinals made a number of practical suggestions to set the work of the Council in motion. But already the danger of its ending in stalemate could be felt. Under the presidency of John it was difficult to discuss the removal of the schism since John insisted that the two other Popes had been deposed ever since Pisa and that the schism therefore no longer existed: Sigismund, who might have put some pressure on him, was not there. And these proposals all steered clear of reform, the most urgent question of all.

How easily the Council let itself be sidetracked into trivialities was soon crassly apparent. At last the delegation of Pope Gregory arrived in Constance. The papal arms were put up on his residence: John had them removed during the night because he considered himself the only Pope. This quarrel obscured all else for the time being. A plenary session of the cardinals had to be called. This meeting did not go to the root of the papal question, which had only reached the stage of secret underground work, but simply patched up the public quarrel about the coat of arms by a trivial compromise. The Council was already in danger of dissipating its opportunities in unessentials. How welcome, then, was the Hus case which offered a chance of serious work without any of the more risky questions being broached. Thus the inclination to tackle it before the arrival of Sigismund grew from day to day.

Hus did not see the danger. He quietly worked at three sermons which he intended to preach to the Council. He called them, "The adequacy of Christ's laws for the guidance of the Church," "The declaration of my faith," and "On the peace or the unity of the Church." In them he expounded his faith, but revealed very clearly his intention of remaining within the Church. Even the third sermon which castigated the immorality of the clergy was not more severe than similar sermons before other Councils. They would have convinced many of the well-intentioned cardinals were Hus only allowed a hearing.

The letters to Prague at this time, too, were more like sermons intended to console and hearten his congregation. He was a little oppressed by material cares. " I reckon therewith," he wrote, " that I shall soon be in need of the most important things. Share this care among our friends. Many of our people used for the journey what money they had and are already in need. I suffer with them but I cannot give to all." But this did not play a substantial part for him. How firmly he believed in a satisfactory development was betrayed when he continued, " I have retained for myself only one horse, that of Rabstein, which is stronger and livelier than the others, in case I must ride out from the town to meet the king."

At the same time Palec and Michael de Causis had succeeded in convincing the cardinals that the case of Hus could be treated as a vital issue for the Church. They had distributed among the cardinals the most objectionable passages of Hus's militant writings : and thus they were believed when they exclaimed pathetically in the accusation, " If Hus somehow were to return from the Council, throughout the whole Kingdom of Bohemia one house would rise against another, and this evil would soon spread throughout Germany, and souls would be poisoned in the most deadly fashion. There would arise such a persecution of the clergy and the faithful as there has not been since Constantine : for he will never cease inciting the laity against the clergy and all true believers." They closed with the urgent warning, " If the prelates abuse or do not rightly apply the full powers of the Church which have devolved upon them, they themselves and their flock with them will be plunged into the abyss."

When the ground had thus been prepared, rumour began to play its part. On November 9, on the very day that the Pope lifted the ban, posters proclaimed in Constance that Hus would publicly preach on the following Sunday and give a ducat to all who attended. Hus once again failed to realise the danger of this attack. " We do not know if friend or foe has done it," wrote John of Reinstein. The rumour that Hus would preach could not be scotched and increased the dissatisfaction at his daily celebration of Mass. Finally, a false and senseless rumour brought the whole town into an uproar. Hus was alleged to have attempted to flee from Constance in a hay wain. This gave the cardinals a chance to intervene.

In the name of the Council the bishops of Augsburg and Trient and the Mayor of Constance called on Hus on November 28.

They said they had come to fetch him that he might be given the hearing he had so long desired. John of Chlum, scenting mischief, vigorously opposed them. He referred them to the letter of safe conduct and the promised public hearing and to the order that Hus should not speak before the arrival of Sigismund. "Know that you are acting against the honour of our lord the king!" To the mayor he said, "Even if the devil came to have his cause examined he would have to be given a hearing." The bishops sought to appease him. "We have come peacefully and not to arouse a tumult." Then Hus intervened, "I have not come only to the whole Council. To them will I say what God will put into my mouth and what I am asked. I am nevertheless prepared to come to the cardinals at their request and if I am asked anything I hope to choose death rather than to deny the truth." And so he went with them. On the stairs the widow Fida took leave of him, weeping: she knew nothing of the hypocritical envoys, but she had seen the armed men who surrounded the house. Perhaps she had also heard the bishop murmur, "Now you will read no more Masses."

In the episcopal palace Hus appeared before the cardinals. But instead of a hearing there was only a brief exchange of words. The cardinals made the familiar reproaches and Hus answered, "Know, reverend fathers, I would rather die than be conscious of one, or, as you say, many, errors. For this very reason have I freely come to this Council and am prepared in all humility to receive instruction." The cardinals saw that they could make no headway in this direction as they sought an excuse for imprisoning him: they therefore hastily praised Hus's words and withdrew. Instead a learned minorite brother appeared, pretending to be a simple monk, and asked Hus for instruction: dangerous confessions were to be lured out of Hus by this trick. But Hus noticed the trap contained in the question and said to Chlum, "He is truly no uninstructed monk when he demands information on so deep a question," and to the monk himself he said, "You call yourself a simple man, but I can see your duplicity." Nevertheless, he answered all the questions put to him, but his answers gave no loophole for action against him.

Now Hus and John of Chlum were alone: the hours slipped by and they saw ever more clearly that they had been trapped. In the meantime the cardinals were in consultation. Palec and the others urged that Hus should be arrested: others hesitated to take this step. Finally, however, the Czechs prevailed. Michael de Causis danced triumphantly round the room, "Now we have him. Now he shall not get out of our clutches till he has paid the last heller ! " It was evening. Hus and Chlum were detained by armed men when they attempted to leave. At last the Master of the Papal Court appeared. He told John of Chlum that he might go. Hus, however, must remain in the episcopal palace.

John of Chlum was the most faithful advocate and friend of Hus. His love and enthusiasm could not be checked. He hastened to the Pope. In the presence of the cardinals he made bitter reproaches about their hypocritical and false conduct and shameful breach of word. The Pope answered in their presence, " I not : my brothers ordered the arrest." Then he took Chlum aside. " You know," he said, pointing to the cardinals, " how badly my own affairs stand with them. They handed him over to me and nothing remained for me to do but to take him into custody." Was the Pope only trying to cover himself or could he really do nothing ? At any rate, he did not help. Chlum thereupon wrote to Sigismund who in an angry letter demanded the immediate release of Hus. He displayed the royal safe conduct on all sides in Constance. He publicly posted notices protesting against the imprisonment of Hus. " I proclaim and make known," he wrote, " that Hus, in spite of the letter of safe conduct of our lord the Roman and Hungarian King, has been taken prisoner and is still being held. And although the Pope and the cardinals have been earnestly requested through formal envoys of my lord to release the Master, they refused and still refuse to release him, in scorn and contempt of the empire and of the royal majesty." He declared " in the name of the king " that the arrest " was completely and utterly against the will of my lord and in contempt of his safe conduct, and were he not far from Constance but were present he would not have tolerated it. If he comes here later, then all will feel that he is most violently enraged at the contempt of his and of his empire's letter of safe conduct and protection." But even such vigorous language did not help. The cardinals would not release their prey. There was nothing left but hope in the king.

In the cruellest manner Hus was plunged into the depths of despair from his confidence and trust and newly-aroused hope. He had come freely as an equal to equals who could promote a public hearing and ask for him the opportunity to preach his sermons. His task appeared to him, and not to him alone, as no less important than that of the cardinals. He had come under the protection, nay, as an ally, of the king : he had only just been pondering how he might enter Constance a second time and more worthily at the side of the king. And suddenly he saw himself handed over without defence to sinister powers : in the midst of a great and responsible piece of scholastic work he had been slyly set about and treated like the commonest criminal.

For the first days his confinement was half honourable : Hus began to be reconciled to it. After all, it was possible to work in a guarded cell. But eight days later he was sent to his real prison in the Dominican monastery on an island in Lake Constance : and this dungeon was loathsome. It was a dark, miserable cellar, deep under ground, dank and unhealthy and infested with a pestilential smell as the drains of the monastery there gave into the Lake. Work was impossible in this gloom even had he had the things he needed, and all contact with his friends was cut. Horror alone was there, and the smell of decay. Hus was physically unequal to this confinement. He was soon in a high fever, racked with rheumatism, gall-stones, vomiting and all other possible ills. The Council seemed desirous of torturing him to death. How embittered and fearful he must feel of a death that cheated him of bearing witness to his faith.

The Council now showed its true face. Hus lay in his vile dungeon, tortured by every bodily pain, oppressed by every spiritual need, and the Council did not protect him because it wanted to wear him down.

The order of procedure prescribed that the witnesses must take the oath in the presence of the accused, and just when his illness was at its most painful Hus had to watch ten or fifteen people file past him daily. A ghastly dance seemed to be taking place : he was in a fever. Was not the whole thing delirium ? All those who had so long wished to be revenged on him passed through his cell, the whole past rose up against him. How had they all been collected so quickly ? Had the grave of time or the portals of hell opened ? There was Palec : had he not once been his friend ? Now he could not suppress his loathsome scorn. " Since the birth of Christ there has never been a worse heretic than you, Hus, with the exception of Wyclif," he shouted to the sick man. And how Michael de Causis, the wretched cheat, rejoiced to see Hus lying there. John the Iron, the militant bishop, had come too. The clergy of Bohemia had imposed a tax upon themselves to make the journey possible. Wenceslas Tiem of Passau, whom Hus had attacked as a trafficker in indulgences, had in the meantime been made a provost for his services ; but even that did not prevent him from entering this pestilential cellar to vex his enemy. The German universities had sent those Masters and Doctors who had had to leave Prague on account of Hus. They had not yet reconciled themselves to living in Germany and longed to be back in Prague, and they vented on the sick man their longing and anger. And the Prague parish priests who had so often complained of Hus suddenly appeared in Constance, too. How had they got there? There, too, was John Peklo, who claimed to have been in hell: perhaps this was already hell? Monotonously the oath was repeated. But Hus heard only, "Revenge, revenge, revenge." This was happening at the highest assembly of Christendom.

In this dungeon full of feverish faces the last hope, that in Sigismund, could not survive. Nothing but death, a tortured, senseless death, stood before Hus. In the outside world, however, from which Hus was cut off, the Council still seemed unable to begin their work. The second public session, fixed for December 17, had to be postponed as the results of the conferences were all too scanty, and could not be held till three months later. Almost four months elapsed between the first and second session of the Council. That was bad for Hus's cause as a whole, but at the moment it was his salvation. For how unwelcome would it have been for the Council to have this most delectable case cut short by Hus's premature death. The Pope sent his personal physician to Hus "that he might not lose his life in the usual way," as Mladenovic reported. The physician succeeded in helping Hus.

Yet whether Hus was dangerously ill or simply suffering in health, whether in despair or sustained by a last hope, the Council could not get from him what it wanted. Hus's spiritual resistance remained unbroken even in the face of this diabolical test. His body might be destroyed by tortures: the words with which Hus greeted death were unyielding. The Council had appointed a committee of investigation to which belonged the Patriarch of Byzantium and the Bishop of Lebus: adhering to the letter of the regulations and yet with planned malice they plagued the sick man uninterruptedly with examinations. They wanted to exploit his illness. Hus, who could hardly speak, demanded an advocate. His request was rejected. A heretic had no right to it. "Well, then let the Lord Jesus be my advocate and defence, who will settle all things shortly," Hus answered. "I have commended my cause to Him as He did His to God the Father." The commissioners pestered Hus to submit himself to the verdict of twelve or thirteen Masters. Hus refused. He wanted to be heard by the whole Council. They held up to him the appeal to Christ, which was charged against him. He recognised it "joyfully and with laughter" as his. They insisted more and more upon a recantation: Hus answered unflinchingly, "I leave it for the Council." A single word, a slight yielding, could have rescued him from the revolting dungeon: but even in a state of physical collapse Hus did not think of his comfort. He strove only for the public hearing that would give point to his life or death. The triumph of his inner steadfastness proclaimed itself even at the most terrible moments of his trial, which had also its milder interludes.

Thus Christmas approached and then Sigismund at last reached Constance. On December 24 he was in Uberlingen. He let the Pope know that he should not begin the Christmas Mass until he arrived. This solemn Mass began at four in the morning and was celebrated with the greatest pomp. To the right of the Pope a throne had been erected for the king and queen. At its foot German princes held the golden imperial orb and sceptre. The Elector of Saxony, the Marshal of the Empire, stood with a drawn sword beside them. The king was vested as an evangelist and himself read the Gospel. The Mass lasted well into the day. Then the Pope handed the king a consecrated sword and called upon him to protect the Church. The king solemnly vowed to do this. For the first time he was to keep a promise to this Pope. The sword would smite John XXIII himself. But it would not free Hus.

At first the king did indeed try to save Hus from prison. He was honestly angry and did not spare his threats: he would break open the prison doors by force, he would restore his wounded honour at any price: he even left Constance to coerce the cardinals. His resistance lasted exactly one week. On New Year's Day, 1415, the chronicles of the Council report: "The king most graciously ordered that a free hand should be given to the fathers in the case against Hus." Sigismund had yielded and the year of Hus's death had begun.

WITH his health Hus regained the forces which he believed he had lost in confinement. He began to prepare his answer to the charges against him. His astonishing memory made up for the books he lacked. His quotations were exact and no less numerous than was usual in his writings. The papal physician obtained a substantial improvement in conditions for him, too. On January 8, 1415, he was transferred to a healthier and less horrible prison. The strictness of his confinement was also relaxed to some extent. The papal guards began to carry correspondence between Hus and his friends, and visitors were occasionally admitted.

Hus was now able to write and receive letters, and several books, including the Bible, were smuggled in to him. His guards were bribed by his friends, but the deep impression made by Hus's personality seems to have been more important than the bribes. Soon the guards could be numbered among his friends, and they asked of him instruction in true Christianity. Hus wrote several short tracts for them, "On Penance" for Jacob, "On Marriage" for Robert, "On the Seven Mortal Sins" for George, and still others. This is one of the simplest but most impressive testimonies to Hus's ennobling influence. The authorities of the catholic world assembled there condemned Hus and accused him of heresy: but the simple guards turned to him to learn true Christianity. They, unprejudiced and impressionable, were overwhelmed by Hus's true piety. The unlearned had no doubt as to where living faith was to be found in the struggle between Hus and the Church. Even while he was in prison the hearts of the simple people were drawn to him.

At the same time the situation of John XXIII was growing worse. On February 7, 1415, he suffered his first big defeat. Until then the Council had voted by persons, each member having one vote. This had been of great advantage to John, for the representatives of the Italian Church, materially dependent on him and therefore loyal to him, were in the majority. John had purposely brought a number of poor prelates to Constance with him. Now, however, it was decided that voting was to be by nations. Each nation, independently of the number of its representatives present, received one vote. The Italians, the Germans, the French, and also the English, for the first time at this Council, had a vote each. The Spanish at first could not vote since no representatives of their country had come to Constance. This decision was a turning-point in the course of the Council, and by it John was indeed lost. Only the Italian nation was inclined to vote for his proposals. From this day onward the nations met more and more frequently in session without John's being present. The resolution to force him to resign matured among them. And from this day the most fearful accusations against John began to circulate secretly among the members of the Council.

March 3 saw the second defeat of John. In the second public session of the Council which could at last take place, he had to swear on his knees that he was ready to retire if the two other Popes renounced their claims and the weal of the Church demanded his retirement. The meeting was so touched by this self-sacrifice that Sigismund himself hastened to John and bowed down and kissed the hem of his garment. A great victory seemed won. For weeks there was a struggle over the formula of resignation. John tried to formulate it in such a way that his own readiness was couched in vague terms while the condemnation of the other two Popes was roundly expressed. Even Sigismund's request did not immediately influence him. But finally the Pope accepted the formula of the Council on oath. He was even compelled to announce his decision in a bull to the whole of Christendom.

The second defeat of John was more striking than the first. Actually, however, it had no conclusive results and indeed even weakened the effect of the first defeat. By their decision to vote by nations the Council had John at their mercy : the long negotiations showed that the Council found difficulty in exercising its newly-won power. The formula of resignation forced on John also betrayed weakness. It still lay in John's discretion to say when the Church was served by his resignation and when it should be made. He could seek excuses if the situation chanced to change to his advantage or if the two other Popes resigned and power was in his hands alone. The Council had chosen a voluntary resignation of the Pope because the Council of Pisa had achieved nothing by deposing one Pope. This maintenance of an appearance of free-will had a purpose only if the Pope's promise was binding and could be enforced at the Council's discretion.

The Council later tried to correct its mistake. Negotiations with the two other Popes seemed to be going well. Gregory XII had sent more envoys and apparently would yield. Benedict XIII was shortly to meet Sigismund in Nice to negotiate with him about his resignation. John was therefore asked to empower the king and the cardinals accompanying him to Nice to announce his resignation. In this way both Popes would be unable to create new difficulties. The Council knew well that each Pope had blamed the other for the breakdown of negotiations at Pisa. But now the Council was punished for its weakness. John stubbornly refused any further concessions. He refused to name a plenipotentiary: he would himself arrange his own resignation and decide on the most suitable moment. No threat and no request could weaken him. Thus the apparent victory of the Council had led to a deadlock. The Council still demanded a voluntary resignation: it did not order, but negotiated. But John was concerned only with further chances of intrigue and subterfuge.

The Council was outwardly strong and impressive: but internally it was torn with dissension. The cardinals did not take part in the sessions of the nations, but held a separate session and schemed to frustrate the decisions of the nations. This went to such extremes that it was even proposed to exclude the cardinals from the Council. The French nation shared the interests of the German and the English. But when the two latter nations began to assume the leadership, the French began to approach the Italian nation whose interests were the very opposite of its own. And that although Gerson was already present. There was almost a breach with Sigismund whose demands actually coincided with those of the French. The German nation had insisted that every question should first be discussed by each nation singly and then between the nations, and should only be put before the public session after agreement had been reached. Thus a dignified impression might be made. But the German nation was the first to break this understanding because it was not united in itself. The West German princes of the Church still adhered to Pope Gregory.

This concern for external dignity, instead of internal, deprived the Council of its most effective weapon against John. The secret accusations against him were frightful and could justify any compulsion, but they were not welcome to the Council because they might injure the reputation of the Church. Many of these accusations were not new to the cardinals, but if they became generally known what a lurid light they would throw on the cardinals themselves who placed this man at the head of the Church.

The charges had finally to be used, however, for John was afraid of them alone. Faced with them he declared himself ready to resign: when the Council suppressed them he drew out for weeks the talks about the formula. He only yielded at last when the charges once more began to circulate. Yet even further resistance did not lead to the Council's resorting once more to them.

It is monstrous that the Council could negotiate at all with such a man. The charges against him were such that it is morally incomprehensible that general indignation did not sweep aside every political consideration. The charges made against the head of the Catholic Church would have cost any other person his life and yet they were glossed over. It was later attested by witnesses that the Pope had poisoned his predecessor, Pope Alexander V: that he had bought his cardinal's office: that he had neither fasted nor prayed: that he had sold six churches to laymen: that for six thousand gulden he had appointed a five-year-old child preceptor of the Order of John: that he had sold the benefices of six chaplains to a fourteen-year-old layman: that he had installed merchants in the Curia to assess and sell any benefices that fell free: that he had several times sold false bulls: that for gold he had sold extreme unction, absolution, indulgences and bishoprics: that he had sold the head of St. John the Baptist for fifty thousand gulden: that he was a murderer, a poisoner, a simonist and a heretic: that he had asserted that there was neither an eternal life nor a resurrection and that the soul dies with the body: and thus the charges go on: they later mounted to seventy-two articles. In the official document, to minimise the impression, the worst points were suppressed: in their place was a comprehensive summing-up that was almost more damning. "He is regarded throughout the world," it ran, "as an oppressor of the poor, a persecutor of the just, support and stay of the unjust, the prop of the simonists, an adorer of the flesh, the paragon of vices, enemy of every virtue, mirror of meanness: he neglects the general assembly because he is always sunk in sleep or in the midst of his pleasures, and all who know him speak of him as the devil incarnate." And negotiations with this Pope went on and his crimes were secretly condoned.

With Hus, on the other hand, no quarter was given: he had dared publicly to describe the Pope as Antichrist. He must be broken and crushed. His premature death was to be avoided, but incessant hearings were to follow upon each other's heels in his new prison until he was cornered. Hus once described one such hearing, and this terse description is impressive because the undertone of complaint in it is very rare in his letters. "Michael, too, was there," he wrote to his friends in Constance, "he held a sheet of paper in his hand and spurred the Patriarch on that I should answer these questions. In the meantime several bishops came. Again Michael did me an ill turn. The Patriarch said above all that I had very much money. Thereupon an archbishop said to me during the hearing, 'You have seventy thousand gulden.' Michael cried out before them all, 'Ha ha, where has the sack full of money got to? What large sums do the lords in Bohemia owe you?' Truly I had a heavy vexation on this day. One of the bishops said, 'You have set up a new law.' Another said, 'You have preached all these articles.' But with God's help I also gave them hard answers and said 'Why do you do me wrong?' Palec and Michael de Causis could not rest. Palec brought up all the old matters that we spoke of years ago in the form of articles.'" Michael set to work on the letters of Hus and also worked out a number of articles from them, not caring whether they were forgeries. He even tried to cut any possible line of retreat for Hus. He asserted that Hus had written to the people of Prague that they should not believe any recantation he might make because he would swear with his lips and not with his heart. And naturally the Council was indignant when Hus wrote that he would allegedly only obtain a public hearing if he paid two thousand gulden, for it touched them all too nearly. Simony went on undisturbed in the Council in many forms and John had not ceased selling benefices.

But the letters of Hus did actually offer a new weapon against himself. Against the will of Hus a new development had occurred which told against him and yet he had to shoulder responsibility. Shortly before he left for Constance Jacobellus had discovered the verse in the Bible, "Except that you eat of the flesh of the Son of Man and drink of His blood there is no life in you." He concluded from it that the laity must receive communion in both kinds, bread and wine. The Church reserved the chalice, the wine, for the priests, and offered the laity only the bread, the host. Jacobellus demanded the chalice for the laity, too. Hus had foreseen how sorely this disputed point would tell against him and on taking leave of Jacobellus had said, "Dear Jacob, be not overhasty. If by God's will I return I will truly help in this." For Hus it was not a question of this cup now: he might at any moment have to drain another.

Jacobellus, however, would not be restrained. He, the rigid, knew no consideration. He called a debate in the University and many masters declared themselves on his side. In November 1414, communion was administered in both kinds in many churches. Hussite learning began to have a visible life of its own. A prohibition by the Archbishop followed but it had no effect. The measures of the Church had no further force. On the other hand, discord grew among the followers of Hus and not all accepted this innovation. As a split was feared Hus was urged to express his views on this subject : his words alone had sufficient authority to restore unity.

Hus was in favour of the chalice since " the words of the Gospel sound very definite," but the question still did not seem to him so urgent that it should bring him into fresh danger : he found the chalice " not necessary but helpful " : the possibility of a split, on the other hand, frightened him to the depths. He was still alive and yet dissension had begun ; even the thought of his fate did not suffice to keep unity. Had he falsely chosen the hour of death ? Once again he set his fate behind him and offered himself for the cause. From his prison, in the face of all dangers, he defended communion in both kinds for the laity. This alone could remove dissension. He thus laid himself open to a new and serious charge. The accusations of John the Iron were based almost entirely on the new form of communion, which is described only as the result of Hus's teaching. Now his letter to Jacobellus was intercepted through the latter's fault and thereby these charges could immediately be brought home to Hus. Once only did Hus allow himself a reproach to a friend. " I am bowed with grief over Jacobellus," he wrote. " He more than any others preaches that people should be on their guard against hypocrites and yet he most easily allows himself to be misled and believes hypocrites." For the future of the Hussites Jacobellus' act had a decisive meaning. In the chalice he gave them the symbol that united them : but at that particular time he placed on Hus, who already had so much to bear, a new and oppressive burden.

Hus did not break beneath this load. He again began to hope. " God rescued Jonah from the belly of the whale, Daniel from the lions' den, the three disciples from the fire, Susanna from the sentence of false witnesses : He can also save me for the glory of His name." He did not build on this hope, however. He looked death calmly in the face and continued, " If death, precious in the eyes of the Lord, is chosen for me, however, may the Lord's name be praised." Anger against his enemies was softened by a readiness to forgive. " For my sins God has allowed Michael and Palec to rise up against me." He pressed ever more urgently for an interview with Sigismund, reminding him of his broken promise and mysteriously hinting that he had something important to impart. But obviously his spiritual experience was more important to him. " Now at last I learn to understand the Psalter, I really learn to pray and do penance and comprehend the mockings of Christ and the sufferings of the martyrs," he often wrote.

At first his nights were so tormented that he hardly dared refer to his dreams. Now peace pervaded them. " Interpret for me last night's dream," he wrote to John of Chlum. " I saw how they destroyed all the pictures of Christ in the Bethlehem Chapel. When I stood up the following day, I saw many painters who were painting ever more beautiful pictures upon which I looked with pleasure. And the painters and many people said : 'Let only the bishops and priests come now to destroy them.' " The interpretation of John was so confident that it was later regarded as a prophetic announcement of Luther. He joyfully described how " tomorrow, when the sun of righteousness arises," Hus's life and teaching would be splendidly renewed. " And if now the goose, destined for sacrifice, is brought low in its weak flesh, as soon as it awakes from the dream of this miserable life, it will, we hope, together with Him who is in Heaven, laugh at the destroyer of pictures and writings."

That was a great consolation to Hus. " The writing on the wall of the Bethlehem Chapel will never pass away," he answered his loyal " Doctor of Biberach." And as his friends implored him to prepare himself for his hearing, he was not troubled that he could not since he did not know the questions that would be put : again and more calmly he placed his cause in the hands of God.

The Council, however, was suddenly taken by surprise. On March 20, 1415, Frederick of Habsburg arranged a festal tournament in which the king took part. The whole town was afoot in order not to miss the great spectacle. But the tournament ended with a sensation for in the evening it was found that Pope John had escaped from Constance. His flight had been feared for some days and so the city gates had been closely guarded and the Pope kept under discreet observation by means of one visit after another. The tournament had been arranged by Frederick, who was in the Pope's service, to distract attention. While all of rank and name were at the tournament, the Pope, supposedly ill, had disguised himself in a cape such as squires wore, thrown over his shoulder a crossbow which later aroused more excitement than the escape itself, and succeeded in fleeing

B. Picart Inv. 1723.

from Constance on a wretched horse and accompanied by a boy and a chaplain in disguise. In the midst of the tournament a servant appeared before Frederick and whispered to him through his visor that the escape had succeeded. Frederick allowed himself to be rapidly defeated and then vanished inconspicuously, following the Pope to Schaffhausen. The existence of the Council seemed called in question at one blow, as was John's intention. The Pope, having vainly tried to bribe even Sigismund, saw at last that there was no way out and thus dared a last coup that might save him. He reckoned that the weak Council would disperse once he, the official head, was no longer there.

But John had overestimated his power. His flight compelled the Council to proceed against him with the energy they had hitherto failed to show. The confusion was great at first. Constance was excited as never before. All were ready to leave. The merchants were the first to pack since they feared they might be plundered. The decision of Sigismund, however, saved the assembly. He himself rode through the town to the cardinals and the envoys, to the princes and the merchants, and pealing trumpets procured him a hearing. He announced that the Pope had fled, but no one should take fright or depart, since he guaranteed security and the continuance of the assembly. He succeeded in preventing the dissolution of the Council. On March 26 there was the third public session. It was declared that the Council would continue, and, freed from the drag of John, Sigismund and Gerson could better persuade it to act more energetically. Public sessions became more frequent.

Sigismund's deed is, however, stained by his final betrayal of Hus. On March 24 Hus begged his friends to appeal to the king on his behalf. Secretly the papal servants left one by one to follow the Pope: Hus received no more food: he did not know if they would kidnap him and take him to the Pope or if they had simply forgotten him. At any rate something must happen quickly to him. The same day the servants handed over to the king the key of the prison. Once again the fate of Hus lay completely in the hands of Sigismund. Now he could use his new power to keep his promise and liberate Hus. Sigismund, however, thinking only of holding the Council together, sacrificed Hus to his false caution. He handed over the key to the Bishop of Constance with the order that Hus was to be kept a close prisoner. What did his word matter when success was in the balance.

Now all the horrors of the first confinement were exceeded.

The bishop sent Hus to his castle of Gottlieben outside Constance. There he was once more put into a dark dungeon where he had to sleep on two boards to which he was chained during the day by his feet and at night by hands and feet. The food was scanty and bad and the guards cruel, although later, under Hus's influence, they became kinder. Hus fell ill again there, but this time no notice was taken. He was not allowed to see his friends or receive visits and letters, and he could not even write letters. He remained seventy-three days in this frightful prison, cruelly shackled, abandoned to illness and cut off from the world. Only the torment of the examinations began again soon. But nothing seemed now to touch Hus, and all the members of the many commissions confessed how serenely he endured these malicious questionings.

The Council, however, that thus treated Hus, seemed more magnificent and powerful than ever to the outside world. At a meeting of the nations Gerson made the long-prepared speech in which he placed the Council above the Pope. In the fifth public session on April 6 his proposal was accepted and the Council declared itself the highest instance of Christendom. " The Synod has its power immediately from Christ and every rank and dignity, including the papal, must obey it in all matters concerned with the faith, the extirpation of schism and the general reform of the Church of God, root and branch."

All three Popes were overthrown by this resolution. Later, indeed, Gregory XII was moved to a voluntary resignation. Benedict XIII, however, had to be deposed and fled to the remote sea-fortress Peniscola, and the Council began to take immediate steps against John. He was summoned to appear at Constance and when he failed to do so he was condemned for his flight and suspended from office. Then at last the charges against him were taken up and confirmed by witnesses. On May 29 in the twelfth public session he was solemnly deposed. This event was hailed as a liberation and a thanksgiving procession went through the streets of Constance. The Council felt it could boast of great deeds, after all. As the highest instance it had reaffirmed allegiance to the constitution of the Church, it had deposed three Popes and ended the schism.

But the Council had only undertaken these actions because John had left them no other way out, rejecting any easy compromise which they would have welcomed. For long weeks there were even discussions with John about a voluntary return. These weeks saw the papacy at its lowest depth of abasement : but the Council was still unwilling to take clear-cut action.

From Schaffhausen John wrote a cringing and evasive letter to Sigismund whom he abused in the commonest terms in other letters written at the same time. The climate of Constance had been unfavourable to his health, he wrote, and he had been forced to remove to a healthier place. And this was not simple mockery : it recurred in all the defences of the Pope as a serious argument. A few prelates and cardinals obeyed his call and removed to Schaffhausen. Those remaining in Constance opened negotiations with him and attempted to persuade him to return.

Meanwhile, however, Sigismund had outlawed Frederick of Habsburg and summoned the princes of the Empire to war with him. John had to flee again. It was Good Friday. He, the Pope, had not taken part in any service and he would not allow himself to be kept from his carousals for one moment. Clad in his papal vestments he went in the pouring rain to the fortress of Laufenburg. Now the cardinals and the important prelates left him and only Frederick and a small retinue accompanied him. In Laufenburg he fell to quarrelling with Frederick. John wanted to go to Burgundy where he could find safety and protection, but Frederick would not let him. The person of the Pope was a pledge that he would be reimbursed for his wars and he did not intend to let such a valuable pledge slip through his fingers before he had received his money. Soon the approaching enemy forced them to leave Laufenburg. The Pope left the fortress two hours before sunrise, disguised with bow and quiver, accompanied only by six men. Day and night he was pursued over the mountains, a hunted beast.

On April 9 John arrived in Freiburg. This town was firmly in the hands of Duke Frederick. Here John could rest for a month. He paid the monks who looked after him with indulgences and the few loyal ones who remained with him were rewarded with new benefices. But the Council rapidly got into touch with him again. John declared himself ready to receive envoys and a large mission was prepared to bring him the demands of the Council. When it arrived in Freiburg John had just fled to Breisach. The mission followed him and John promised an answer the next morning. The next morning he had vanished once more. During the night with one of his people he had let himself down with a rope from the fortress, and then he had wandered from one gate to another and none of the guards had wanted to let him through : it was finally the Chancellor of Frederick who assisted his escape. John went to Neufchâtel : across the Rhine he could see the Burgundian cavalry who awaited him. But that was a challenge to Frederick of Habsburg. He staged a revolt of the citizens and John had to return to Breisach the next night. Then he wandered for an hour and a half from one gate to another before he was admitted. He finally collapsed in fits of tears.

The fooled envoys of the Council had returned to Freiburg, but they were still waiting for their Pope. Frederick, on the other hand, saw that John's party had lost and he had still not received his money. He therefore sought reconciliation with Sigismund. He led John back to the envoys in Freiburg. Now John was watched like a prisoner. The envoys still encountered him with reverence, however, which encouraged John to resort to subterfuges once more. He declared himself ready to resign, but only in Burgundy or Italy. On May 5 Frederick of Habsburg submitted. Kneeling in a public place he gave himself and his fate into the hands of Sigismund. Sigismund punished him ruthlessly. He lost all his lands and from then on was the "Duke of the empty pockets." To save life and liberty he had also to hand over John. On May 17 John was taken to Radolfzell as a captive. Even there negotiations on his voluntary abdication still continued for twelve days before he was deposed.

How the Council should have behaved was seen when they turned to the case of Jerome.

As long as he could write, Hus had warned all his friends in Prague, and Jerome in particular, against coming to him in Constance. For many Czechs began to make pilgrimages to Constance at this time in their anxiety about their beloved Master. Christian of Prachatice had visited him in prison, and this visit, which had drawn tears of emotion from Hus, had been a great joy. But even this old and venerable Master was arrested and only released after long efforts on the part of the Bohemian nobles. In what danger must Jerome then stand!

Jerome did not heed the warning. When Hus left Prague, Jerome had just returned and he had said to Hus, "My Master, in what you have written and preached according to divine law, especially against pride, greed and similar vices, you are in the right. Be steadfast in it and be firm and strong. So soon as I learn that you are in need or if it should further the cause itself, I will follow you of my own free will and help you." He kept his word and went to Constance, arriving on April 4, 1415. Here his friends speedily made it clear that he could not help and could only destroy himself: it was no longer even possible to visit Hus. Jerome, too, had believed in right, in free discussion, in scientific instruction. It took three days to convince him of the contrary and then at last he left the town. But he did not even now return but only went to Uberlingen. From there he wrote to the Council and had his letter nailed up in Constance. When after two days he had still received no answer he set out on his journey homeward. But it was too late. The Council had barred his way.

The letter betrayed what hopes had been aroused by the Council, for Jerome wrote, " I hereby bring to the knowledge of everyone that I, on account of my slanderers and accusers, and also on account of the malicious contemners of my country, am prepared of my own free will to come to Constance and to prove the purity of my belief and my innocence, not only in hidden corners and to private persons but openly and freely before the whole Council. If then I am found in any false doctrine or heresy, then I do not refuse publicly to pay the penalty as is due to one who teaches falsely or is a heretic. Therefore, I beg of our lord the King and also of the Council that I receive a free and safe conduct to this purpose." But the letter showed how the Council had disappointed hopes already, for Jerome concluded, " Should, however, arrest or such force be exercised against me before the proving of any guilt, let herewith the whole world know that this general Council would not be proceeding with right and fairness if it refused me, who of his own free will offers to come, what is fair and nothing but fair : which, moreover, I believe I shall not have to assume of a Council of wise men."

As Jerome was not one of their own, the Council did not hesitate, feeling in no way shamed by the concluding sentence of the letter. What did it matter that the charges against Jerome did not remotely approach those against John. The Council answered. The words " safe conduct " did indeed occur but in reality it was a stern summons to appear. " As it is our duty above all," it ran, " to catch the foxes that destroy the vineyard of the Lord God of Sabaoth, we therefore summon and cite your person as suspected and of ill repute of manifold false doctrines and their audacious assertion, within a period of fifteen days to answer for all in Constance that one person or another will then upbraid you with. To this end we offer you, in as far as orthodox belief permits, a safe conduct against violence, but ever with the reservation of justice. At the same time notice is given that whether you appear within the due period or not, nevertheless steps will be taken against you by the Holy Council without regard to your disobediently absenting yourself."

Shortly before he reached the frontiers of Bohemia, where

he would be safe, he was recognised and seized in Hirschau in the Upper Palatinate. On May 23 he was brought into Constance in a cart, heavily loaded with chains. With iron handcuffs on his hands and fettered with a long clanking chain he appeared before the fathers. To the reproach that he had not obeyed the summons he replied that he had not learnt of it and that he would have returned from Bohemia, whereupon all the fathers so cried out against him that his words were drowned. At last Gerson re-established quiet and then attacked him on his activities in Paris : Jerome answered with dignity and precision. There was a similar exchange of words with the Masters of the Universities of Cologne and Heidelberg. Many interrupted with cries of " He must be burnt, burnt ! " " If my death gives you pleasure, then, in God's name." The Bishop of Salisbury sought to mediate, " It is written, ' I do not wish the death of a sinner but that he may live and repent'," but his words were lost in the tumult.

That evening Jerome still remained under the guard of the town magistrates. Mladenovic tapped on his window. " Be steadfast, Jerome, and do not fear to suffer death for the truth for which formerly, when you were free, you said such splendid things." Jerome answered confidently, " Indeed, brother, I do not fear death, and as we once talked so much about truth, so let us now see what it indeed knows and does." His confidence was soon put to the hardest test, however. The next day he was taken to the dungeon in St. Paul's tower which had been assigned to him. It was a wretched, dark, unhealthy hole. Jerome was bound by his feet to a block that was so high that he could not sit. His hands were weighed down with heavy chains and he had nothing but bread and water. His friends did not for days learn of his whereabouts. Then they managed to get better food for him. But on the eleventh day he was so mortally ill that he was even granted a confessor, who succeeded in getting his conditions of arrest somewhat alleviated. But till his death Jerome remained in this revolting dungeon and remained fettered. He never again saw Hus whom he had wanted to help.

Hus's case too was being energetically tackled. In the same session at which the Council was declared the highest instance in Christendom a new commission was appointed to examine him. And when it turned out that the cardinals appointed had too little time to devote to it a new commission was shortly afterwards set up. With the help of fifty doctors it worked at the drawing up of the charge. In addition, on May 5, the legal basis for Hus's sentence was created. The Council solemnly condemned the forty-five articles of Wyclif and two hundred and sixty others that the University of Oxford had drawn up from the books of Wyclif. Seventeen of them tallied word for word with assertions of Hus. All the books of Wyclif were condemned to be burnt and his remains to be dug up and scattered. Hus's fate was thus foreshadowed.

The Bohemian nobles were making every effort in the meantime to help Hus. From Bohemia and Moravia letters of protest arrived, sealed by two hundred and fifty of the most powerful nobles, while those who were in Constance protested to the Council themselves. They received two answers. John the Iron Bishop described the alleged chaos in Bohemia: since the chalice had been handed to the laity the blood of Christ was carried in bottles through the streets, and one Hussite woman had publicly administered communion to herself. The Council repeated the falsest of complaints, that the safe conduct had not been written until fourteen days after Hus had been imprisoned, that Hus had preached in Constance. John of Chlum corrected these mistakes, he distributed among the Council Hus's confession of faith in 1411 which had verged so nearly on a recantation. But all was in vain and he no longer received any answers.

In despair John of Chlum made a fresh attempt on May 31. He learnt that the commission of investigation had almost ended their work. He feared that Hus's mind must be suffering under the heavy confinement: he demanded at least a public hearing for him and his temporary release that he might recuperate and collect himself. Chlum offered himself and the other Bohemian nobles in Constance as bail for Hus. He once more asked Sigismund to intervene, and this time he found Sigismund more ready. For in the meantime a new letter had arrived from the Bohemian and Moravian nobles in which they used unveiled threats against him. They reproached Sigismund with not having released Hus after the flight of John, that Hus "already under your power and in your town was arrested, provided with your agreement and your letter of safe conduct" and they implored Sigismund that Hus "when he is free according to your will may even so freely return to us in Bohemia, first for the sake of God and the spreading of His truth and then for the good name of your Grace and for the quiet and honour of the country of Bohemia, and finally for the sake of our loyal service which is ever ready for your Grace." They reminded their "Gracious King Elect and Lord" that he would soon be dependent on them. Sigismund therefore exerted himself in favour of the public hearing which was still the easiest way out: and the

Council answered Chlum, "As regards the application for bail, the deputies of the Council could not accept that with a clear conscience even were a thousand people offered, for the man for whom it is asked can in no way be accorded faith and credulity. Yet they will do this, that on June 5 Hus is again brought to Constance and receives before the Council a kindly public trial, for they wish to proceed mildly." At least a public hearing seemed to have been secured, but would this change Hus's fate?

The external splendour of the Council grew ever more dazzling. Since John had forced them to depose him, he had been treated as a wretched prisoner: the Council seemed to recognise only submission to its will. Its strength was now negatively great and clear: its secret weaknesses and dissensions would only become apparent again when it had positive problems to solve. Then reform would fail miserably. Then too the disgraced Balthasar Cossa, the former Pope John XXIII, who was so severely condemned by the Catholic world that no Pope after him might assume the name of John, would remain a cardinal after a long imprisonment and another disgraceful flight, and would be reinstated in many of his offices and honours.

But first the Council was to reach the climax of its power. On June 3 John was despatched to the castle of Gottlieben. The gloomy walls now held them both, the first head of the Council and its first victim: John received as loathsome a dungeon as his former captive with whose sacrifice the decline of his own power had begun. Involuntarily the Council created an urgent symbol of Hus's rightness: this proximity alone completely justified him and his struggle.

But this time the Council kept its word: they were neighbours for only two days. On June 5 Hus was taken to the Franciscan monastery in Constance for his trial.

On June 5, 1415 all the prelates and theologians of weight were crowded into the narrow refectory of the Franciscan monastery. The proceedings against Hus were to begin. The air of the overfilled room was clammy and oppressive. The Czechs who longed to see their Master once again were among the many who were not admitted. The fathers made yet another attempt to avoid the unwelcome public examination and Hus was not fetched from his nearby cell. They hastily began to read the articles as a preliminary to condemning them. Mladenovic learning what was afoot rushed to John of Chlum who hastened to the king. The king intervened to prevent this new breach of faith. He sent the Elector Ludwig and the Burgrave of Nuremberg to the monastery to insist that Hus must be heard. He also demanded a copy of the charge against him in order to examine it himself. This was refused him, but Hus was called forth before the assembly.

Snatched from terrible loneliness to a fearful publicity he stood almost unprepared. He had first to accustom himself painfully to daylight. Then the suffocating air dazed him. He dimly saw a confused throng before him. Gradually individuals emerged and he saw that he was before an assembly of Church dignitaries such as the world had seldom witnessed. Fifteen cardinals, envoys from twenty universities, innumerable archbishops, bishops, monks, doctors and masters were present at the hearing : the spiritual and intellectual rulers of the Catholic world were ranged there against him. He was alone. Seventy-three days of inhuman confinement, with all the attendant phantoms of loneliness, had worn him down. Illness racked him, he was unrested, and rudely thrust back into the hurly-burly, not slowly reaccustomed to life as his friends had desired. And not one of these friends was there to say an encouraging word or give him a kindly glance. But he stood erect : they should never bend him. And so the sick man proved a match for this glorious and mighty assembly.

But they did not prove a match for him. The sound of voices almost drowned the first article of the charge as it was read again. Hus wanted to reply. At once a deafening noise broke out as they threatened, mocked and scolded him. Hardly a word could be distinguished. The words of the charge and Hus's answers were lost in the din. He did not know where to turn : from all sides people pressed in on him—the cardinals who had examined him, strangers whom he did not know, Palec and Michael de Causis, Stokes and Gerson, who had drawn up the most damning nineteen articles against him. He exerted all his strength to make himself understood. But hardly had he said a word before they fell upon him, " This is not the place for that," " Say yes or no," " Leave your sophistries," and would not allow him to proceed. At last he realised the hopelessness of the situation and was silent. Then they fell upon him once more. " See, now you are silent, so you agree with this heresy." Hus burst in with the words, " I had thought to find more goodness, order and decency at this Council."

Hus saw the fervently desired hearing for which he had hoarded his strength transformed into a travesty. What was the meaning of this tumult ? Was it an outbreak of long-repressed anger or simply a shameful plan to cheat him ? Even his noble rebuke did not bring them to their senses. On the contrary, the Cardinal of Ostia shouted, " Do you speak thus now ? In Gottlieben you spoke more modestly." Hus defended himself desperately, " In the castle nobody shouted at me. Here you all shout." But his brave steadfastness did not help. The unworthy tumult grew ever louder. There could be no thought of answering the charge, let alone of preaching the long sermon on which he had set his heart. The noise was finally too much even for the fathers themselves. As quiet could not be restored, the hearing was broken off and postponed. Hus was led back to his prison. His first hearing was over.

In prison Hus had a little quiet. He heard again from his friends and could himself write to them. His letters betrayed no hope. " By the love of God the return to Prague is not impossible, but I no longer yearn for it, unless it be the will of the Lord." He begged his friends to pray that God might give steadfastness to him and Jerome, " for I believe that he will suffer death even as I shall, in so far as I have understood the envoys of the Council." The examinations in Gottlieben must have been shattering, but his letters show how unbroken he remained. " If they would give me pen and paper I would write : I, John Hus, as I hope a servant of Christ, will not admit that any article of my writings is false, lest I thereby reject the opinion of holy teachers : secondly, I will not confess that I have asserted, taught and held the articles which are ascribed to me by false witnesses : thirdly, I will not swear upon oath lest I be perjured." He was still ready to be convinced of error by scientific proofs but not to obey arbitrary orders and accept false evidence and even confirm it. All that he did he must be able to justify before his own conscience.

Despite all his sufferings he now shed the vacillation and hesitancy that formerly beset him. He fought fearlessly with a complete awareness of all that was at stake. He had indeed abandoned hope but without it he fought as purposefully as ever. He wanted the world to understand the true meaning of his words and have a clear picture of him. His friends had given into the king's care those of his writings especially dangerous to him, although not actually touching on the essence of the conflict. He asked them to get certain books back. He wrote out a detailed list of which were to be left with the king and he advised his friends to hide others to save them from burning. To pass on letters was particularly dangerous at this time : he kept on urging his friends to be very cautious so that none should be brought into danger. Many of his friends had given him money for Constance at great cost to themselves. In the very days that were settling the fate of his teaching and his life itself, he gave instructions as to how money was to be repaid. He began to take leave of his friends, reviewing their present position and advising them for the future. In mortal danger and cut off from all help he conducted his struggle with decision and foresight. It was overwhelmingly clear what a leader the Hussite movement lost prematurely in him.

On June 7 the second hearing took place. The Czech friends of Hus had begged Sigismund to be present to prevent a second tumult and also that they themselves might attend in his retinue. Express orders were given that peace and quiet were to be preserved. This hearing too was late in beginning, for throughout the morning the sun was almost totally eclipsed. The Council saw with dismay this sign which instilled confidence in Hus. When the London Synod was condemning Wyclif's articles they had been interrupted by an earthquake. Was God now warning Hus's tormentors ? In Prague, too, the eclipse was almost total : there, however, it was regarded as a sign of the suffering that would break over Bohemia from Constance.

When the hearing could at last start it was somewhat nearer the wishes of Hus. Michael de Causis read the charge while the Council listened. Hus was able to answer most charges quietly. He refuted two charges so successfully that they were dropped. One was on the Wyclifian interpretation of communion. Hus denied emphatically that he had ever preached it. The president of the court tried to prove to him that realism necessarily led to this interpretation : Hus convincingly opposed his arguments. " The cardinal was reckoned one of the mightiest theologians : when however he was clearly proved ignorant of this subject he was silent," Hus reported afterwards. The English thereupon took up the charge. Hus dealt with one of them like a schoolboy. To Stokes he simply said, " That is not true ! " Only with the third was there a more serious argument but his opponent gave up with the words, " Why dispute longer ? As far as I have heard, he thinks rightly about the sacrament of the altar." The second charge he refuted was based on the doctrine that a priest in mortal sin was no priest. Hus asserted that he had only written that such a priest could not worthily celebrate the sacraments. This was disputed. Hus cried out, " I will suffer death if that is not to be found in my writings." One of his books was brought and opened, and there was this reservation. Other charges however were maintained in spite of Hus's defence, such as his championing of Wyclif, his non-appearance in Rome, his fight for the University. Here the Council certainly seemed in the right : it would have taken much goodwill to bring Hus's arguments into harmony with ecclesiastical law, and this good will, so singularly lacking, was not a prerequisite for a court of law. But had this Council, summoned in the name of Jesus Christ, simply to regard itself as a court of law ?

How little the court was justified in this attitude was shewn by incidents which were more typical of the proceedings than were the discussions. Twice the court broke out into derisive laughter and mocked Hus. The first time was when Hus admitted that he had wished that his soul were there where that of Master Wyclif was, since he hoped that Wyclif was in bliss. The second time was when he defended his appeal to Christ with the words, " I confess that there is no more just and efficacious appeal than to Christ. Who is a juster and more effective judge, who can better help the oppressed and wronged than Christ who does not deceive and is not deceived." Both these expressions of simple faith provoked laughter. Previously Hus had perplexed the whole assembly when he had confessed to a belief in the miraculous. Perplexity and laughter, these typified the reaction of the Council. Hus was the one believer facing the ranks of the unbelievers. The roles of accused and accusers might well have been reversed for Hus alone fought in the name of Jesus Christ, for him alone was the gracious figure of the Saviour still a living reality.

The cardinals believed that they were merely summoned to

condemn and sentence. This was plainly shewn by the intervention of Cardinal Zabarella, one of the most honest of the cardinals. The charge about communion had already collapsed and he broke in once more to say, "We must however still trust the many reliable men who have testified against you in this matter." This objection might still stand in an ordinary court of law, but was this one? Witnesses for Hus were not allowed, nor was an advocate: what else remained for him but to say, "I attest before God and my conscience, that there has never come into my mind what they claim to have heard and have dared to witness against me. If none but enemies testify, what can I do?" Naturally Zabarella did not admit the validity of Hus's own evidence. "We cannot judge you according to your conscience, but only by what is partly proved against you here and partly admitted by you yourself. You might well call them all enemies and opponents who testify against you with a clear conscience and on good evidence. But them we must believe." And he did not let pass an opportunity of expressly defending those men who had clearly betrayed their hatred of Hus. "You have called Palec a suspect witness and yet he acted humanely and without passion, and drew up articles more mildly than they appeared in the books. Yea, you have even declared suspect the Lord Chancellor of Paris, Gerson, the most respected Doctor in all Christendom." But what was the use of respect when a fanatically-held idea demanded a victim?

The cardinals also sought to give such a turn to the proceedings that Sigismund should be called against Hus. Peter d'Ailly asked Hus, at a moment when he was sure of Sigismund's attention, "You say that you came here of your own free will, and had you not wanted to come neither the King of Bohemia nor the Roman King here present could have forced you." Hus answered truly although it could only harm him. "I have said so: I came here freely and had I not wanted to come neither the one king nor the other could have compelled me, for the Bohemian nobles who love me are so many and so powerful that they could easily have defended me in their castles." In emphatic indignation d'Ailly shook his head. "What depravity!" But brave John of Chlum sprang to his feet, ready to sacrifice himself. "That is quite true. I am but a minor lord in our country and yet I could shield him a whole year long against any. But there are many and mightier lords there who have strong castles. They love him and could shield him as long as they liked against both kings." Hus was justified. But the question had achieved

B. Picart In. 1713.

its purpose. Sigismund could see that he was dealing with dangerous rebels.

The Council wanted to wring a recantation from Hus. His self-betrayal would best serve their purpose, enhancing the glory of the gracious Council and defeating the rebellious Bohemians. Once again it was d'Ailly who in conclusion said to Hus, " You recently assured us in the castle that you wanted in all humility to submit yourself to the decision of the Council. I only advise you to do so, and the Council will deal indulgently with you." The king himself now joined in urging Hus : how agreeable it would be for him if a recantation by Hus soothed both his own conscience and the Bohemian nobles. He talked some time to Hus, publicly confirming his safe conduct. He said, " The fathers of the Council have now given you a public, peaceful and seemly hearing and I thank them for it. And I too advise you, as did the cardinal, not to persist in hardness of heart, but in all things here proved against you and self-avowed, to throw yourself completely on the clemency of the Council. For my sake they will incline to mercy, and may you take upon yourself penance for your heresies." At the same time these words betrayed something else. Sigismund wanted to clear himself, whatever might happen, and to wash his hands of any blame. The public hearing he had insisted on was to save appearances. With this achieved, Hus had nothing to expect from Sigismund, who now blamed Hus for the consequences of his own betrayal of him. " If on the other hand you obstinately cling to your errors, then truly the fathers themselves know what they have to do with you. I have told them that I will protect no heretic. On the contrary should someone obdurately persist in heresies, I would myself kindle the fire to burn him." With these words Sigismund at once revealed and screened his treachery. Yet he could still seek to persuade Hus to recant. " But I would advise you to throw yourself completely on the grace of the Council and the sooner the better, that you may not be still more deeply ensnared in your errors."

Hus remained firm even when confronted with this king who should have protected him and now so skilfully dropped him. Sigismund should at least have secured the promised hearing. He boasted indeed that he had already done so but in reality this formal examination in which Hus was allowed only brief answers did not in the least resemble the desired hearing in which discussion and a connected sermon would be permitted. It was certainly an improvement on the opening farce, but it did not rise so very much above it. Hus thanked the king for the safe conduct and refused to recant and once again called for the instruction which was possible only in a debate. " May your grace know," he answered the king, " that I did not freely come here to make an obstinate defence, but humbly to improve myself wherever I might be convinced of error." With these words of his the second hearing closed.

A third was to follow. What could Hus expect of it? The cleavage between the outlook of Hus and the Council was clear. The Council insisted on a strictly legalistic attitude in spite of the doubtful legality of the proceedings. The evidence of the witnesses had already condemned Hus. Only a recantation could change the situation for him. There was no reason why he should be granted a scholastic debate or even permitted to preach. Hus on the other hand was fighting for his faith and for a pure Church. He still believed that all he had asserted was strictly loyal to the Church but perhaps he might be convinced in a debate, and he must insist on this debate, both for the sake of his conscience, which could not yield to force, and for the sake of the Church. For this Church was facing perdition; only if it abandoned its rigidity, only if it returned to the pure truth that Hus defended, could it be saved. A recantation would also be a betrayal of the Church. In a debate he might convince the fathers as they might convince him. Before this last attempt had been made he could not retrace one step. But this very insistence was interpreted as obstinacy; and obstinacy was the worst offence in the mediæval courts for heretics.

Hus again wrote an account of the hearing. He joyfully recorded his victory. " Almighty God today gave me a strong and brave heart. Two articles have already been refuted." But he did not yield to any illusions. He knew that in the next hearing, if it were on similar lines to the last, the doctrine of predestination would be brought up. In despair he cried, " Oh, if only I might have a hearing in which I could dispute its grounds, I believe that many would be silenced who now shout." His despair got the better of his joy and he concluded his letter, " What temptations I was later faced with God alone knows." Had he thought of a recantation? We do not know, for this hint, recurring several times, is the only suggestion of surrender; it never found expression in his speech or deeds. Hus was no dogged fanatic; he was vulnerable and sensitive and he had to pay the price of his steadfastness. The more precious therefore was this steadfastness which did not spring from blind heroism but from a victorious conscience. How easily Hus could have been silent on his temptations. He was not seeking glory, however, but truth.

The third hearing on June 8 resembled the second. It was long. Thirty-nine articles extracted from the writings of Hus were read. Gradually an atmosphere of weariness and indifference permeated the whole gathering. Hus had to fight with all his strength against it. Again he was only allowed short answers ; sometimes a more lengthy exchange of words developed, but these exchanges never resembled a learned discussion. Hus was only attacked and reprimanded ; whatever he might say his answers were arbitrarily rejected. Often he was interrupted in mid-sentence. The fathers were eager to close the hearing as its outcome was now clear. Again that jeering laughter broke out when Hus expressed his belief in God, in Christ, and in the other world.

Proceedings were now plainly directed towards securing a death sentence. The similarity between the teachings of Hus and Wyclif, true enough in itself, was repeatedly stressed with mischievous intent. Sentence had already been passed on Wyclif, and why should Hus be allowed to defend, however learnedly, doctrines already denounced ? Palec showed particular malice towards Hus, but once again he was shielded, this time by d'Ailly. The vices of the clergy were also publicly defended, and an attack on them by Hus was described as wicked.

The hearing often lost itself in scholastic subtleties, the rights and wrongs of which it is now difficult to assess. Once at least a lightning flash lit up this artificial darkness. Hus's assertion that only he who led a Christian life could " in truth and in a worthy fashion before God " be Pope was under discussion. The corrupt could only be Popes " according to the office and not truly and worthily." When the Council would not recognise this principle, Hus cried out, " That has pointedly proved itself in the case of the former Pope John XXIII. Tell me, was he a true Pope or not rather a thief and a robber ? " The fathers looked at each other and smiled. " Naturally he was a true Pope." Why did they smile, could they deny it ? Hus persisted. " Then why was he deposed if he was a true Pope ? " he continued. Thereupon Sigismund answered, " The lords of the Council firmly held that Balthasar Cossa was true Pope, but for the notorious acts of shame with which he offended the Church of God and for his misuse of church goods he was deposed." The Council was well pleased with this help from Sigismund. In this way it avoided saying how a true representative of God on earth, a true successor of Christ, could be a murderer and a scoundrel. And thus this article too remained as a proof of Hus's heresy.

This article also served to range Sigismund still more firmly on the side of the fathers. Hus had to confess that this article also implied, " He who lives in mortal sin is not worthily king in the sight of God." Sigismund, bored with the long session, was no longer listening. He was talking in a window niche to the Burgrave of Nuremberg. But a sudden shout arose, " Summon the king ! " Hus had to repeat his words in front of him. The king for the only time rose above the assembly and the attack failed. Not that it mattered, for the Council had long ago won Sigismund to their side. The king simply said, " John Hus, no one lives without sin." This human tone, heard on this one occasion from the adversaries of Hus. might perhaps have influenced the zealot, but the fathers gave it no chance. D'Ailly cried out, " Was it not enough for you to bring the clergy into contempt, but that you must also overthrow the kings from their thrones ? "

Hus steadfastly held his ground in the dispute on the papacy which was not yet finished. Hus asserted, " The apostles and the true priests of the Lord ruled the old Church very well in all that was necessary for its salvation before ever a papacy had been introduced. And they would have been able to do it without a Pope, as might easily have happened, to the end of the day." Again the fathers laughed. " Lo, he is among the prophets real ! " But again there was no cause for laughter as Hus continued, " Yes, that is indeed possible. I maintain that the Church was infinitely better ruled in the days of the apostles. Why should not Christ rule better through His true disciples than through such monstrous heads as we have just had ? Now we have no such head and yet Christ has not ceased to rule His Church." But the recent experience of the Council that had just declared itself the highest instance of Christendom had taught it nothing. Instead of accepting the article which strengthened its authority, it did not hesitate to reject it as heretical.

If the fathers really intended the reform they continually promised they must have listened to Hus. Hus insisted on the debate because he felt he would share the responsibility for the decline of the Church if he acquiesced in such articles being brushed aside with laughter, with a wave of the hand, with a few noncommital, formal words. How would the Church be snatched back from the abyss when it ignored the signs of the times ? " That is out of place here," Hus was told again and again as soon as he attempted to expound his doctrine in detail. What then was in place, if not this conception of Christianity as a living force ?

But the Council limited its task to extracting a recantation from Hus. When the hearing was finished d'Ailly once again appealed to him to recant, promising that the Council would proceed against him " with true grace and mildness." This appeal unleashed a storm. The members of the assembly thronged around Hus crying " Truly, better to throw yourself upon the grace of the Council than to persist in obstinate heresies!" Hus defended himself against the charge of obstinacy, saying to the fathers, " I beseech you only for God's sake that a hearing be given me to expound my ideas, and if my reasons and my scriptural proofs be untenable I will gladly submit to better instruction." But then a real commotion broke out. None felt the courage of this man who dared to make a stand against the whole world when he could easily save himself with a few words. " What, you will submit to instruction by the Council but not to its reprimand ! " they exclaimed. " That is subterfuge, that is obduracy ! " Hus would not quibble about the term ; he would accept the rebuke and the decision of the Council if it were only bound up with instruction. This d'Ailly seized upon. He announced the formula of recantation prescribed for Hus. " Know hereby," he said to him, " that your instruction as proposed by the Council consists of this ; firstly, that you humbly confess that you have erred in those articles which you have hitherto asserted ; secondly, that you swear upon oath that to all eternity you will never more assert, teach or preach these articles ; thirdly, that you publicly recant all these articles ; and fourthly, that you now accept, write and preach the contrary of them." The Council, too, was obviously no stickler for words if this formula was called instruction. It could only appear a mockery to Hus.

Once again he proved his greatness and maturity ; clearly and firmly he made the demand, the fulfilment of which was more important to him than his life. " Revered fathers," he beseeched them once more, " I am ready to obey the Council in humility and to accept instruction. But I beg for God's sake that you do not lay the snares of damnation upon me, do not attempt to force me to lie and to abjure articles of which nothing is known to me, as God and my conscience are witnesses, and which have never entered my heart. As for the articles which are mine and stand in my books, I will gladly retract them as soon as I am taught better. But to abjure all the articles of which many are falsely ascribed to me would be to lie, and I should encompass myself with the snares of damnation and would be acting against my conscience." Sigismund attempted to smooth the way for him. "Why will you not abjure all the false articles which, as you say, have been wrongly alleged against you? I would without a second thought abjure all possible heresies, but it would not follow therefrom that I had formerly confessed them." But Hus would not cheat his own conscience, not even for the sake of the king. "To abjure means to recant of a heresy formerly cherished."

The tumult continued. Zabarella promised to soften the formula. Sigismund repeated the promise of d'Ailly and at the same time plainly threatened Hus that death at the stake faced him as a heretic; they thought they could bargain with Hus as they had done with John. The fathers continued to reproach him with obstinacy for insisting on instruction. Hus could do nothing but repeat, "I cannot insult God and my conscience. I beg that I may be given another hearing in which I may expound my opinions in more detail!" Once instructed he would submit to the decision of the Council. Then Palec rebuked him, "And suppose I protest never so much that I shall not box the ears of the Master sitting next to me, and then do so, what is the assurance worth? Thus you keep on assuring us that you do not wish to assert any error, especially any of Wyclif's, and yet you are defending them!"

They were talking different languages; Hus must test by his own conscience what was true and what was false but they regarded as refuted anything repudiated by the authority of the Church, this questionable authority of a degenerate Church which Hus rejected for the sake of the true Church. Two ages were confronting each other; the Church who claimed the conscience of the individual and demanded unconditional obedience, and one of the first of these individuals who was aware of his own conscience as a voice that no authority could silence. A new age with new demands was dawning in this narrow room; and the old age, the Church, should have accepted it for its own salvation. Did they not understand Hus's cry of fear; he did not yet know that he was the herald of the new and only wanted to save the Church. He suffered the spiritual torments of the man with sight who despaired because the blind would not let themselves be snatched back from the abyss. To the Council this terrible urgency appeared as malicious obstinacy. And death was the meed of obstinacy.

Hus was suddenly silent. What could he say when a fat, richly-clad priest shouted the old lies at him, "He must not be allowed to recant. Even if he recants he will not keep to it. He wrote that himself to his followers." Hus had been unable to sleep all night for toothache, headache and fits of ague ; he had summoned his last strength for the endless hearing, doubly and trebly tiring because he was never allowed to speak freely. Now he was as pale as death and could hardly hold himself upright. Palec however seized on this momentary lull to declare to the assembly, " I call your Majesty and your Reverences to witness that I have been led, in my accusations against Hus, by no personal hatred or passion. God is my witness. I have done it only to fulfil the vow that I, as Doctor of Theology, although unworthy, have made." Michael de Causis hastened to make a similar protestation. A guilty conscience was speaking loud and clear, but d'Ailly praised them both for their mildness and humanity. Hus wearily parried them with the remark, " I leave all to the verdict of God who will judge you and me according to our deserts." Then he was led away.

The Czechs, however, when no one supposed that they were still present, heard King Sigismund close the assembly with the following words : " You have heard of many and heavy crimes which are not only proved against Hus by reliable witnesses but also confessed by him. I deem that each one of them is worthy of death. If he does not retract, I am of the opinion that he should be burnt. But even if he does what he is told to do, even if he retracts, do not believe him. I should not believe him. I advise that he be not allowed to teach or preach in the Kingdom of Bohemia." Sigismund had become the most dangerous enemy of Hus.

Hus still placed hopes in the king, however, for at the second hearing Sigismund had told him that he would receive the charges in writing so that he could prepare his answer. Hus did not yet know that the king had incited the fathers against him and thus clung to the words which gave hopes of another hearing. Immediately after the third hearing he wrote to his friends, " See to it that all the lords apply to the king and the Council that what the king has promised may come to pass. Spur him and the Council on with this promise for with God's help I shall there speak the truth. I would rather that my body were destroyed by fire than that I were so unworthily silenced by them. May the whole of Christendom thus learn what I said at the last. I beg the lords in God's name to do this. Oh, that you might rather see them place me at the stake than slyly muzzle me." All the great sacrifices he had made, all his fearful sufferings, would be outweighed by a worthy hearing.

Then he learnt that Sigismund himself had encouraged the fathers to sentence him to death. Only then was the first complaint against the king wrung from him. "His shame will be great," he wrote, "if he forgets this last promise too. But now I believe that his word is as trustworthy as his safe conduct of which they warned me in Bohemia to beware. Others said, 'He himself will deliver you over to your enemies.' I thought he had understanding of the laws of God and of truth. Now I recognise that he has no understanding. He sentenced me sooner than did my enemies. If he would only be guided by the heathen Pilate who, when he heard the accusation said, 'I find no fault in this man.' Or if he at least would say, 'Well, I have given him a safe conduct; if he will not himself leave the decision to the Council I will send him back to the King of Bohemia with your verdict and the evidence of the witnesses, that he may judge him with his clergy.' For he told me through Heinrich Lefl and others that he would procure for me an adequate hearing and that if I would not submit myself to this court he would send me in safety back to Bohemia." How moderate is even this complaint, written in the depths of despair, in comparison with the magnitude of the king's treachery.

Anger had now lost all power over Hus. The old sacred passion that made him scourge the corruption of the clergy now but seldom swept him and only for a moment. He did not indulge in vain regrets. When he knew of this fatal betrayal and that he would receive no further hearing he devoted himself fervently and firmly to his new task, preparation for death.

It is one thing to fear death or long for it when it is uncertain and fresh hope or fears constantly distract; it is another thing to face the certainty of death. Clarity of vision might be obscured by this certainty. But Hus did not lose his. He could still save his life by a short letter, by a few words; and certainly the temptation came upon him once or twice. But he never lost his certainty that this would be wrong. And thus the loss of his fallacious hope brought him the final enlightenment.

As long as he fought for instruction he had to promise submission and bear the possibility of conversion in mind; he need not betray that it was in reality the conversion of the Church that he hoped for. This often made his obstinate professions appear confused. His battle of conscience, which must burst the limitations of the Church, could clearly be seen by those outside the struggle. Hus however did not want to break with the Church and he sought harmony with a purged Church. Consciously he remained to the last entangled with the Church, although his feelings had carried him far beyond it. But now that the Church had cast him out, he became more aware of the new demands.

A doctor came to his cell to advise him to recant, saying to Hus, " If you submit yourself to the Council, then all that you do will be good and lawful. If the Council says that you have only one eye, although you know you have two, you must confess, ' Thus it is.' " But Hus answered him, " And if the whole world told me so, as I have understanding I could not assert such a thing without arousing the resistance of my conscience." Now Hus was plainly stating what his conduct had already proclaimed. The opinion of the whole world could not silence the individual conscience.

But Hus's final certainty had to undergo a severe test. For weeks the Church laboured to extract a recantation from him. The well-intentioned and the malicious besieged him, the cardinals and commissions who had heard him and other fathers who wished to save him. He was even instructed that a recantation was lawful. The arguments were stale, but often they were seductively unfolded. One of his well-wishers wrote, " Do not fear that you might deny the truth, for not you but they pass judgment who are your fathers. And should you commit perjury, the guilt would not fall upon you but upon those who had forced you. If only your stubbornness ceases, no more heresy will attach to you. I write briefly because I write to a learned man. You will not cause trouble but will accept teaching." Threats were mixed with the seduction. The constant assault was meant to wear Hus down. Then the formula of recantation was made less drastic. Hus never wavered. " Better were it if a millstone were laid upon me and I were sunk in the depths of the sea. It serves me better to die than, fleeing the punishment of the moment, to fall into the hands of the Lord and then perhaps into the fire and eternal shame."

In the face of certain death his attitude was the same as at the beginning of the hearing ; all his hopes had collapsed, but his conviction remained unchanged. Recantation was not to be hoped or feared. To show that he knew what lay ahead of him, Hus signed one letter, " Written in chains, in expectation of death, on the day of John the Baptist, who was fettered, imprisoned and beheaded because he castigated wickedness" ; others were similarly signed.

On June 23, 1415, the books of Hus were condemned to be burnt, thus foreshadowing the way that he was destined to tread. The sentence was designed to make Hus more compliant, but it did not shake him, for he had made his peace with death. He was only troubled that the sentence might confuse his followers in Bohemia, and this he must prevent. " Beloved," he wrote to them, " do not be frightened that they have condemned my books to be burnt. Remember that they also burned the writings of the holy Jeremiah who wrote at God's command, and yet they did not escape that which he had prophesied. Remember that and stand firm, for I trust in God that the school of Antichrist will be in dread of you and leave you in peace. The Council of Constance will not come to Bohemia to demand the books of you, for I believe firstly that many of them will die before that, and the others will be scattered in the world like the storks, and when winter comes they will not recognise what they have done in summer. Do not be intimidated by their resolution which will bring them no good, as I hope in God. They will scatter even as butterflies and their decisions will be like cobweb."

To lend emphasis to his words, which he feared might pass unnoticed, he described the Council as it really was. In the last resort he once again went over to the attack. It was not the danger to himself looming ahead but the threat to his teaching that forced him to speak in the old ringing tones of his denunciatory sermons. This outburst of passionate accusation showed more clearly than any defence how right he was.

He first stated bitterly, " They have also condemned my Czech books, which they have neither seen nor heard, and if they had heard them they would not have understood. For on the Council were Italians, French, English, Spanish and Germans; the books could be understood only by John, the Bishop of Litomysl, who was also here, and by the other Czechs from whom proceeded the slander of divine truth and of our country of Bohemia, of which country I believe that it is the land of the best faith because it so insistently demands God's Word and good morals." And then he went on, " Oh, if only you could have seen the assembly which called itself the most holy of

Councils and held itself for infallible. Proud it was, and greedy, and full of abominations. You would see excessive deeds of shame, of which I have heard the Swabians openly say that Constance cannot in thirty years expiate the sins committed by the Council in this town. Note that they have condemned their own head as a heretic. Well then, answer me, you priests who preached that the Pope is God on earth, that he cannot sin or commit simony, as their lawyers prove; and that he is the head of the entire holy Church which he administers well, their heart that nourishes them spiritually, the spring of all power and goodness, the sun, the refuge without fail in which each Christian may hide himself. Holy Church they call themselves, and most holy Council which cannot err; well, they already erred when they adored John XXIII with bent knee, kissed his feet and called him Most Holy Father, knowing him to be a loathsome murderer, an obdurate sinner, a simonist and a heretic, as they pronounced him in their sentence. Woe to them, for the head is already cut off, the God on earth fettered, proclaimed a sinner, and the refuge has fled from Constance and been closed down that none can flee to it. The Council has declared him a heretic because he sold indulgences and bishoprics and other offices for money. But those who condemned him had bought from him and others had trafficked with them. There is John of Litomysl, who twice chaffered for the Archbishopric of Prague but was outbidden. Ah, why did they not first draw the beam out of their own eyes? Their own law says: if someone has bought a position for money, it shall be taken away from him. Shame upon buyer, seller and middleman. There is another bishop in Constance who sold, and another who bought, and the Pope took money for the confirmation of this. If our Lord Jesus should say to the Council, 'He among you who is without the sin of simony shall cast the first stone at Pope John,' I believe one after the other they would turn and flee. And why did the cardinals elect him Pope since they knew that he was an evil murderer who had slain the Holy Father? Why did they traffic in simony with him when he was Pope, for they are chosen to be his advisers and to advise him to good. And are they not therefore guilty who committed simony with him? Why had everyone to say to him Most Holy Father as long as he remained in Constance? They still feared him. But when the secular arm intervened with God's forbearance or will, they all vowed that he must never be released again. Truly in the Pope and in the members of the Council were patent the evil, the abomination and the shame of the Antichrist!"

He spoke with the same unsparing candour about the condemnation of communion in both kinds which had taken place on June 15. Through the resolution of the Council this question had become of vital importance for Hus. For the Council said expressly, " Although Christ ministered this holy sacrament to His apostles in both kinds—bread and wine," and " although in the early Church this sacrament was taken in both kinds," yet it decreed that in spite of these assertions communion should be given to the laity only in the form of bread. " As this custom was introduced by the Church and the fathers not without reason and has long existed "—in reality it had existed only two hundred years—" it is to be respected as a law that may not be overthrown or changed at will without the authority of the Church. He who persists in this will be regarded as a heretic and punished." The Council which had laughed and mocked at belief in Christ thus put itself above Christ in a public statement. " What madness," wrote Hus, " to condemn thus as heresy the Gospel of Christ, the epistles of Saint Paul, yea, the deeds of Christ and His apostles and of the other saints. Saint Paul says to all the faithful, ' As oft as you eat of this bread and drink of this wine '—but lo, now we are told that the custom of the Church demands the contrary."

Fearing dissension among his colleagues, he once more wrote to Gallus, his successor at the Bethlehem Chapel, who rejected the chalice for laity, " Do not oppose yourself to the sacrament of the cup of the Lord for Christ Himself and His apostles have spoken for it. No passage in the Scriptures speaks against it but only custom which has, I believe, through negligence only, taken root. We must not follow custom but the example of Christ and His truth. I pray to God that you may not further contend with Jacobellus, so that no cleavage may grow among believers over which the devil would rejoice. Beloved, prepare yourself for suffering, drop all fear." For Hus already had a premonition of what lay ahead for Bohemia. " I believe that in Bohemia there will set in a great persecution of those who serve God truly if God does not intervene through the temporal lords who are more enlightened in His laws than the clergy."

Hus fought angrily and bitterly only where his followers and his teachings were concerned; he no longer fought for his life. Quietly and peacefully he prepared himself for his death. Copies of the charges against him were allowed him for a written answer; he now answered them as he had from the beginning desired. But before all else he used every day now granted him for his farewells. He wrote to his friends in Constance and

Prague, and to the University. He greeted many of his followers by name and distributed his few belongings among them. He thought of Jerome and was anxious for him, but not for himself. With an ever-increasing mystical fervour he detached himself from life.

Thanks, comfort and advice were sent to each friend separately. After the last hearing John of Chlum had managed to press his hand. Now he wrote, " How dear to me was the handshake of John, who did not fear to give his hand to me in my wretchedness, an outcast heretic led in chains, cursed by almost all." He advised him, " Leave the service of mortal kings and remain at home with your wife and children and abide firmly in the service of God. You see how the wheel of mortal vanities revolves, now raising one, now overthrowing another. Short is the consolation of the one who is raised ; soon follows eternal punishment in fire and gloom." He instructed his pupil, Martin, " Live according to the laws of Christ. I beg you, in God's name, do not grow to love splendid garments such as I alas loved and wore, setting a bad example. Beware of confidential talks with women, above all be cautious in the hearing of confessions, do not be caught in the snares of excess, for I believe that you are a pure boy whom God has had in his care. Do not fear to die for Christ if you wish to live with Him." Nevertheless, Hus sought to guard him against any dangerous consequences of his discipleship. " When they press you on account of your adherence to me, then say, 'I believe that the Master was a good Christian, but what he has written and taught in the schools, that I have not understood completely and have not read it all'. " Before all he was giving thanks again and again. " I beg all of you that you be thankful for the zeal of the lords from Bohemia, Moravia and Poland, for they often tried to assist in my liberation by opposing the Council as brave defenders of God and supporters of the truth, especially Wenceslas of Duba and John of Chlum." He added, " Believe what they will report for they were at the assembly before which I answered." He cherished the hope that his friends in Constance would protect his memory from all slander. Full of joyous certainty he wrote to them, " I firmly hope that God will allow me to share the crown of life together with you, lovers of truth, most sincere ones ! "

His large heart now found room even for his enemies. Formerly he had reported all that Palec had done against him, but now he added, " Perhaps I should not have written so lest it appear that I hate him." He forgave even Sigismund, and as he was able to choose his own confessor he chose Palec. Palec would not agree to this, but he came to visit Hus and made every effort to persuade him to recant. " Do not heed the shame of retracting," he said to Hus, " but think only of the good that will arise from it." Hus answered him, " The shame is greater if one is condemned and burnt than if one abjures. How should I fear it? But tell me, what would you do if you knew for a certainty that you had never held the errors ascribed to you? Would you abjure them?" Palec began to weep. He only said, " That is hard," and weeping they took leave of each other as Hus said, " Forgive me if I have ever scorned you with one word and that in my writing I have called you a liar." The whole time that they were talking to each other Michael de Causis had been striding up and down before the cell, Michael who had always increased the hardships of Hus's imprisonment. He had just forbidden the wife of the warder to visit Hus. Now he cried loudly and triumphantly to the warders, " Thanks be to God's favour we shall at last burn this heretic for whom I have already spent so much money." Hus heard him and wrote, " I demand no revenge. I leave that in God's hands, and urgently beg God for grace for him."

Hus often believed that the last day had come. " I think," he wrote, " that this letter is the last to you, for tomorrow, as I hope in Christ, I shall be purged of all sins by a fearful death." But there are no signs that this certainty of death ever diverted him from his purpose, although he did not hide the price his firmness cost him. " What I encountered this night I cannot write. How graciously God has proceeded with me and how He remained with me in strange temptations, that you will learn when we meet again in Him through His grace."

In spite of these torments, he prized every day that death still left him. " God knows," he wrote, " why He postpones my death and the death of my beloved brother Jerome. He has given us long in order that we might be better aware of our sins and bravely lament them; He gave us time that great and long temptation might take away from us our great sins and bring us solace; He gave us time that we might contemplate the terribly mockery and the cruel death of our King Christ Jesus and suffer it the more gladly." The horror of these undisclosed temptations, however, appears clearly when Hus faced them and wrote: " We ought not to forget that the saints have achieved the heavenly kingdom through countless sufferings; some were torn to pieces, others broken on the wheel, others roasted, others boiled, others flayed alive, buried alive, stoned, crucified, crushed between millstones, others drawn, drowned, burnt to death, hanged, quartered—and previously mutilated, incarcerated, flogged, and fettered ; who could count all martyrdoms which the saints suffered in the old and new Testaments for the sake of God's truth—and particularly those who castigated the clergy for their vices and preached against them." But in it lay solace, " It is a strange truth that if someone suffers here below he will really prevail against badness and in particular against the wickedness of the clergy, which cannot otherwise be touched." This solace was so strong that Hus reconciled himself to the idea of having his books condemned : " Now I already rejoice that they had to read my books in which their wickedness is laid bare : I know that they have read them more diligently than they have done the Holy Scriptures because they wanted to find false doctrines."

On July 1 and 5 the last attempts were made to move Hus to recant. Solemn delegations led by the worthiest cardinals appeared in the narrow cell in order to smother Hus's conscience. He answered as he had always answered and he declared again in his last letter that he could not recant if he were not instructed in something better and that he could not abjure what was falsely imputed to him.

On July 5, by order of the king, the Czech nobles arrived with the cardinals and bishops in an attempt to shake Hus. But brave John of Chlum said, " Master John, we are simple, uninstructed men and cannot give you advice. Therefore judge for yourself ; if you believe that you are guilty of some part of that with which you are reproached, do not shrink from accepting instruction and recant. But if, in your conscience, you do not believe that you are guilty of that they charge you with and of lies in the eyes of God, stand fast unto death with the truth you recognise." Hus replied with tears in his eyes, " John, know if I were aware that I had written or preached anything erring against the law and against the holy Mother Church I would retract it humbly, God is my witness. I ask constantly that they should show me better and more acceptable passages than those which I have written and preached—if they are shown to me I shall readily retract." A bishop interjected, " Do you want to be wiser than the whole Council ? " Hus replied, " I do not want to be wiser than the whole Council, but I pray that the lowliest of the Council should show me better writings and instruct me convincingly and I shall be at once ready to recant." The bishops thereupon cried out, " Lo, how obstinate he is." If a recantation could not be obtained, at any rate Hus's obstinacy was finally proved.

On July 6, judgment against Hus was pronounced. The Council assembled solemnly for its fifteenth public session in the cathedral. Sigismund was present, seated on a raised throne and in full regalia. At his feet were again the dignitaries of the Empire ; the Count Palatine with the imperial orb, the Burgrave of Nuremberg with the sceptre, the Prince of Bavaria with the crown, and a Hungarian Magnate with a drawn sword. In the centre of the church was a strange wooden structure looking like a table and a complete set of vestments for the mass hung above it on a wooden peg.

The session opened with a Mass ; during the Mass Hus, closely guarded, had to wait in the vestibule of the cathedral, for having been excommunicated he could not be present. Then he was led in and placed on the wooden structure for all to see in comfort. He listened to the preaching of Bishop Lodi from the text, " The body of sin must be broken." He could not protest when the bishop appealed with pathos to the king, " The triumph, the crown and the magnificent prize of victory await you, O most Christian king, who unites again the torn Church, removing long schisms and extirpating heretics. For this end God has given you the wisdom of divine truth, the power of royal majesty and true justice. Therefore destroy new heresies and false doctrines, and especially this obdurate heretic, through whose malignity many a region of earth has been infected with the heretical plague and brought to ruin. This holy work has been entrusted to you, glorious prince, and it behoves you as the one to whom the principality of justice has been entrusted. And thus out of the mouths of babes and sucklings you have ordained praise, and praise will ever be sung you that you destroyed the enemies of the faith." Thereupon followed a decree as typical of the Council as was this florid sermon. Under penalty of excommunication and two months' imprisonment people of whatsoever rank or position were forbidden to interrupt the session by cries, interjections, contradictions, applause or signs of displeasure. This severe decree did indeed save the dignity of the assembly. Why in any case should there be tumult when the issue was already decided ?

The programme was worked through quickly and without a hitch. The prosecutor of the Council demanded that as Wyclif had been condemned as a heretic, so too should Hus. The papal judge-advocate read again sixty articles of Wyclif and their condemnation. Then the articles extracted from Hus's writings were read. There were now only thirty of them, nine having been dropped. After the first article Hus said aloud, " Yes, that

I doubt not." A cardinal cut him short with the words, " Be silent now, and afterwards you can answer them all at once." Hus protested, " How can I answer them all at once ; I cannot carry such a heap of them in my head." After the next article he again attempted to speak, but the president called out to him, " Now finally be silent. We have heard you enough." Hus besought him, " I beg you for the sake of God to hear me so that the assembly here may not believe that I have asserted false doctrines. Afterwards do with me what you will." This had no effect. Thereupon he fell to his knees and prayed aloud, his hands folded, his eyes raised to Heaven, paying no further heed to the articles.

The evidence of the witnesses against him was then read out. Each testimony concluded with the words, " Proven by a Doctor of Theology," " Proven by a priest," " Proven by a Master of Arts." According to the custom of the Church, names were not given. This gave a chance for the most senseless charges to be maintained, even after Hus had successfully refuted them in reference to his writings. The charge about communion, about priests in mortal sin, and several new and improbable ones never previously submitted to Hus were now produced. Hus could no longer remain calm ; he begged so urgently to be heard that at last he was allowed to make brief answers, and again he convincingly disproved them.

Suddenly a new charge appeared : Hus had described himself as the fourth person of the Godhead. Even in his last hours Hus had to defend himself against such nonsense. He could hardly believe his ears and cried, " Tell me the name of the Doctor who has witnessed this against me." " That is not necessary here," the reader answered coldly. " Far be it from me, a poor wretch, to name myself the fourth person of the Godhead," Hus asserted. " Such a thing has never come into my mind." What could be more convincing than this simple assertion? It did not change the charge or the verdict.

The appeal to Christ was once more brought up against Hus. He stood by it and repeated it. " See, Jesus," he cried, " this Council holds Your deeds and laws for error and condemns them. But when You Yourself were oppressed by Your enemies You commended Yourself to God the Father as the justest of judges and thereby gave an example to us weak and poor creatures." Once more terrible laughter broke out over Hus. But he continued unwaveringly, " Yes, I say it once again, the surest appeal is to Christ Himself. No man's presents deter Him from justice, He is not deceived by false witnesses or ensnared by cunning.

To each and all He metes out what he deserves." The appeal to Christ had no practical effect, but thereby Hus proved his faith to be more real to him than life this side of the grave.

Unshaken he once more declared that he had not obeyed the summons to appear in Rome because he did not wish to stake his life uselessly. His appearance in Constance showed that he was not thereby seeking to evade the Church. "For that very reason have I freely come to this Council with the intention of attesting my innocence and to give an account of all my beliefs, having been promised a safe conduct by the king here present who should protect me against all might." Sigismund heard these words. Did they strike home?

Mladenovic here reports, "As Hus said this he turned his eyes sharply towards the king, to whose face a deep blush of shame mounted." A hundred years later this blush is said to have saved Luther; at the Council of Worms the clergy urged Charles V to arrest Luther but he, having promised Luther a safe conduct, answered them, "I will not have to blush like my predecessor Sigismund." It is, however, probable that Sigismund listened unmoved, that this passage was later interpolated in the report, and that the remark of Charles was later attuned to it; but it is certainly true that the death of Hus saved Luther's life. The glory of Hus's martyrdom suffused the German reformation. Later attempts were made to establish a direct relationship between Hus and Luther. Hus is supposed to have said: "Now you are roasting a goose, but in a hundred years' time there will come a swan whom you will not roast." The link between them did indeed exist: Luther wrote, "We are all Hussites without knowing it"; but Hus's remark is only an invention. He was no prophet. Sufficient for him was the support of faith in his fight for truth.

He never doubted the victory of truth, but he had to die for it; the sentence was read. "Under an appeal to the Name of Christ, the holy Synod of Constance decides, announces and declares, that John Hus has been and still is a proved and open heretic who has taught errors and heresies long denounced by the Church, and also much that is troublous, objectionable, audacious and seditious, preaching all this to the no small offence of the divine Majesty and the whole Church and to the damage of Catholic belief; that he has scorned the keys and censure of the Church and has persisted in such obduracy for many years, and thereby, with a contempt of the Church authorities, has in an insulting and annoying way appealed to the Lord Jesus Christ as the highest judge. In view of this the holy Synod declares John Hus to be a heretic and as such judged and condemned. It also decides because it recognises him as a stubborn, incorrigible man who is not ready to abjure his false doctrines and heresies that he shall be deprived and degraded of all the priestly and other dignities with which he is invested."

When Hus heard this sentence he fell on his knees and prayed, "Lord Jesus, forgive my enemies. You know that they have accused me falsely, brought false witnesses against me and drawn up false articles. Forgive them for the sake of Your great mercy." The Council, which claimed to speak in the name of Jesus once again answered him with laughter.

Two verdicts had been prepared, the second for use should he recant. In this case he would have been taken to a Swedish monastery to be walled into a narrow cell for the rest of his life, only a small aperture being left through which food could be handed him. That was the "true grace and mildness" that the Council wanted to extend to the penitent Hus. Without knowing it he had chosen the better way; his steadfastness, fearful though its consequences were, was rewarded.

The degradation demanded by the sentence was carried out in the Cathedral. It was a fearful ceremony. Hus was outcast from Christendom, that is, from the whole world of those times, from every human community; even the doors of Heaven were to be shut on him by it. But through this he found his path completely merging into that of his beloved Saviour. First he had to take down the vestments from the wooden peg and robe himself as a priest. As he did so he said, "My Lord Jesus, too, when he was sent from Herod to Pilate was robed in a white garment and mocked." Once again he was called on to recant. But he turned to the people, "Lo, these bishops demand of me that I should recant and abjure, but I fear to do so lest I lie in the eyes of my God and offend my conscience and God's truth. For I am aware that I have never taught what is falsely ascribed to me, and that I have written and taught the contrary. I cannot abjure lest I give offence to the souls of so many to whom I have preached and to others who proclaim the Word of God." Was nobody stirred by the courage and truth that lay in these words, spoken during the most frightful commination, spoken in the face of a death which might still be averted? The six bishops who were unfrocking him simply cried, "Now we see how obdurate he is in his heresy and malice."

Hus had to climb down from the wooden platform. First they took the chalice from his hand and as they did so cursed him, "Damned Judas, as you left the council of peace and made one with the Jews, lo, we take from you the chalice of salvation." Hus answered them with great firmness, " But I trust in the Lord, Almighty God, for whose sake I patiently bear this blasphemy, that He will not take the cup of His salvation from me. I have the firm hope that I shall today drink of it in His kingdom." Garment by garment the vestments were stripped from Hus, and every touch was accompanied by curses. Hus answered aloud, " I willingly bear this blasphemy in all humility for the sake of our Lord Jesus Christ." At last his tonsure, too, had to be destroyed. The bishops could not agree as to whether one cut with the scissors was enough or whether his head had to be clipped bare. Hus appealed to the king, " See, the bishops are not even united in their blasphemy." Then his hair was cut crosswise. As they did it the bishops uttered the words, " The holy Council of Constance hereby deprives John Hus of his priestly dignity and of the glorious offices he held, and declares that from now on they have nothing more to do with him. We now give him over to the secular arm." Thereupon they placed on his head a tall cap of paper on which were painted three small devils tearing the soul of a sinner with their claws. " That is the arch-heretic," was written underneath in large letters. They said, " We now give your soul over to the devil." " But I give it over to my gracious Lord Jesus Christ," Hus answered. And pointing to the paper cap, " My Lord Jesus Christ had for my sake innocently to bear a much heavier and harder crown of thorns. Why should I, a wretched and sinful man, not bear this much lighter one for His name and His truth." Impatiently the bishops repeated, " We give him over now to the secular arm."

The sentence was immediately put into effect. It changed nothing that Hus had long previously shown the hypocrisy of these proceedings in which the Church, professing unwillingness to shed blood, handed over the heretic to the secular arm with the express understanding that he was to be burnt. This article of Hus's too had been condemned as heretical. To the Latin appeal of the bishops Sigismund answered in German by ordering the Palgrave Ludwig, " Take him in our name, and do with him what is done to heretics ! " The Palgrave called Heinrich of Ulm, the Mayor of Constance, and ordered, " Take hence John Hus, who in accordance with the sentence of our most gracious king and our own command is to be burnt as a heretic." The mayor called to the municipal servants and the executioners, " Lead him out and burn him ! "

First Hus had to watch the burning of his books in the courtyard of the episcopal palace. He only smiled. Then he was led to the common place of execution on the marshes. Thousands of armed men accompanied him and a vast concourse followed, " three thousand men at arms without the unarmed folk and the women," Richental reported. At the Gelting Gate of the town the crowd could only pass over the bridge in driblets as it was feared that the bridge might otherwise give beneath them. Hus prayed aloud :

If I have walked with vanity
And my foot hath hastened to deceit,
Let me be weighed in an even balance
That God may know my integrity.

Then he cried out, " Jesus Christ, Son of the living God, have mercy upon me." Whenever the procession was brought to a halt, he turned to the people and cried that they should not believe that he was burnt for heresy for he had been falsely accused, a victim of false witnesses and of his bitterest enemies. And again he prayed :

In thee, O Lord, do I put my trust ; let me never be ashamed. Deliver me in Thy righteousness. Bow down Thine ear to me ; deliver me speedily ; be Thou my strong rock, for an house of defence to save me.

The procession had reached the place of execution. In view of the stake, Hus fell to his knees and prayed. The devil's cap fell from his head. The executioners set it on him again with the words, " May you burn together with the devils your masters whom you have served here." Once again Hus only smiled. The executioner brought his prayers to an end. Hus had to rise to his feet. Loudly and with a joyful face he cried, " Lord Jesus Christ, gladly and in humility I will bear this shameful and cruel death for the sake of Thy holy Gospel. Forgive my enemies."

The people standing around were moved. Some were heard to say, " We do not know what this man formerly taught or preached, but we see and hear nothing but holiness from him." They demanded that Hus should be granted a confessor. A priest on horseback cried out, " He is not worth it for he is a heretic." But Hus was nevertheless asked if he wished to confess. " Yes, gladly," he answered, for in prison the last confession had been a great consolation. When Palec had refused, another priest had come, and had not urged him to recant. The priest who was now called demanded a recantation since a heretic must have no share in divine grace. Hus refused, saying, " It is not necessary, I am not in mortal sin." He wanted at least to thank the people, but the Palgrave forbade him to speak to them in German. Hus was only allowed to take leave of his warders. He said, " Thank you, my beloved brothers, for all the goodness you have shown me. For you were true brothers to me and not warders. Know that I believe firmly in my Redeemer in whose name I will bear death, comforted with the certainty that this day I shall reign with Him."

Now the executioner led him to the stake. Hus was bound to it with seven wet ropes and chained by the neck with a heavy rusty chain. When he saw it he said tonelessly, " My Lord Jesus Christ was for my sake bound with one much heavier; why should I, poor wretch, not let myself be bound with this for His holy name's sake? " He repeated earlier words almost mechanically. Was a last temptation approaching? His face was turned to the east. Many found this unseemly for a heretic and he was turned to face westwards. Under his feet two bundles of wood were pushed and hay and straw were piled round him up to his neck and soaked with pitch.

At this moment the Marshal of the Empire, von Pappenheim, sprang melodramatically towards him and demanded him in the name of the king to recant. He could still save his life. But Hus had overcome his last moment of weakness and his voice had all its old force as he answered, " What heresies should I recant when I am not aware of a single one? I call God to witness that I have neither taught nor preached what false witnesses have charged me with. The foremost aim of all my deeds and writings was to turn men from sin. This truth of the Gospel I preached in the words and with the explanations of the holy doctors, and in this truth will I today gladly die! " God had fulfilled his most fervent desire; at the last moments, in the midst of the faggots and with death imminent, he stood firm to truth, to Christ.

The Marshal and the Palgrave threw their hands above their heads and the Marshal galloped off, the Palgrave turned away. With bated breath the gigantic crowd stood there. The flames rose. Hus prayed, " Oh God, have mercy upon me." Then he sang in a loud, clear voice, " Jesus Christ, Son of the living God, have mercy upon me." He sang it once, twice, thrice. Then a puff of wind blew smoke and flame into his face and he could sing no more. Was he suffocated at this moment? Some believed that they could see his lips still moving as he vanished behind the fire and smoke.

No one moved, no one spoke a word, as long as the flames burnt. As they died down, the upper part of his body was seen hanging by the chains from the stake. The executioners overturned the stake and started the fire afresh to burn him completely. They broke every bone separately and cleft his head so that the fire might destroy them more rapidly. They stuck the heart on a spit and held it in the flames until this great brave heart was ashes. The excutioner had, as was his acknowledged right, kept Hus's mantle for himself. But he was forced to burn this too ; the Palgrave promised to compensate him for it. Not a relic must reach Bohemia. And when the second fire had died down, all the ashes were carefully collected, loaded on a cart and thrown into the Rhine nearby so that not a fragment of his dust should remain on the earth ; the Czechs must not be able to rescue one sacred particle. And the river carried the ashes down to the sea, the sea that would receive the ashes of Wyclif.

That night however the Czechs dug up the earth where the fire had been and carried it to Prague. There it was to set ablaze a still more fateful flame that would eat into this Church. One of the Czechs who brought back the earth may well have been Zizka, the Hussite general who never knew defeat.

B. Picart del. 1712.

When Sigismund spurred the fathers on to burn Hus, his speech rose to an excited peroration. " Truly I was but young when this sect appeared in Bohemia, but see what a strength it has waxed to. And therefore make an end of the secret disciples and friends, and especially of . . . the man who is now held here under arrest." " Of Jerome," the fathers broke in. " Yes, Jerome," cried Sigismund. " Oh," they said complacently, " we shall rid ourselves of him in a day. He will cause us little trouble, for Hus is the master and Jerome only the pupil." Thereupon they parted " joyfully."

The fathers were mistaken. The trial of Jerome lasted longer than that of Hus. For a year it occupied their attention. For Jerome was of a different character from Hus ; pliant, restless, often vacillating or impulsive, and then again tough and consistent. For him it was not loyalty and steadfastness that were at issue, not the purity of his ideas, but the freedom essential for his questing nature. And to regain his freedom he felt any means were justified. He had practised this often enough before. He had recanted and abjured whatever might be asked of him only to escape his captors ; once free, he could mock the credulous and defend his old doctrines more fervently than ever. He would have gambled away his life long previously had he not followed this rule. Now he tried it again. He yielded, performing all that was demanded of him and going to the utmost limits of self-abasement. Then when he found that this did not bring him freedom he proved once again and more overwhelmingly than ever the inner greatness which was the foundation of his being beneath all his superficial instability.

His case was suspended as long as Hus was being tried and the rover who had scoured Europe in his unwearying search for truth had to wait passively in his terrible prison. On July 19 he was brought out for a short hearing that led nowhere. Then the work of the fathers began. They urged him to recant even more vigorously than they had Hus. In Bohemia the news of the burning of Hus had let loose a storm. The nobles had written an even more indignant and threatening letter. " The venerable Master Hus," they wrote, " without being convicted of any error, merely on the malicious evidence of traitors and his and our enemies was condemned by you and deprived of life in the cruellest fashion, to the eternal affliction and shame of ourselves, of the Kingdom of Bohemia and the Margravate of Moravia. Moreover you have seized and fettered the worthy Master Jerome, a man of pleasant eloquence and an excellent philosopher; and this without having first seen or heard him, at the instigation of a few slanderers. And perhaps even now you have had him killed like Hus." The Council could not but shrink from a second burning; the recantation of Jerome on the other hand could pacify Bohemia and save all for the Council, for the Church and for Sigismund. Every effort was therefore made to elicit a recantation from Jerome.

These efforts were successful. Jerome complied in order to escape. He felt he must be there when the fight began in Prague. What did it matter that he had to deny even Hus. He could defend Hus's memory and teaching better in Prague than in prison, and only there could he complete the work of his master. On September 11, before an assembly in the Cathedral, Jerome made a long declaration in which he repudiated Wyclif and Hus. He did indeed introduce several reservations in order to preserve some shreds of dignity and his tortuous phraseology betrayed shame and perhaps even inner conflict, but his declaration was in essence the recantation demanded of him. "I stand and shall ever stand with the holy Council," it ran, "in condemnation of the forty-five articles of Master Wyclif and the thirty articles of Master Hus and I confess here directly and sincerely that those articles are rightly and blessedly damned as being dangerous to believers in Christ and confusing the Church of God; without however intending to impinge on those sacred truths which the said men may scholastically or popularly have written or preached. As for the thirty articles of Master Hus in particular, I say in truth that when they were first put before my eyes in the form in which they now stand I could not believe that they were his. But later on I was completely convinced that they were. In order to remove all scruples I urgently demanded the books of the said Hus. And there I found the articles from the first to the last, and in the same wording in which they were condemned, in the books written by his own hand. And it is only now that I declare with comfort and security that the sentences refuted, rejected and condemned by the present holy Council should be rejected and condemned by all believers in Christ, although not without exception as heretical and false, but some as heretical and some as false. I invoke God as witness that I do not thereby intend to detract from his person or his good conduct, in my opinion, or from the numerous holy truths which I have heard from him. Rather, to tell the truth, I was a close friend of his person on account of his impeccable conduct and above all for the sake of the holy truth which he preached, zealously interpreting the Word of God to the people ; and for the sake of truth I was ever a defender of his honour wherever I might be. But now being enlightened as to his writings I do not wish to be a friend of his errors, for in accordance with my true and sincere principles I do honour and have always honoured the truth."

The Council next demanded that he should send his recantation to Bohemia. Painful though it was he obeyed. His letter to the leader of the Moravian nobles was almost more outspoken than his words to the Council. He wrote, "I hear that there has been a mighty tumult in Bohemia and Moravia because of the death of Hus, as though he had been unjustly sentenced and his burning an act of violence. Therefore I write of my own free will to you, my Lord, that you may know what you should believe. And I beg you that you will not consider that an injustice has been done him. To my knowledge what happened had to happen. Do not think, Lord, that I write this under compulsion or that I have fallen away from him through fear. I am indeed in fast custody and many great Masters laboured with me without however being able to bring me over to their opinion, but on the contrary I was of the opinion that an injustice had been done him. But when the articles for which he was condemned were laid before me for my scrutiny, and after I had very diligently examined them and weighed them and not with one Master alone, I became completely convinced that some were heretical, some false, and some objectionable and hurtful. So will I now, as I was his friend and with my own mouth have championed his honour on all sides, no longer be the champion of his errors, as I have made known voluntarily to the whole Council in far more circumstantial words."

This too was not sufficient for the Council. The scanty reservations in the long declaration seemed suspect ; the undertone of the letter, stressing so often freedom of decision, aroused their doubts since in its final effect it sounded constrained. Jerome was commanded to express himself still more plainly and unreservedly in a long statement to the Council and in a letter to King Wenceslas, the Queen and the University of Prague, and he had also to make a proclamation to the whole of Bohemia. For fourteen days he fought against it. Then he was ready to buy his freedom at this price. He abandoned the last shreds of his self-respect and abased himself to the full.

This new declaration of September 23 admitted of no further doubt. " I, Jerome of Prague," it began, " Master of Arts, confessing the true catholic and apostolic faith, anathematise all heresies and in particular those of which I have been accused until now and which Wyclif and Hus have previously taught. I confess in particular that several of the articles mentioned are heretical and long ago rejected by the holy fathers, and some blasphemous, others false or objectionable and still others presumptuous and causing disturbance, and others offensive to devout ears." He explicitly repudiated Hus. " Formerly, often hearing Hus preaching and lecturing, I believed that he was a righteous man not deviating in any way from the traditions of holy mother Church and the holy fathers. Now however I understand that he and his teachers and disciples are rightly rejected and condemned by the holy Council as heretical and senseless. I state this freely and unconditionally as I have already been sufficiently enlightened on the verdicts passed by the Council on the teachings of Wyclif and Hus and against their persons, which verdicts I, as a devout Catholic, do in all approve and adhere to." As regards himself Jerome asserted, " I swear by the Holy Trinity and this book of the Holy Gospels that I will remain firmly forever in the truth of the Catholic Church. I declare that all who may be against this belief are worthy of eternal anathema together with their teachings. Should I myself, though far be it from me, ever preach or believe aught against it, I will submit myself to the rigours of the law of the Church and confess myself as worthy of eternal damnation."

Was the Council satisfied? The activities of Hus seemed suddenly blotted out; Jerome was about to obliterate an epoch with his words. But then hotheadedness prevailed over common-sense and the Council, who might have exploited the recantation to further their Bohemian policy, simply squandered all the advantage they had gained up to date and continued the proceedings. Jerome was to have written still another letter; but this time he did not comply. He wanted first to see some results. He complained bitterly that it was an injustice for him to continue under arrest. The longer he had to wait for his freedom the stronger grew the resistance which he had only abandoned for the sake of regaining freedom. " I will write no more such letters," he finally told the assembly as they urged him.

He had actually satisfied the investigating commission to whom his case had been entrusted and they were in favour of his release. But a new, or rather an old, party then intervened. With eager malice the Czechs once again took up the cudgels against him. Palec and Michael de Causis besieged the cardinals, and Doctor Naso, a German leader from Bohemia, did not shrink from publicly reproaching the commission. " We cannot be sufficiently astonished, reverend Fathers, that you accept such an evil heretic on whose account Bohemia has already suffered so much harm, as you yourselves may yet have to suffer. I almost fear that you may have received gifts from this heretic or from King Wenceslas." Once again the powerful Gerson made common cause with them. On October 28 he published a treatise " On Declaration and Recantation in Matters of Faith," in which he proved that in spite of a recantation a heretic must nevertheless remain suspect of heresy. These intrigues assumed such proportions that the investigating commission resigned. Its place was taken, on February 24, 1416, by a new commission consisting only of enemies of Jerome. Under the influence of this commission, which destroyed any hope of freedom, Jerome made magnificent amends for the harm he had done.

The new commission ignored his recantation. It began at once to draw up the charges against him. As Jerome had written little they had to base their accusations almost entirely on the evidence of witnesses. Naturally only hostile evidence was accepted. The commission wanted to examine Jerome, but he refused to answer them and demanded a public hearing. On April 27 the charge against him was ready. The commission laid before the Council a hundred and fifty articles which Jerome must answer. They were sent to him in prison that he might prepare his reply. He once again demanded a public hearing in which he could defend himself. This hearing was granted. Did the Council expect that Jerome would sink to still greater depths of abasement?

Jerome wrote little. No works reveal to us his ideas in detail and we can only indirectly reconstruct his life. No letters betray what he experienced and suffered in prison. To a much greater extent even than Hus he was an orator. But the new age of the renaissance and humanism, to which he more clearly belonged than Hus and for which he was an unconscious trail-blazer, had also its representative at the Council. And he described the last speeches of Jerome and his path to death in one of the most beautiful letters that have survived to us from the early humanists.

Poggio Bracciolini, one of those scholars to whom Europe owed the rediscovery of the antique world, had come to Constance as papal secretary. He used this chance to seek old manuscripts in Germany and Switzerland. During the Council he discovered in a monastery in St. Gallen the writings of Quin-

B. Picart del 1713

tilian, believed lost. The fate of Jerome suddenly gripped his attention in the midst of his work, moving him so deeply that he wrote an account of it although the rest of the Council made no impression on him. This case alone seemed to stand out for him " especially on account of the eloquence and learning of this man." Accustomed to finding greatness only in antiquity he was forced to admit, " I confess that I have seen no one speaking at a trial in which his own life was at stake reach, as he did, the eloquence of antiquity which we so much admire." Poggio was completely detached from the religious quarrel. The more valid is, therefore, his account, written on the very day that Jerome was burnt and under the immediate impression of events. Poggio was wholeheartedly for Jerome and wrote a moving memorial of that resurgence of inner greatness which cleansed him of all stain. The few reservations made by Poggio to preserve himself from any suspicion of heresy only reveal more clearly where his respect and sympathies lay.

On March 23, 1416, just a year after his arrival in Constance, Jerome was brought to his hearing. The four nations were assembled in the cathedral to hear his defence. He was to answer the articles one by one. Jerome found this unjust ; he wanted first to explain his case in outline before answering individual charges. When his accusers would not agree he cried, " What unfairness ! For three hundred and sixty-six days while I have been in the hardest prison, in dirt, in filth, in muck, in chains, in direst need, you have continually listened to my enemies and slanderers, and you do not want to listen to me for one hour ! As the ears of each one of you were open to them for such a long time they have persuaded you that I am a heretic, an enemy of the faith, a persecutor of the clergy, while I have been given no chance of defending myself. And so you have condemned me in your minds as a godless man before I can confess what I am. And yet you are men, not gods, not eternal but mortal, you can err, you can be deceived, cheated and seduced. Here the lights of the world, the wisest of the earth, are said to be assembled. You must strive to the utmost that you do nothing hasty, nothing foolish, nothing unjust. I, indeed, whose life is at stake, am but a poor man. I say that not for my own sake, who am mortal, but that to me it seems unworthy of the wisdom of so many men that something unfair be decided against me, causing harm not so much through the cause as through the example." The fathers seemed perplexed by this outburst, which was a new type of argument. Jerome had some success. He must indeed still first answer the individual charges, but at the conclusion he would be allowed the long consecutive speech for which Hus had striven in vain.

The answers of Jerome to the separate articles won the greatest admiration of Poggio. He wrote, " It was wonderful to see with what words, what eloquence, what reasons, what expression of countenance, what a voice, what confidence, he answered his adversaries and later delivered his speech to the end, so that one could not but regret that so noble, so excellent a spirit should have indulged in such heretical endeavours, if the reproaches against him are true. It is not my business to decide such important matters and I satisfy myself with the opinion of those who are regarded as wise. It is incredible how wittily he answered, with what reasons he defended himself. He brought forth nothing unworthy of a good man, so that if one believed of him what he confessed in his words, one would have lacked not only just grounds for a death sentence but even the smallest cause of offence. All was false, he said, all the charges had been invented by his adversaries. When he was reproached among other things with being a slanderer of the apostolic see, an enemy of the Pope, an opponent of the cardinals, a persecutor of prelates, an antagonist of the clergy and indeed of the Christian religion, he rose and began in a plaintive voice with outstretched hands, ' To whom can I turn now, Fathers assembled here ? Whose help shall I beseech ? Whom shall I implore ? You perchance ? But my enemies have estranged your spirit from my salvation for they have branded me the enemy of all those who are to pass sentence on me. For they thought, even if what they have invented appeared unimportant, you will nevertheless by your sentence destroy in me the common enemy and opponent into which they have wrongly transformed me by their lies. If then you believe their words I must despair of being saved ! ' He dealt with many matters with a witty saying, many with a rebuke ; many times he forced laughter in the midst of so serious a matter by joking about the charges against him. Asked what he held of the sacrament, he said, ' First it was bread, but during consecration and after, the true Body of Christ.' Someone demurred : ' But you are alleged to have said that it remains bread after consecration.' Whereupon he answered. ' To the baker it remains bread.' To a Dominican who violently attacked him he cried, ' Silence, hypocrite ! ' And to another who swore to something against him by his conscience, ' That is the best way of deceiving the people.' "

Still more impressive and important was the great speech of Jerome. The first session was not enough for all the articles to be dealt with. On May 26 there was a second hearing. When the reading of the articles was finished Jerome rose and said, "Since you have listened so zealously to my adversaries it follows that you must also listen to my speech in the same frame of mind." This caused a mighty uproar, the fathers protested, shouted and murmured, but finally he was allowed to speak. When Jerome began to speak the noise had hardly perceptibly subsided and many fathers wanted to drown him by talking aloud and laughing and shuffling their feet, but gradually they all fell under his spell and he mastered all their occasional outbursts. His speech destroyed any hope of his ultimate submission ; but he almost succeeded in doing what Hus had dreamt of—in swaying the whole Council through the power of his speech and leading them on to the right road.

The speech was above all a testament of a new way of thinking. Hus had fought for a sermon ; but it was impossible to give this name to the speech of Jerome. If his remarks during his hearing were always an appeal to humanity or a demand for justice and not a defence of a doctrine, in this speech all scholastic subtleties were finally shed. It revealed what the death of Hus and the death of Jerome, freed from their temporal implications, meant for all time. The contemporary forms of belief, which formed the entire contents of the charges, were hardly mentioned; in a vast philosophic survey Jerome placed himself and Hus in the long chain of men who in all ages and of all creeds had died for the truth. He showed that Hus's and his own suffering were part of the eternal struggle for truth and freedom of thought. The barricades of the Middle Ages fell. Thanks to this speech the fires of the second martyrdom lit up the path to the new age. A wealth of human detail, of reasons and demands understandable in any age, a longing for simple clarity and straightforward justice, lift his defence from the obscurity of the past and bring it home to us.

It was at the same time a warning to the new age. Jerome could demand freedom of conscience because he stood firm on the ground of faith ; he wanted to save Christianity. The new freedom was to serve to re-establish the rule of Christ. Only because Jerome was the friend and pupil of Hus was the weakness of his character suddenly transfigured with such glorious steadfastness in the face of death. Whenever he was far from Hus he again fell victim to his own instability. We understand him better than Hus, perhaps, but he alone was not capable of preparing the way for reformation. He was nearer the new and unbelieving times than was Hus and therefore his appearance was more dazzling, but of slighter importance. Already the first humanists, among whom Poggio included him, will not stand the test of history so gloriously because they lack a religious background. The Church is thereby the more blameworthy. A Church that had embraced Hus would have been a support and stay in the dawn of the new freedom. In his speech Jerome re-affirmed his allegiance to Hus. The impression he made was overwhelming ; and not simply because it happened to be the humanist Poggio who gave an account of the speech. There are several other accounts of it, and the following version was obtained by collating them :

" I know, most learned Fathers, that many excellent men have suffered unworthy fates in spite of their virtues, have been oppressed by false witnesses and condemned by the most unjust sentences." That was Jerome's text. Poggio's report and the official minutes of the Council record, " Then he began with Socrates and recounted how he had been unjustly sentenced by his age, but although he might have fled, did not want to do so that he might take the terror out of prison and death, the two things that seemed most loathsome to mankind. Then the imprisonment of Plato, the torturing of Anaxagoras and Zeno, and the unjust sentencing of many heathens. Then he passed to the example of the Jews. First he said that Moses, the liberator and law-giver of his nation, was repeatedly slandered by his own people as leading them astray and despising them. That Joseph was even sold by his brothers out of envy and then thrown into prison under suspicion of adultery. That Isaiah, Daniel and almost all the prophets were unjustly sentenced as mockers of God and leaders of rebellion. Then he proceeded to John the Baptist and to our Saviour, who, as everyone knows, were sentenced through false witnesses by a false verdict ; to Stephen, who was killed by the college of priests ; to the apostles who were all condemned to death not as good men but as rebels and agitators, as contemners of God and misdoers. And if the same thing happened to him, he would not be the first or the last in this world." How different was this from the recital of the horrors of the martyrs with which Hus prepared himself for death. " All spirits were moved and inclined to mercy."

Jerome continued, " It was of old the way of the most learned and most sacred of mankind that they differed from each other in their opinions on matters of faith, not in order to annihilate belief but in order to find true belief. Thus Augustine and Jerome were of different, nay, not merely different but contrary opinions, without coming under suspicion of heresy." Having created this philosophic basis for his point of view, which went far beyond the horizon of his times, Jerome went over to his own defence. But it was no defence in the meaning of the Church, not the recantation which the fathers again expected. This recantation had only been intended as a fraudulent payment for freedom ; now that Jerome recognised that he could in no way obtain freedom his own concern was to justify himself before history. He felt guilty only about his double-dealing with the recantation, and this alone did he feel the need to expiate.

And what a fine and brave expiation. " Everyone expected that he would clear himself by refuting the charges and begging forgiveness for his errors. But he protested that he did not err and would not withdraw from crimes falsely imputed to him by others. And then he launched out into praise of John Hus, naming him a good, just and holy man in no way deserving of death at the stake. He too was ready to accept any martyrdom in a brave and steadfast spirit, and not to yield to his enemies and the shamelessly-lying witnesses who one day must give an account before God, whom they could not deceive, for what they had said. Great was the sorrow of those around for they wished that such an excellent man might be saved and that he had been assisted by a right understanding. But he seemed to strive for death by his insistence on his opinion."

The speech was conscious and deliberate suicide. Even one of his enemies, Dietrich Frey, had to admit, " All had pity for him save he himself, for he wanted no pity." Jerome explicitly withdrew his recantation ; he had acted against his conscience when he declared himself in agreement with the condemnation of Hus and in addition had written to Bohemia. " Hus taught nothing against the existence of the Church, but only against the abuses of the clergy, against arrogance, the haughtiness and the pomp of the prelates. For the property of the Church belonged first and foremost to the poor, the sick, and the maintenance of the Church ; it must seem unfitting to every good man when it was squandered for whores, banquets, fodder for horses and dogs, fine clothing and other things unworthy of the religion of Christ." Of all sins " with which he had ever insulted the majesty of God, none weighed so heavily upon him and for none had he such pangs of conscience as the sin he had committed from that unholy and accursed chancel when for fear of death he had spoken against the teaching and person of that holy man and had approved his condemnation." And of Wyclif he said, " he had never learnt to know a man who had written with such good and deep meaning." He solemnly declared that he would remain true to the teaching of Hus and Wyclif. " What they hold, that will I also hold. And I believe that I shall thereby believe what is right."

Poggio was impressed, above all, by the form of the speech. He wrote : " It was the sign of an exalted spirit that he, when his speech was oft interrupted by a manifold noise and he was irritated, did not spare any of them but compelled them all to blush and keep silent. When murmurs arose, he remained silent, occasionally uttering a rebuke. Then he continued, entreating and imploring them to let him speak, since they would never hear him again. Firm and resolute of spirit, he was never frightened by their noise. He gave wondrous proof of his memory. He had passed three hundred and sixty-six days at the bottom of a dark and stinking tower. He complained of the loathsomeness of this, but he assured his hearers that, as became a brave man, he was not sighing because he had had to bear unworthy things, but because of the inhumanity of man over which he could not but be astonished. In such a place he had not only been deprived of any chance of reading but even of seeing. I leave out of account the spiritual fears that daily tormented him and might even have robbed him of his memory. Nevertheless he quoted so many highly learned and wise men as witnesses of his views, so many doctors of the Church supporting his opinion, that there would have been enough and more than enough if he had spent the whole time in complete quiet and leisure dedicated to study. His voice was agreeable, full, ringing, and with a certain dignity ; his gestures those of an orator, suitable, now expressing revulsion, now arousing pity, which he however neither wanted nor demanded. Unafraid, unshaken, he stood there, not only despising death, but fighting for it, so that one could not but call him a second Cato." Unlike the fathers of the Church, Poggio exclaimed, " A man worthy to live forever in the memory of mankind."

Jerome had gloriously risen from the depths into which he had fallen. Four days were allowed him still to recant. The most respected of the cardinals visited him to seek to persuade him. But now Jerome remained firm. He was happy that he had expunged his shame ; he had lost his wish for freedom, and death had no more sting for him. All the attempts of the Council were in vain. And so on May 30, 1416, sentence was pronounced and carried out.

The procedure was the same as with Hus. Only King Sigismund, travelling on behalf of the Council, was absent. Once again a fanatical sermon by the Bishop of Lodi rang forth. " O happy Bohemia, if this man had not been born ! Of how much ill was the presumption of these two peasant men the cause, these wretched plebeian, low-born men of unknown origin ! " And turning to Jerome, " And yet you have not been proceeded against with the severity due to such a proclaimed heretic as you, worse than Arius, Sabellius, Faustus and Nestorius ! " Only reputable men had been allowed as witnesses ; all should have been allowed, " Even the dishonoured, usurers, robbers, prostitutes." " You have not been tortured ; you should have been and then you might have humbled yourself and spewed up your false teaching. Punishment might have opened your eyes, sealed now by guilt. In what a friendly manner have the lord cardinals and others, moved by compassion, called on you and entreated you to come to your senses. How graciously were you granted public hearings. O that you had not received them, for I fear this has given you overweening insolence."

Jerome defended himself for the last time. " I call God to witness that I confess and adhere to all the articles of belief of the holy Catholic Church, but I will not concur in the condemnation of those holy men whom you unjustly sentenced. You know that you are condemning me unjustly and maliciously since no fault has been found in me. But after my death I shall leave behind a thorn in your consciences. I appeal to the highest and most just Judge before whom you will render account." And as the tall paper cap was set upon his head, " The crown of shame, the abomination of hideousness," he, like Hus, said, " Our Lord Jesus who died for such wretches as I was crowned with thorns for my sake ; shall I not willingly, for his honour, wear this crown."

He was led through the same streets as Hus. He prayed, " *Credo in unum deum*," and said in German to the people, " As I have prayed, no other do I believe. But now I must die because I would not agree with the Council and would not say that Master Hus was sentenced in a right and holy way. For I verily knew him to be a true preacher of the gospel of Christ." His last care was to bear witness to the purity of Hus ; he subordinated his own death to the memory of his friend.

Before the stake he prayed quietly. When he was stripped and bound to it with wet threads and with a chain at his neck, he sang triumphantly :

Hail thee, festival day,
Blest day that art hallowed for ever,
Day when our Lord arose
High in the heavens to reign.

The executioners wanted to spare him by lighting the fire behind him but he called to them, " Come here and light the fire before my eyes. Had I feared it I should never have come to this place for I might well have escaped." With a serene mind he saw the fire creeping towards him and prayed aloud, " Lord God, Almighty Father, be merciful to me a sinner, for You know that I have sincerely loved the truth." Then the flames closed round him.

His death must have been more difficult than that of Hus for he was a large, strong man, with a physique hardly broken even by his terrible imprisonment. The old chronicle says, " When the fire began to burn his body, blisters the size of an egg showed all round it, and thus he lived a while in the fire in the greatest martyrdom, even for as long as a man might go from St. Clement's in Prague over the bridge to the Church of St. Mary." The stone bridge over the Vltava, erected by Charles, was famous for its length and to walk that distance through fire would seem an endless way.

Yet Poggio could report, " With a glad brow and joyful countenance he went to meet death ; he did not shrink before the fire. No stoic was ever of so firm a spirit, none has ever met death so steadfastly as he did. When the fire was kindled, he began to sing a hymn which even the fire and the smoke could scarce interrupt. I saw this death with my own eyes and all its separate acts. Neither Mucius let his hand be burnt with such a confident spirit as he his whole body nor did Socrates so readily drink the hemlock as he embraced the fire."

Hardly had the second fire died down before the Czech enemies of Hus, Palec above all, were transformed into the most zealous champions of reform. They knew their own country and knew that if things remained as they had been, Bohemia was lost to the Church. But this time they were unsuccessful. The cardinals insisted that the new Pope should be elected before reform was undertaken. The election of the new Pope produced fresh scandals. Three Popes were all but elected once again. To prevent this the cardinals agreed upon an Italian, the aristocratic Roman Colonna. They thus betrayed the cause of reform. As Pope Martin V, Colonna dissolved the Council almost before the most scanty preliminaries to reform had been broached. And there the business had to rest for the time being.

But long before its dissolution the Council saw the complete failure of its policy towards Bohemia. The news of the death of Hus was a signal for disturbances which hit the Church before all. In Prague priests were persecuted and churches plundered and the enemies of Hus were killed with the sword or drowned in the Vltava. In the country parishes Hussite priests took the place of the catholic ones. Hus and later Jerome were venerated as martyrs, their pictures were put up in churches, and masses for martyrs read for them. The Czech service and communion in both kinds prevailed more and more, and innumerable hymns celebrated Hus and Jerome as true Christians. Four hundred and fifty-two of the most powerful nobles of Bohemia and Moravia joined to form a league to defend the demands of the Hussites.

The Council made repeated attempts to intervene but all its measures were unavailing. The nobles in league together were summoned to appear in Constance but in their strongholds they mocked this futile challenge. John the Iron was sent with special powers to fight the Hussites in Bohemia and he formed a counter-league of catholic nobles, but only fourteen rallied to him. John himself could not appear publicly, his property was laid waste and divided, and soon there remained nothing for him to do but to leave Bohemia. The Council proclaimed an interdict because John of Jesenice, long under the ban of the Church, remained in Prague, but the interdict only caused fresh unrest which brought Prague almost completely into the hands of the

MARTINUS. V. PONT. ROM.
MARTIN
CINQ.
B. Picart del. 1713.

Hussites. King Wenceslas, wavering till then, now declared himself with them. He sequestrated the incomes of the catholic clergy because they continually slandered Bohemia abroad, and he kept John of Jesenice in Prague.

After his great successes Sigismund now saw all called in question, reform as well as his future rule in Bohemia, and he attempted to mediate. He prevented the proclamation of a crusade against heretical Bohemia which had been intended, he prevented the citing of King Wenceslas, and of Queen Sophia who openly confessed Hussitism, as heretics although proceedings had already begun against them, and at the same time he tried to spur Wenceslas on to energetic measures against the Hussites. Wenceslas half agreed and brought about some agreement in Prague between the rival parties, now favouring one side, now the other ; but all his efforts were equally ignored in Constance.

Thanks to this shilly-shallying and the continued mediation of Sigismund everything remained in a fluid state for years. The Hussite movement gained time to consolidate itself and train new leaders, a task it mastered thanks to the influence of Hus. In Ousti, a little town in Southern Bohemia, where Hus had preached most frequently during his exile, persecuted Hussites were given asylum by an enthusiastic follower of Hus, a rich weaver. Here was formed a sort of academy which, at first together with the University of Prague and later against it, legislated for the new faith.

When the Council was ended Sigismund intervened more energetically. In December of 1418 he issued a public manifesto to Wenceslas. He threatened to summon a crusade against Bohemia and to depose the king. This threat frightened Wenceslas and he proceeded seriously against the Hussites. John of Jesenice had to leave Prague. The catholic priests who had been driven out were brought back again and replaced in their offices and catholic services were again introduced. At first these measures seemed successful. The catholic party was still strong in the country which had a considerable German population. Soon the catholic priests began to persecute and suppress the Hussites. The Hussites were even driven from Ousti. The king packed the New Town Council with violent anti-Hussites to give the Church secular support against the Hussite court. He wanted to change the other Prague magistrates in the same forcible fashion. But this increased pressure caused open rebellion.

The Hussites driven from Ousti fled into the country to a fortress-like hill to which they had given the name of Tabor. Here they held their services and dwelt under canvas. They gradually transformed their camp into a fortified town. On

July 22, 1419, they summoned the first great Hussite assembly. Forty-two thousand people came from all sides in solemn procession carrying before them a chalice, their holy symbol. The Taborites went out to meet them and in the spirit of Hus they all greeted each other as brothers and sisters. Any other form of address was forbidden, all differences of rank were wiped out, the poor were cared for by the rich. The times of the early Christians seemed to have returned. On all sides the Hussite priests preached, the believers listened in quiet reflectiveness, communion was distributed in both kinds and from serious talks about the true faith a new community developed. The vast assembly maintained exemplary order while it lasted and quietly and peacefully dispersed again. None had any premonition of the imminent battles in which this new Christianity would have to defend itself with its blood.

In Prague the spirit of Jerome was prevailing. In February three churches had been conceded again to the Hussites as a result of popular demonstrations and in June another one was forcibly occupied by them. When the new Council of the New Town introduced sharp measures, the Hussites organised a solemn procession on June 30 to ask God's help. John of Selau, a true and fanatical disciple of Jerome, led the procession past the Town Hall. There it was held up whilst the Councillors mocked it. From all sides armed men suddenly streamed, led by Zizka. The Town Hall was taken by storm. Seven Councillors who could not escape were thrown from the windows on to the lances of the troops surrounding the Town Hall.

King Wenceslas swore to be revenged and sent to Sigismund for help. But he was no longer equal to the excitement and was seized by a stroke. He died on August 16, 1419, and with him perished the last obstacle to open insurrection. He could not even be publicly buried ; and Sigismund could not enter his kingdom. The coffin of the wretched king was lit up by the flames of the revolt kindled in Constance.

With the first defenestration of Prague the epoch of the Hussite war had begun. Almost exactly two hundred years later, on May 23, 1618, the Thirty Years' War was to begin with the second defenestration. It would sweep away all traces of the reformation in Bohemia. But the Bohemian reformation would have finished its task, preserving the seeds of reformation, dead in England, until the German reformation had taken up the fight and could assure its ultimate success. "The Gospel that we have," wrote Luther, "was bought for us by Hus and Jerome with their blood." Bohemia nourished the doctrine, smothered in England, until it could return to England across Germany. It may be regarded as symbolical that among the first Hussite leaders was an Englishman, Peter Payne, who played an important part. He was a Master of Oxford University and a Wyclifite who had made good his escape.

The seed sown by Hus was not lost. But the memory of Jerome was lost. In the course of time the two figures were merged into one ; the terrible death which they had both faced with the same steadfastness and almost with the same words helped this process. At last there was only the one figure bearing the name of Hus. From Jerome was borrowed the violent impulsiveness that seemed to suit the Hussite wars better than the hesitating conscientiousness of Hus while the steadfastness of Hus cloaked the instability of Jerome. Hus's fervent faith blotted out the part played by the modern humanist philosophy which Jerome was one of the first to profess. Even their pictures were interchanged. Hus had a broad peasant face and was beardless ; the traditional portraits of Hus however reproduce the bearded face of Jerome which seemed to later ages to be more worthy of a prophet.

This book has attempted to separate the two figures from each other and to destroy the conventional picture of the fanatical nationalist which is false and has no message for this age. The real struggle of Hus and Jerome, on the contrary, is still of urgent importance for us. We are still faced with the unsolved problem of whether it is right, heedless of external success, to preserve purity and steadfastness, or whether the end justifies the means. Freedom, it seems, has not proved its worth. Almost more seductive to us appears obedience, however unworthy it may be, if it can safeguard order and internal peace. But the certainty of Hus and the stability which Jerome, in spite of all his failures, found ever again in Hus and in Hus only, shows us, too, the only way to overcome false obedience and give freedom its true fulfilment.

We must not reject freedom. The abuses of the Roman Church were corrected only after the reformation had been successful and thus forced the counter-reformation. And today order will degenerate if the counter-weight of freedom is lacking.

The liberation from mediæval bonds is clearest in the intellectual breadth of Jerome, but nevertheless Hus's share in the struggle for freedom is more important. Jerome failed as soon as he was cut off from Hus. For freedom must not be misunderstood as a liberation from Christianity ; today, as then, the world would sink into chaos if freedom were robbed of its mainstay of religion.

INDEX

Abraham, *see* Velemovice
Ach, Peter of, 78-79
Ailly, *see* d'Ailly
Albert, priest of St. Sebald's at Nuremberg, 184
Albik, Archbishop of Prague, 119, 125, 151-52
Alexander V, Pope, 94-95, 101, 103, 121, 203
Andrew, shoemaker, 181
Anne of Bohemia, wife of Richard II of England, 4-5, 54
Anne of Schweidnitz, wife of Charles IV, 9
Augustine, St., 147

Ball, John, 5
Barbara, wife of King Sigismund, 33
Benedict XIII, Pope, 38, 85, 94, 162, 163, 202, 209
Bernard, St., 54
Bohuslav, Dean, 14
Boniface IX, Pope, 18, 37
Bracciolini, *see* Poggio
Brancas, Cardinal, 139
Brod, Andrew of, 93, 99, 102, 128, 136, 188
Byzantium, Patriarch of, 198

" Cardinal," Hus's, *see* Reinstein
Causis, *see* Michael de Causis
Charles IV, King of Bohemia and German Emperor, 4, 7-9, 19, 21, 31, 36, 44, 46, 54, 55
Charles V, German Emperor, 239
Chlum, Henry of, 183, 187
Chlum, John of (the " doctor of Biberach "), 183, 186, 187, 192, 195-96, 206, 214-15, 216, 220, 233, 236
Chotek, Bernard, 144
Clement VII, Pope, 4
Colonna, Odo, Cardinal (later Pope Martin V), 109, 111, 139, 166, 168, 260
Constance, Bishop of, 192, 208-09
Constantine Porphyrogenetos, Emperor of Byzantium, 24
Cossa, Balthasar, Cardinal (" il diavolo cardinale " ; later Pope John XXIII, *q.v.*), 95, 100, 105, 121, 215

d'Ailly, Peter, Cardinal, 61, 169, 173, 222, 224-28

" Diavolo cardinale," *see* Cossa
" Doctor of Biberach," *see* Chlum, John of

Dola, the Prior of, 115, 151
Duba, Wenceslas of, 183, 185, 186, 187, 234

Eliae, John, 93, 99, 102, 128, 136, 154

Faulfisch, Nicholas, 81
Fida, 187, 195
Fondulo, Gabrino, 163
Frederick (" with the empty pocket ") of Habsburg, Duke of Austria, 168, 178, 206-08, 210-11
Frederick of Hohenzollern, Burgrave of Nuremberg and Elector of Brandenburg, 169, 216, 237
Frey, Dietrich, 256

Gallus, 233
George of Podebrady, King of Bohemia, 5
Gerson, John Charlier of, 61, 91, 94, 160, 169, 173-77, 191, 202, 208, 213, 217, 220, 250
Gregory XII, Pope, 85-87, 94, 121, 122, 135, 162, 163, 193, 202, 209
Grillenperg, 119

Harrasser, Walther, 74
Hasenburg, *see* Zbynek
Helwel, John, 184
Herben, Jan, 2
Holubar, 144
Hradec, Marcus of, 52, 101, 128, 131
Hubner, 74
Huler, Master of Worlik, 16, 24
Hus, John : origins and early youth, 22, 24 *sqq.* ; student years, 23 *sq.*, 29-31 ; becomes a priest, 40 *sq.* ; influenced by Wyclif, 60, 65, 73 ; Rector of Prague University and preacher at the Bethlehem Chapel, 69 *sqq.* ; preacher to the Prague Synod and Court Chaplain to the Queen, 75 ; conflicts with Archbishop, 81 *sqq.*, 87, 94, 102 *sqq.*, 106, 115 *sqq.* ; elected Rector of the Czech University, 96 ; decision to accept a martyr's death, 104, 107, 158, 164, 180, 186, 243 ; excommunicated by Cardinal Colonna, 111 ; refuses to go to Bologna, 114 *sq.* ; begins writing in

Hus, John (*cont.*)
Czech, translates Bible, 122 *sq.*, 157; fights papal bull of indulgence, 125 *sqq.*; defends the "fifty-one articles," 138; banned by the Church, 139 *sqq.*; refuses to go to Rome, 142 *sq.*; withdraws from Prague, 145 *sqq.*; at Kozi Hradek, 156 *sq.*; visit to Prague, 159; at Krakovec, 161, 180; cited to Constance, 163; Sigismund's letter of safe conduct, 163, 171 *sq.*, 180; journey, 171, 180-87; attitude adopted at Constance, 177, 190 *sq.*, 218; refuses to submit silently, 192; arrested, 195 *sq.*; imprisoned in Dominican monastery, 197 *sqq.*; transferred to Gottlieben Castle, 209; indicted, 213 *sq.*; trial begins, 216; second hearing, 218 *sqq.*; refuses to recant, 223, 226 *sq.*, 229 *sq.*, 235, 236, 243; third hearing, 224 *sqq.*; his books condemned to be burnt, 231; sentenced, 237 *sqq.*; degraded, 240 *sqq.*; burnt at the stake, 243

"Iron Bishop," *see* John "the Iron"

Jacobellus (Jacob of Stribro), 52, 68, 124, 128, 181-82, 204-06, 233
Janov, Matthew of, 44-52
Jenstejn, John, Archibishop of Prague, 13-19, 37-38
Jerome of Prague, 27, 66, 68, 73, 87-92, 94, 105, 114, 119-20, 128, 131, 141, 154-56, 211-13, 246-59, 260, 264
Jesenice, John of, 110-11, 114, 135, 153, 182, 260-61
Jicin, John of, 133
Jistebnice, Sigismund of, 83
Johanna of Bavaria, first wife of King Wenceslas, 10
John of Nepomuk, St. (Vicar-General John of Pomuk), 13-17, 69, 188
John XXIII, Pope (*see also* Cossa), 105, 109-10, 115, 121-22, 124-25, 135, 139, 152, 153, 161-63, 166, 170, 171, 172, 178-79, 191, 192, 193, 196, 200-04, 206-08, 210-12, 215, 224
John "The Iron," Bishop of Litomysl, 118, 140, 197, 205, 214, 231, 232, 262
John of Luxembourg, Duke of Goerlitz, 9, 32
John, Provost, son of King Otakar II, 24
Jost of Luxembourg, Margrave of Moravia, 9, 32-33, 36, 40, 105-06, 111

Kbel, 82, 84
Knehnice, George of, 81
Knin, Matthew of, 82-83, 93
Kojata, 50-51
Kreutz, 82
Kromeriz, Milic of, 44-47

Laboun, Zdenek of, 101
Ladislas, King of Naples, 86, 121-22, 127, 135, 161-62
Landulf, Cardinal, 93
Lebus, Bishop of, 185, 198
Lefl, Heinrich, 229
Litomysl, Bishop of, *see* John "the Iron"
Litomysl, Nicholas of, 74
Lobkovice, Nicholas of, 92
Lodi, Bishop of, 237, 257-58
Louis II, Duke of Anjou and King of Naples, 135
Ludwig III, Count Palatine and Elector, 216, 237, 241, 243-44
Ludwig of Magdeburg, Archbishop, 15
Luther, Martin, 64, 206, 239, 263

Mainz, John of, 86
Martin V, Pope (*see also* Colonna), 166, 168, 260
Martin, a pupil of Hus, 234
Martin, John and Stanislav, the first Hussite Martyrs, 132-34
Masaryk, T. G., 5
Michael de Causis (Michael of Nemecky Brod), 139-40, 154, 188-89, 192, 194, 195, 197, 204, 217, 218, 228, 235, 250
Milic, *see* Kromeriz
Mladenovic, Peter, 183, 198, 213, 216, 239
Muhlheim, John of, 71

Naso, John, 250
Nassau, John of, 38
Nemecky Brod, Michael of, *see* Michael de Causis
Nepomuk, St. John of, *see* John of Nepomuk
Nicholas, a Carmelite monk, 141

Olbram, *see* Skvorec
Ostia, Cardinal of, 217
Otakar II Premysl, King of Bohemia, 24

Palec, Stephen, 52, 74, 100, 127, 128, 135-36, 138, 151, 153, 188, 194, 195, 197, 204, 217, 224, 227-28, 234-35, 242, 250, 260
Pappenheim, von, Marshal of the Empire, 243
Payne, Peter, 264
Peklo, John, 198
Poggio Bracciolini, Gian-Francesco, 169, 250-59
Pomuk, John of, *see* John of Nepomuk, St.
Prachatice, Christian of, 182, 211

Prague, Jerome of, *see* Jerome
Prokop of Luxembourg, 9
Protiva, John, 69, 101, 102, 188
Puchnik, Nicholas, 13-14, 16, 38

Rabstein, Pflug of, 183
Reinstein, John of (Hus's " cardinal "), 52, 182, 183, 192
Richard II, King of England, 54
Richental, Ulrich of, 166, 178, 187, 242
Rohle, Wenceslas, 19
Rupert, Count Palatine and German King, 34, 82, 86, 105

Sagan, Ludolf of, 160
Salisbury, Bishop of, 213
Selau, John of, 263
Sforza, Giacomuzzo Attendolo, 135
Sigismund, King of Hungary and German King and Emperor, 8, 9, 32-36, 40, 86, 105, 111, 118, 121, 122, 162-63, 165, 168, 169, 170-73, 187, 191, 192, 193, 196, 199, 201, 202, 208, 210, 211, 214, 216, 218, 220, 224-29, 234, 237, 239, 241, 246, 262, 263
Simon, Cardinal of Rheims, 160
Skvorec, Olbram of, Archbishop of Prague, 37-38
Sophia, wife of King Wenceslas, 92, 99, 112, 183, 262
Stanislav of Znojmo, *see* Znojmo
Stitny, Thomas, 25
Stokes, John, 118, 217, 219
Stribro, Jacob of (" Jacobellus," *q.v.*)
Sybart, John, 156, 158

Tiem, Wenceslas, 125, 197
Trevelyan, G. M., 5
Trinkaus, 36, 76
Tyler, Wat, 2, 5

Ulm, Heinrich of, Mayor of Constance, 169, 178, 194, 241
Urban VI, Pope, 4

Vechta, Conrad of, Archbishop of Prague, 152
Velemovice, Nicholas of (" Abraham "), 83-84
Vserub, Peter of, 81

Waldhauser, Conrad, 43-44, 45
Waldstein, Voksa of, 106, 131-32
Wenceslas, King of Bohemia, 1, 4, 7-19, 32-36, 40, 54, 75, 82, 85, 86, 92-93, 105, 108-11, 116, 131-32, 136, 140, 145, 153, 154, 170, 183, 262, 263
Witold, Prince of Lithuania, 155
Wyclif, John, 2, 53-54, 57-60, 64-65, 73-75, *et passim*

Zabarella, Cardinal, 220, 227
Zbynek Zajic of Hasenburg, Archbishop of Prague, 75, 76, 78, 81-84, 86-87, 94, 96, 101-02, 104, 105, 106, 111, 116-19
Zizka, John, 2, 108-09, 244, 263
Znojmo, Peter of, 154
Znojmo, Stanislav of, 52, 68, 74, 81, 100, 136, 151, 153, 154
Zul, Nicholas, 76